THE ROMANIZATION OF AFRICA PROCONSULARIS

THE ROMANIZATION OF AFRICA PROCONSULARIS

BY

T. R. S. BROUGHTON, PH. D.

GREENWOOD PRESS, PUBLISHERS
NEW YORK 1968

Reprinted with the permission of
The Johns Hopkins Press

Reprint edition, 1968

LIBRARY OF CONGRESS catalogue card number: 68-23279

Printed in the United States of America

Patris Memoriae
Sacrum

PREFACE

This essay has been written in an attempt to describe in their social and economic setting the principles which governed the development of the province of Africa under the Roman régime. Despite the many excellent studies which exist of the development of Roman Africa there may yet be room for one which attempts to define the municipal institutions of the Roman province in relation to their indigenous background, and to show the processes of slow growth and of adaptation which characterize the relation of Rome to her African subjects. The results of such a study, even if they should be neither very startling nor very original, may help us to realize a little more truly the mode of operation of the Roman genius.

The study has been restricted to the Proconsular province in which the fusion of Roman, Carthaginian, and indigenous influences was most apparent, and has been limited to the period from the destruction of Carthage to the reign of the Severi in which the province developed to its greatest prosperity and in which Rome's organizing and civilizing genius was most operative.

I must confess my obligations to the many scholars who have written upon North Africa, particularly to M. Gsell, whose Histoire ancienne de l'Afrique du Nord and whose commentary to the maps of the Atlas Archéologique de l'Algérie are indispensable to all students of North African history. I owe much also to the studies of Messrs. Schulten, Cagnat, Barthel, Toutain, Carcopino, Poinssot, Rostovtzeff and numerous others my debt to whom I shall express in the notes.

I am grateful to the authorities of the Harvard College Library for the use of books, maps, and atlases, to the authorities of the American School of Classical Studies in Rome for the use of their library, to the authorities of The Johns Hopkins University library for the courtesy which assisted my study, and to Professors Miller, Robinson, and Mustard of The Johns Hopkins University for their interest and suggestions. Special thanks however are due to Professor Frank of The Johns Hopkins University, who first suggested this subject, for his direction and advice.

T. R. S. Broughton.

Bryn Mawr,
Pennsylvania.

CONTENTS

INTRODUCTION

The Social and Geographic Background

Northwest Africa, in which are included the modern states of Tripoli, Tunis, Algeria, and Morocco, is as it were an island bounded on three sides by the sea and on the fourth side by the desert. But the country is in no other sense a unit and never has been. Its natural conformation as a long narrow fringe of land divided lengthwise by its own chief natural divisions has conditioned the development of North Africa from the beginning, while the broken, diversified character of the country and the immense differences in the economic value of the land and in the basic conditions of life in regions quite near to each other have tended to prevent any genuine unity, political or social, of the indigenous people.[1]

As this study deals particularly with the territories which were included in the proconsular prov-

[1] An account of the physical features and climatic conditions of North Africa is found in Gsell, *Histoire ancienne de l'Afrique du Nord,* I, pp. 1-176; Rivière et Lecq, *Traité pratique d'agriculture pour le nord de l'Afrique.* The best maps for Algeria are those of the *Atlas archéologique de l'Algérie,* 1: 200,000, published by the Gouvernement général de l'Algérie with a complete explanatory text by M. Gsell, and for Tunisia those of the *Atlas archéologique de la Tunisie,* 1: 50,000, with supplements 1: 100,000, published by the Ministère de la Guerre with an explanatory text by Babelon, Cagnat, and Reinach. For general purposes one can use the map at the end of *C. I. L.*, VIII, pt. 2.

ince until Septimius Severus organized the separate province of Numidia we may describe these regions in somewhat greater detail.[2] The northern coast of Tunis and of eastern Algeria is rough and forbidding, broken at the mouths of rivers by indentations which provided harbors for Phoenician mariners to find shelter and build their trading-posts. A coastal range of mountainous country extends inland from thirty to fifty miles. This region is well-watered and well-wooded, and fertile wherever the broken terrain permits cultivation. Succeeding this in eastern Algeria is a region of high plains and some rolling country, extending southward and southwestward from Constantine, where the rainfall is less but sufficient for ordinary cereal crops. In this region culture was at first, of course, nomadic, but agriculture was considerably developed under the Numidian kings. Farther south about a region of salt lakes the land becomes almost barren, but the last few drops of moisture from the northern winds are deposited on the northern slopes of the Aurès and of the Batna mountains and make agricultural life once more possible there. Here when the Roman peace had forced the nomads into settled habita-

[2] The western boundary of the proconsular province seems to have followed the course of the Ampsaga river, Pliny, *H. N.*, V, 22, and to have turned westward along the O. Enndjas. It continued southward west of Djemila (Cuicul), *C.*, 8318, 20144, through Zraia (Zarai), *C.*, 4508, where there was a customs station between Numidia and Mauretania, and west of Tobna (Tubunae), *At. arch. Alg.*, f. 37, 10; *Bull. du com.*, 1901, p. 315, no. 6, toward the Chott el Hodna.

tions and stopped their national sport of raiding grew up about legionary posts such towns as Timgad and Diana. Beyond the mountains lies the Sahara.

In Tunisia there is the same passage as one goes from north to south from the well-watered but mountainous region near the Mediterranean to the arid steppes of the south.[3] But the conditions of development are changed by a different conformation of the country. Tunisia lies open to the east, and the chief regional and climatic division is the series of mountains, valleys, and plateaus which extends southwest from Cape Bon to Tebessa. North of this the valleys of the Bagradas and the Miliana rivers which flow into the gulf of Carthage have always invited permanent settlement and agricultural life, and have been the chief highways of penetration into Africa. To the south except for a strip of land at the coast the country is largely given up to barren steppes where a few nomads eke out a

[3] Ain Drahim in the northern coastal region receives as much as 200 cm. of precipitation per year; the Bagradas valley from 40 to 60 cm., none too well distributed. From Cape Bon southward the rainfall diminishes from 40 cm. to 25 cm. at Sfax and 20 cm. at Gabès. The plateau of Mactar receives 60 to 80 cm. but Sufetula less than 40 cm. South of Nefza, Tozeur, and Biskra the amount of rainfall is negligible. The coastal region receives less rainfall toward the west as the Mediterranean narrows. In eastern Algeria the rainfall diminishes from over 100 cm. at the coast to from 40 to 60 cm. on the Tell about Constantine. In general the variations of temperature increase as one proceeds southward but freezing temperatures occur even at the coast. Snow falls on the mountains and on the high plains.

miserable existence. On the western rim of this region at Sufetula and Cillium a subsoil seepage from the hills gives sufficient moisture for the deep roots of the olive. Here the French by following Roman methods are making the country prosperous once more.

At the sea-coast the amount of rainfall steadily diminishes as one goes south. Some compensation is secured by very careful processes of conservation of moisture and constant cultivation of the ground to prevent evaporation.[4] Under these conditions agriculture necessarily becomes arboriculture, and hardy drouth-resisting plants, chiefly the olive, are cultivated. It remains to be seen how far inland from Sfax into regions which Rome never developed the application of these principles will bring agricultural life. To the far south lies a region of salt lakes, mountains and sand with scattered oases such as Nefta, Tozeur, and the old and important town of Gafsa which has always been the strategical center of the region. But for the phosphate mines much of this territory would be absolute desert. Nearby in the Matmata mountains a cliff-dwelling eneolithic culture survives.

Such are the chief regions of the territory once included in the proconsular province of Africa. It is necessary however to stress the fact that within each of these regions considerable diversities may occur. The plains are not plains in the western sense of the

[4] See Frank, *A. J. P.*, 1926, pp. 69-73.

word, but often little pockets of level land among the hills. The regions drained by the systems of the Bagradas and of the Miliana rivers are, apart from the district immediately about the city of Tunis itself, a maze of hills, plateaus, and little plains, while stretches of level land near the rivers themselves continually narrow or widen as the hills close in or recede. From the northern coastal range a spur of hills projects into the region of the high plains along the eastern border of Algeria and cuts them off from the basin of the Bagradas. The high massifs of Kef and of Dj. Gorra rise in between the Bagradas river and the courses of its tributaries. In the best regions of Africa conditions of elevation and of soil cause diversity of character even where the necessary rainfall comes. Africa can never be considered as a unit.

Scholars and travellers seeing the remains of large and prosperous towns of Roman date in regions in which in modern times desert conditions have prevailed have sought to explain the difference by the assumption that the climate of North Africa has changed. There has however been little, if any, change in the climatic conditions of North Africa within historical times.[5] The physical features which have been largely responsible for the diversities of climate have remained unchanged. Herodotus,[6] Sal-

[5] Gsell, *op. cit.*, I, pp. 40-99
[6] IV, 191.

lust,[7] Mela,[8] and Tacitus[9] during the years preceding or shortly after the Roman conquest speak of desert conditions in regions where desert conditions have existed in modern times. The great French survey[10] proves that the Roman development was not due to any notable use of irrigation, since there was usually not sufficient rainfall to provide water for irrigation, but to a very careful conservation of water in all parts of the country in cisterns and reservoirs. Today the consistent application of the Roman principles of the conservation of moisture and the cultivation of plants adapted to the locality is bringing back to productivity after centuries of barrenness regions which were fruitful under the Roman régime.

The basic element in the African population was the indigenous Berber stock which seems to have occupied the country since prehistoric times. Their origins and racial affinities are not definitely known.[11] They were a people emotionally intense but individualistic and without power to cooperate in large groups. They were unoriginal and appear to have had little capacity for self-development. It is doubtful even if they had remained untouched by foreign influences if they would have evolved any advanced political or social organization. As

[7] *Jug.*, 17, 5; 75, 2; 78, 5; 89, 4-5.

[8] I, 41-2.

[9] *Ann.*, II, 52, 3.

[10] *Enquête sur les installations hydrauliques romaines en Tunisie.*

[11] Gsell, *op. cit.*, I, pp. 275-308, discusses the various possibilities.

it was, they clung conservatively to their own small village or family groups, slowly yielding to Carthaginian and Roman influences.[12]

Before the influence of Rome was felt in Africa Carthage [13] had performed an important civilizing mission in certain portions of the country. The foundation of Utica by Phoenician traders in the twelfth century B. C.[14] was followed by the establishment of trading-posts along the north coast of Africa and along the shores of the Syrtes.[15] Carthage, founded in the ninth century B. C.,[16] outgrew her mother city of Tyre and became the leader of the colonies previously founded. She also sent out many of her own.[17] Although her interests were primarily mercantile, the need of the agricultural land necessary to every ancient city, and of a supply of mercenaries to defend her interests led her to a degree of interference in the affairs of the interior. The Bagradas valley was an avenue of trade inviting penetration and was probably occupied at an early date.[18]

[12] On the social and political institutions, and on the cultural development of the Berber people, see Gsell, *op. cit.*, V, and VI.

[13] Gsell, *Hist. anc.*, I-IV, is the best treatment of the Carthaginian period; see also, Melzer-Kahrstedt, *Gesch. d. Karth.*

[14] Pliny, *H. N.*, XVI, 216. Gsell, *op. cit.*, I, p. 360.

[15] Gsell, *op. cit.*, I, p. 361 ff.

[16] For a discussion of the contradictory sources, see Gsell, *op. cit.*, I, p. 397 ff.

[17] Gsell, *op. cit.*, I, pp. 458-9.

[18] By 400 B. C. Libyans were recruited, not merely mercenaries in her armies, Diodorus, XIII, 44, 54, and 80; Gsell, *op. cit.*, I, p. 464. They were therefore subjects.

The exact limits of the territory she subjected to herself are not known.[19] Her arms had penetrated to Theveste during the first Punic war,[20] and Sicca Veneria is known to have been subject to her shortly afterwards.[21] It is probable that little land beyond the present Algerian frontier was actually occupied.[22] It is possible that her influence extended to Capsa in the south [23] but more likely by way of commercial relations than actual conquest. Carthage was not primarily anxious for a great land empire, and even if she were, the African hinterland was much less promising ground than Sicily or Spain. For the rest therefore she left the Berber people to their natural disunion and internecine strife. Beyond the area drained by the valleys of the Bagradas and the Miliana rivers, and the coast towns she did not control, hardly even pacified the people.

Within these regions the indigenous people were forced into settled habits as cultivators of the soil, paying tribute to their Punic masters,[24] and in all probability were largely Punicized in language and religion. It is not known how far the indigenous communities thus formed accepted institutions of the Punic type, or, in fact, were permitted an auton-

[19] See Gsell, *op. cit.*, II, pp. 93-181.

[20] Polybius, I, 73, 1; Diodorus, XXIV, 10, 2.

[21] Polybius, I, 66, 6.

[22] It is not certain that Theveste was annexed, but the fossa of 201 B. C. was probably only a short distance west of Souk el Arba, Gsell, *op. cit.*, II, p. 102.

[23] *C.*, 22796; Gsell, *op. cit.*, II, pp. 98-9; V, pp. 278-9.

[24] Gsell, *op. cit.*, II, pp. 299-308.

omous community life at all by Carthage [25] but names of Carthaginian magistracies such as the suffeteship became part and parcel of their own speech.[26] Despite the heavy tribute which Carthage regularly demanded, and the excessive demands which she made in times of stress [27] there seems to be no doubt of the number and the prosperity of the Libyphoenician villages.[28] When Masinissa robbed Carthage of the middle Bagradas territory he took on one occasion more than seventy,[29] on another fifty [30] towns and villages. There were still three hundred in the reduced territory of Carthage in 149 B. C.[31] Many of these especially in the territory near Carthage were probably villas and establishments of Punic landlords, but the majority were indigenous villages.

Only in the region about Cirta did the Punic civilization exert its full influence in Numidia before the fall of Carthage. Masinissa who had himself been educated at Carthage strove to civilize his people by fostering Punic influences. Punic became the language of his court,[32] and he tried to introduce Punic agricultural methods in the land about Cirta.

[25] Gsell, *op. cit.*, II, pp. 300-2; V, pp. 131-2.
[26] Gsell, *op. cit.*, V, p. 132.
[27] Polybius, I, 72, 2; Gsell, *op. cit.*, II, p. 303.
[28] Gsell, *op. cit.*, II, pp. 103-5; 305.
[29] Livy, XLII, 23.
[30] App., *Pun.*, 68.
[31] Strabo, XVII, 3, 15.
[32] On the activity of Masinissa, see Gsell, *op. cit.*, III, pp. 305-8; V, pp. 162, 187-8; VI, p. 109 ff.

For the same reason his successors probably welcomed Punic people into Numidia when Carthage was destroyed. In the regions which border upon the original proconsular province the evidence of Punic influence is very strong but outside of Cirta itself there is almost none from the Carthaginian period.[33] The numerous neo-Punic inscriptions which occur along with Libyan ones in the regions of Mactar, Thugga, and westward [34] point to a considerable influx of Punic people at a later date. The same conclusion is favored by the especial frequency of suffetes [35] and the special popularity of the cult of the Cereres in the same regions.[36] It is probable that all the Punic people who could fled away from the Romans who ravaged the Carthaginian territory and sold all whom they captured into slavery, and found a welcome asylum in Numidia. The hinterland, although it owed a nominal submission to the Numidian kings, had remained uninfluenced. The Gaetulian nomads still roved and raided almost to the sea-coast and as far north as Hadrumetum in 46 B. C.[37]

The general social development of the country as the Romans found it can best be summarized by the

[33] Gsell, *op. cit.*, V, p. 260 ff.; VI, p. 110 ff.; Melzer-Kahrstedt, *Gesch. d. Karth.*, III, p. 108.

[34] See Gsell, *op. cit.*, V, p. 261 ff.; VI, p. 113 ff.

[35] See ch. VI, n. 192; Gsell, *op. cit.*, V, pp. 132-3.

[36] See Carcopino, *Rev. hist.*, mai-juin, 1928, pp. 1-18; for a collection of the evidence and the localities see Audollent, *Mél. Cagnat*, pp. 362-7.

[37] *Bell. Afr.*, 67, 1.

quotation of a passage from Pomponius Mela:[38] "Thus the coast regions are inhabited by cultivators whose customs do not differ greatly from our own except that certain of them differ in language and in cult. For they keep their ancestral gods and worship them in the ancestral manner. The people who border upon them have no towns to be sure, but have dwellings which they call mapalia. Their way of living is rough and they lack comforts. Their chiefs clothe themselves with saga but the common people with the skins of wild beasts and of cattle. They sleep and take their meals upon the ground. Their vessels are made of wood and bark. Their drink is milk and the juice of berries, and their food mostly the flesh of wild beasts since they spare as far as possible the herds in which their only wealth consists. The people farther in the interior are still less civilized and wander about following their herds, moving themselves and their tents as their herds follow their pasture; where the day ends there they spend the night. They are scattered as families everywhere without order and take no common counsel. Since individual men have several wives at once children are numerous and agnatic relations are never few."

We see therefore the social divisions of the country and the physical diversities which conditioned them. The Punic cities along the sea-coast were well developed, civilized, and commercial. Next lay a

[38] I, 41-2.

region in the Bagradas and Miliana valleys where agriculture had been long practiced and the people given a considerable degree of civilized life by Carthage. There followed in the hills and steppes beyond a region in which Carthaginian influence had been somewhat felt and in which Punic people intermingled and became dominant after the destruction of their city, and finally a desert hinterland, untouched and unorganized, peopled by roving nomads. It was Rome's task to organize, administer, and colonize these regions. The following pages are devoted to a study of the principles which actuated the Roman policy and of the adaptations which her administration and colonization made to the basic social and economic conditions of the country.

CHAPTER I

Africa Under the Republic

In 146 B. C. Rome finally satisfied her ancient fear and hatred by destroying Carthage. A senatorial commission of ten men was sent to aid Scipio in the organization of the province.[1] The site of Carthage was accursed, especially the Byrsa and the Megara.[2] Four cities which had supported Carthage to the end were destroyed; [3] seven cities which had allied themselves to Rome at the beginning of the war were confirmed in their territories and given the status of civitates liberae et immunes.[4] One of them, Utica, was given additional territory toward Carthage and toward Hippo Diarrhytus, but under a different legal category from her own.[5] Masinissa's heirs were allowed to retain the seizures of the previous half-century, thus becoming the most important of Rome's client princes.[6] The Carthaginian deserters

[1] Appian, *Pun.*, 135; probably the same as the Decemviri ex Lege Livia of the Lex Agraria of 111 B. C., §81.

[2] App., *Pun.*, 135; Cicero, *De Lege Agr.*, I, 2, 5; II, 19, 51; for the words of the curse, Macrobius, *Sat.*, III, 9, 10-11.

[3] Strabo, XVII, 3, 16; Neferis, Tunis, Neapolis, and Clupea.

[4] *Lex Agr.*, §79; Utica, Theudalis, Uzalis, Thapsus, Acholla, Leptiminus, and Hadrumetum.

[5] App., *Pun.*, 135; *Lex Agr.*, §81.

[6] See Gsell, *Hist. anc.*, III, p. 297 ff. All lands west of the Fossa Regia (note 14) belonged to the kingdom of Numidia. In addition certain lands within the Roman province were granted by treaty to the sons of Masinissa, but only in usufruct; *Lex Agr.*, §81; Cic.,

under Himilco, 2200 in number,[7] were given an allotment of land.[8] All other land became public land of the Roman people,[9] partly allotted to stipendiary settlements of the indigenous inhabitants,[10] partly held subject to sale to private individuals by the praetor or the quaestor, or leased to landlords by censoria locatio.[11]

Rome kept little territory for herself. The indications given by Pliny[12] and the finding of the stones which mark Vespasian's survey[13] of the *Fossa Regia* show how small was the original province of 146 B. C. The boundary ran in a general northwest and southeast direction, perhaps from the Tusca river to

---

De Lege Agr., II, 22, 58. These were probably toward the south of the province and near the sea-shore, Plutarch, *Mar.*, 40, 7; but note the conjecture re Thimida Regia, Gsell, *op. cit.*, V, pp. 265-6.

[7] App., *Pun.*, 100 and 108.

[8] *Lex Agr.*, §76; Livy, *Epit.*, 50.

[9] Rome had not yet adopted the principle that all dependent provincial land was ager publicus. As she had destroyed Carthage and sold into slavery all the Carthaginians she could capture all the public land of Carthage and all the land which had been privately owned by Carthaginian citizens naturally became ager publicus. The inclusion of the land of the stipendiary communities in this class may be exceptional, or may have been an inheritance from the Carthaginian system. As the stipendiary communities appear to have remained upon their allotments comparatively undisturbed there was little difference in the practical effect: see Frank, *Jour. Rom. Stud.*, 1927.

[10] App., *Pun.*, 135; *Lex Agr.*, §77, §80.

[11] See below on Lex Agraria of 111 B. C. This law was intended to clarify a situation which the enactment and subsequent annulment of the Gracchan legislation had rendered obscure. The actual processes of exploitation had probably been valid previously.

[12] Pliny, *Hist. Nat.*, V, 25.

[13] *C.*, 25860, 25967, 23084 (Hr. es Souar); note also 14428, 14451, (fragments of saltus inscriptions about Gasr Mezouar).

Thaenae, but passed east of Vaga by Gasr Mezuar near the Oued Zerga. Thence it crossed the Bagradas and ran along the crest of Djebel Ech-Cheid between the Khalled and Siliana watersheds. Turning eastward near Gaffour it crossed the Siliana and Miliana watersheds near Djebel bou Kril to a point south of Abthugni (Hr. es Souar). Thence it turned southeastward once more, passed east of Djebibina and cut the Sebkhat Sidi-el-Hani on the line to Thaenae.[14] All land outside of this line belonged to the kingdom of Numidia. When we realize that these limits contain an area only of about 5000 square miles, that the territories of the seven free cities probably accounted for about 1500 to 2000 square miles, that additional land was assigned to the free town of Utica, that an allotment was made to the 2200 Carthaginian deserters, and that much of the remainder was broken and mountainous country, we must acquit Rome of any charge of land hunger at this time.

For information regarding the Roman organization and management of Africa during the first years of the occupation we are dependent on scanty information gleaned from various sources, partic-

[14] See Tissot, *Géographie Comparée,* II, p. 14 ff.; Toutain, *Les cités romaines de la Tunisie,* p. 19 ff.; Gsell, *Hist. anc,* III, p. 327 ff.; Cagnat, *Contes rendus Acad.,* 1894, p. 51; Poinssot, *C. R. Ac.,* 1906, p. 467 ff.; Frank, *A. J. P.,* 1926, p. 57 ff. Note also *Atlas arch. de la Tun.,* Béja, 89; Teboursouk, 108, 227, 215; Djebel Fkirine, 52. The Kroumirie was probably not effectively occupied at this time.

ularly Appian,[15] the Lex Agraria of 111 B. C.,[16] Sallust,[17] Caesar[18] and Plutarch.[19] The province was at first placed under an annual praetor, who established his headquarters at Utica.[20] Appian tells us that on all land with the exception of the territories of the free cities, and of the lands allotted to the Carthaginian deserters a tax was imposed, while a tax *per capita* was imposed on women and men alike.[21] This would imply that a considerable population was left. But if the story of the wolves running away with the boundary stones[22] has any factual basis at all it signifies that Gracchus twenty-five years later found the region of the Bagradas above Utica semi-fallow and desolate. It seems hard to believe that the Romans although bent on destroying everything Carthaginian should have evacuated so prosperous a region so completely. But it had been run over by the armies of Rome and her Numidian allies for three years,[23] and what Punic people had been captured within and without the town were sold in slavery[24] while those who could had escaped into the

[15] *Punica,* final sections and *Bell. Civ.* scattered paragraphs.

[16] §§45 to 95 deal with African land.

[17] *Jugurtha.*

[18] *Bell. Afr.,* probably written by one of Caesar's officers.

[19] *Gaius Gracchus, Marius, Pompey, and Caesar.*

[20] App., *Pun.,* 135; Sallust, *Jug.,* 104, 1; Cic., *In Verr.,* II, 1, 70; Val. Max., IX, 10, 2; Orosius, V, 20.

[21] *Pun.,* 135.

[22] Plut., *C. Gracchus,* 11, 2.

[23] App., *Pun.,* 99-101.

[24] Orosius, IV, 23, 7; Cic., *Tusc. Disp.,* III, 22, 53.

hills.[25] The public land of Carthage, and the land owned by Punic proprietors thus became desolate, and only some Libyphoenician folk of doubtful loyalty and uncertain status had been left. Rome completed the work by declaring the whole of the former Carthaginian domain public land of the Roman people and granting some of it to these remaining folk on the terms which Appian records.[26] Orosius mentions a plague of grasshoppers, followed by pestilence in 124 B. C.[27] which caused a huge number of deaths in Africa and Numidia, but how far it was a factor in the depopulation of Africa, his totals are too untrustworthy for us even to hazard a conjecture.

At the conclusion of the war the Romans guaranteed their territory to the seven free cities, their allies, made an allotment to the Carthaginian de-

[25] It is probably in part due to this exodus, the more welcome since the Numidian kings were attempting to civilize their subjects along Punic lines, that evidence appears, dating from the middle of the second century B. C. on, of a strong admixture of Punic influence in such indigenous centers as Mactar, Althiburos, Thagora, and other regions within the borders of the Numidian kingdom. Such a development was, of course, in part due to the extension of the Carthaginian dominion previous to the Second Punic war. It is notable, however, that within the Numidian kingdom hardly any Punic inscriptions are found except at Cirta previous to the fall of Carthage. See Gsell, *Hist. anc.*, V, p. 260 ff.; VI, pp. 110-116 ff. The strength of the cult of the Cereres in the same region bordering upon the Roman province of 146 B. C. points to the same conclusion. See Audollent, *Méi. Cagnat*, p. 360 ff.; Carcopino, *Rev. hist.*, mai-juin, 1928, p. 6 ff. See also Melzer-Kahrstedt, *Gesch. der Karthager,* III, p. 108.

[26] *Pun.*, 135.

[27] Orosius, V, 11; Livy, *Epit.*, 60; see Warde Fowler, *Class. Rev.*, 1904, p. 394; Cagnat, *Armée romaine,*[2] introd., p. xv.

serters, and declared all other land public land of the Roman people. Some of this was assigned to the *homines stipendiarii* of the conquered communities, and the rest was held to be sold or leased for the benefit of the treasury. How much land was involved in each of these categories we have no means of knowing, but a general principle of action regarding the stipendiary land seems discoverable. The strongest indigenous centers of the original province in later times, apart from the Punic coast cities, were almost all in the hill areas of the southern and northern portions, and on the spur ridges and massifs which break the Bagradas and the Miliana watersheds into a maze of small plains and valleys. In a total area available, subtracting the Kroumirie, of not more than two thousand square miles, not much more than half was plain and valley land, most of which had probably been public land of the city of Carthage, or private estates of Carthaginian grandees, while the rest consisted of hill and scrub land fit for pasture or scanty crop. The latter was probably assigned *iure precario* to the indigenous people to be cultivated against the payment of a *stipendium,* while the rest was held for sale or lease. As, however, the interest of the Roman colonist and investor in the third quarter of the second century B. C. was still centered in Italy and in Cisalpine Gaul, it is probable that the treasury realized little from this source and that the land lay for the most part semi-fallow and idle. Rome had not entered

Africa for purposes of commercial and agricultural expansion but to rid herself of a political rival. She gave the lion's share of the spoils to others and turned her attention elsewhere until Gracchus reminded her of the advantages of Africa for investment. She had no thought of Romanizing or of exploiting the country.

The founding of Colonia Junonia [28] by Gaius Gracchus was, as Rostovtzeff says,[29] the beginning of a new era for Africa. A certain amount of Italic settlement resulted, how much we do not know but sufficient to have a permanent effect, and the possibilities of the country were brought to the notice of Roman investors. By the Lex Rubria permission was given to plant a colony on the territory of Carthage of approximately 6000 persons.[30] To these colonists allotments of 200 *jugera* or 125 acres each were made.[31] Later the senatorial party cancelled the charter of the colony [32] but assured the colonists who had already received their allotments the possession of their land in Quiritary right.[33]

The Gracchan legislation aimed quite definitely at an agricultural development, even in its colonial

[28] The chief ancient sources regarding Colonia Junonia are: Plutarch, *C. Gracchus*, 8-11; App., *Pun.*, 135-6; *Bell. Civ.*, 1, 24; *Lex Agr.* of 111 B. C.; Livy, *Epit.*, 60; Vell. Pat., II, 7.

[29] *Social and Economic History*, p. 278.

[30] App. *Pun.* 136 says that there were 6000 settlers but *Bell. Civ.* I, 24 says that 6000 was in excess of the number allowed by the Lex Rubria.

[31] *Lex Agr.*, §§59-61.

[32] *Lex Agr.*, §§59-61: *ex Lege Rubria quae fuit;* App., *Bell. Civ.*, I, 27.

[33] *Lex Agr.*, §§59-61.

foundations.[34] As in Italy Colonia Neptunia was founded to provide a port for the new settlements in Apulia, so in Africa Colonia Junonia was to provide a better port than Utica for the settlement in the hinterland which was the real object of the foundation. The character of the settlement provides more definite proof. Gracchus chose his colonists not from the city rabble but from all over Italy.[35] They were reasonably well to do,[36] probably experienced agriculturalists. They were given allotments of land sufficiently large to be attractive to such people and to allow a certain amount of tenant farming. The survey for the colony covered all the public land available within the limits of the province.[37] Traces of the Gracchan survey have been found in many of the plain and valley areas of the province: in the Carthaginian peninsula, in the plain west of Tunis beyond Djebel Sidi Salah toward Medjez-el-Bab and the fossa regia, in the plains of Goubellat, Mornag, Soliman, Grombalia and Menzel Bou Zalfa. Traces thought to belong to the same system appear near Neapolis, while sure remains are found 60 km.

[34] For discussions of the purpose of the Gracchan foundations, see Rostovtzeff, *op. cit.*, p. 278, and chap. VII, notes 54 and 55; Hardy, *Six Roman Laws*, p. 73; Abbott, *Class. Phil.*, 1915, p. 368 ff.; Heitland, *J. R. S.*, 1918, p. 34 ff.

[35] App., *Bell. Civ.*, I, 24.

[36] Plut., *C. Gracchus*, 9.

[37] The survey within the limits of the original Roman province has been discussed by Schulten, L'Arpentage romaine dans la Tunisie, *Bull. du com.*, 1902, p. 129 ff.; more recently and successfully in connection with a discussion of the Augustan survey by Barthel, *Bonn. Jahrb.*, 1911, p. 39 ff.; see also Schulten, *Arch. Anz.*, 1912, p. 395.

southwest of Neapolis, proving the extension of the survey across the Cape Bon peninsula.[38] It is noteworthy that no traces of this survey are found within the probable territories of the seven free cities or among the hill areas of the regions surveyed. It is probable, therefore, that the survey, though carried through on a consistent plan was applied only to the valley and plain land which was marked for settlement.[39] On the Gracchan scheme there was room for approximately 7500 to 8000 allotments, all of which Gracchus probably intended to fill.[40] The liquidation of the Gracchan program through the subsequent agrarian legislation modified the process of Roman penetration and settlement but Roman interests, financial and commercial, made themselves increasingly felt.[41]

The significance for us of the Lex Agraria of 111 B. C. lies in the information it gives regarding the diverse modes of exploitation of the land, and the general attitude of the Roman government, and in

[38] On these traces see Barthel, *op. cit.*, p. 52 ff., and discussion, p. 76 ff.

[39] This survey would be the basis of all later assignations and leases within these areas. The settlement of the boundary between Thabbora (*At. arch. Tun.*, Teboursouk, 243), and Thimisua (*id.*, Jama, 95), between the time of Vespasian and the second century A. D. by a centurion of the *Coh. XIII Urb.*, Cagnat, *op. cit.*, p. 211 ff., indicates the survey had not been carried into the indigenous stipendiary areas. Note *C.*, 23910.

[40] *Lex Agr.*, §61: *coloniam coloniasve deduci.*

[41] It is suggested that the people of the vicinity who according to Appian's account were added to the Caesarian colony of Carthage were the descendants of the Gracchan colonists, *Pun.*, 136; Gsell, *Rev. hist.*, nov., 1927.

the hints we receive as to the probable effect of the Gracchan and subsequent legislation upon the development of the province. It is an incomplete picture. For the town life and for the commercial penetration of Africa and of Numidia we must secure our data elsewhere. Further, within the law itself, little indication is given of the number of people or of the amount of land affected under each of the different categories mentioned.[42]

The law had two definite purposes: to define, settle, or confirm the land titles which the previous agrarian legislation had rendered uncertain, and to put the land in use for the benefit of the treasury. Several categories of land have already been mentioned but greater clarity may be secured by a recapitulation at this point. The Gracchan colonists were individually guaranteed their allotments in full possession under Quiritary right. The free cities were granted their original territories, and the deserters given land in private possession under peregrine right; all else became public land of the Roman people. Of this the less valuable portion was given and assigned to the former native communities *iure precario*, against the payment of a set

[42] For texts of the Lex Agraria of 111 B. C., see Mommsen, *C. I. L.*, I, 200; Girard, *Textes*,[5] p. 46 ff.; Bruns, *Fontes*,[7] p. 82 ff. Mommsen's introduction and commentary, see above and *Gesamm. Schr.*, I, p. 65 ff., is still the basic study. See also Hardy, *Six Roman Laws*, pp. 35-85, for a useful translation and commentary. On the significance of the law, see also Rostovtzeff, *Gesch. des röm. Kol.*, p. 314 ff.; Barthel, *Bonn. Jahrb.*, 1911, p. 76 ff.

stipendium.[43] Although this class of land was legally subject to resumption of title, it probably never was disturbed.[44] In 75 B. C. a recognition of the moral obligation of the ancient agreement prevented the Roman officials from occupying the lands given under similar right in *usufruct* to the heirs of Masinissa.[45] The additional land assigned to Utica belonged in the same category.[46] With the exceptions of the site of Carthage[47] which was accursed and of the roads and *limites* which remained public,[48] all the rest of the land fell into two classes: first, land which was sold to investors, of which full possession was given, which was heritable, but subject as was usual in all provincial land to a *vectigal;*[49] second, whatever was left could be leased by the censors to the highest bidders whether Roman, Latin, or pere-

[43] App., *Pun.*, 135; Cic., *In Verr.*, II, 3, 12.

[44] Lex Agr., §§77 and 78 provide for compensation if any of the land previously assigned to the stipendiary people should be assigned to others by mistake.

[45] Cic., *De Lege Agr.*, II, 58.

[46] *Lex Agr.*, §81.

[47] *Lex Agr.*, §81.

[48] *Lex Agr.*, §89.

[49] *Lex Agr.*, §45 ff. This was an important class of land, but was not necessarily given prominence in the text of the law because it was the largest class, as Rostovtzeff thinks, *Gesch. Kol.*, pp. 315-6—for many allotments of good plain land had doubtless been made to Gracchan colonists—but because it was the best class of land available for equestrian and senatorial investors and because the treasury wished to sell.

grine.[50] Title to such land could be resumed at any time for any reason; it was non-salable and non-heritable. It is evident then that the Lex Agraria limited definitely the various classes of land in Africa, and confirmed loyally the legal and moral obligations of previous arrangements; it is clear also that the policy of the Roman treasury favored selling what land could be sold to private investors and leasing the rest on the best terms possible.

The chief result of the conditions legalized and established in the Lex Agraria was the rise of landed estates. The Gracchan colonists with allotments of 125 acres each practically began as landlords. As a single colonist with ancient implements could hardly cultivate more than 15 acres himself it is probable that these colonists re-rented all or portions of their allotments to indigenous tenants. Moreover since their land granted in Quiritary right was free from tribute and salable it was especially attractive to the moneyed investors who now became interested in African land. Probably, therefore, in the process of purchase and re-sale, larger and larger holdings were built up, while a portion of the original colonists moved off to urban centers such as Utica. The *ager privatus vectigalisque* since it included some of

[50] The land let *censoria locatio* does not seem to represent as Mommsen and Hardy suggest, the land of the four destroyed cities (note 3), but the residue from the other classes of land; see Rostovtzeff, *Gesch. Kol.*, p. 317 ff. No mention of these cities is made in the text of the law §§83-96.

the best soil in the province was also attractive to investors and was the basis of large holdings from the start. The final class however, the land which remained to be let by the censors to all comers was less desirable as the reference to grazing land shows.[51] While the possessor was assured in practice of protection against undue liabilities,[52] and of reasonably stable conditions of tenure and of payment, the possession of this land could be resumed by the state at any time. During the period from 111 B. C. to 75 B. C. it was probably resumed and sold to meet the demands of investors. For by the latter date pressure for land made provincial officials desirous of reclaiming the territory given in usufruct to the heirs of Masinissa,[53] and in 62 B. C. the abandoned site of Carthage was all the unoccupied ground there was left in Africa for distribution.[54]

Regarding the details of the Roman organization of the indigenous people we are almost without information. The numerous Libyphoenician villages some of which may possibly have had municipal institutions under Carthage [55] seem to have had no legal

[51] *Lex Agr.*, §§83 and 86.

[52] *Lex Agr.*, §85, which protected the lessee against a raise of rent, and §92, which removed the liability for payment of rent upon any of his land which might be sold. There is no suggestion of compensating such an one with other land.

[53] Cic., *De Lege Agr.*, II, 58: *per C. Cottam consulem cautum esse foedere.*

[54] Cic., *De Lege Agr.*, I, 5; II, 51.

[55] Gsell, *Hist. anc.*, II, p. 292, n. 2; pp. 301-2.

recognition under the Roman republic.[56] The mention of the pagi *Muxsi, Gususi,* and *Zeugei* in an inscription of Utica,[57] dedicated to the quaestor of 57 B. C., Numerius Rufus, have inclined some to the belief that these Libyphoenician villages lived on as paganal organizations recognized in law.[58] The mention of the tax per capita of 146 B. C.[59] and the phrase *hominibus stipendiariis* of the Lex Agraria[60] oppose this view. The survey of the province probably did not mark the particular allotment for the individual native.[61] The Roman officials therefore despite the terms of the law doubtless found it necessary to deal with the indigenous people in their natural territorial units, the hill castella, each with its surrounding attached territory.[62] The term pagus in Africa under the republic must refer to these natural units of the Libyphoenician people[63] which through usage possessed administrative validity.

56 The suffetes of the town of Tinismut may date before the fall of Carthage; Merlin, Le sanctuaire de Baal et Tanit près de Siagu, in *Notes et documents,* IV, 1910, pp. 22-3. Note also the Punic commune under suffetes at Hr. Avin, *C.,* 24030 (cf. ch. II, n. 138, and text) which probably dates from 91 B. C.: Gsell, *op. cit.,* VI, p. 115.

57 *I. L. A.,* 422. The sites of these pagi are unknown. The Zeugei may be near Carthage, see Merlin, *C. R. Ac.,* 1913, p. 107, n. 3, but the name has some similarity to Zaghouan, and mons Ziquensis; the district was already termed Zeugitana in the chorographies by the time of Augustus: Pliny, *H. N.,* V, 23.

58 Merlin, *C. R. Ac.,* 1913, p. 108, n. 1.

59 App., *Pun.,* 135.

60 *Lex Agr.,* §§76, 77, and 80.

61 See above, note 39.

62 See ch. II, n. 96 ff., and text; ch. VI, n. 2 ff., and text.

63 See ch. VI, n. 56 ff., and text.

Such also was the pagus of Gurza [64] where in 12 B. C. three civitates stipendiariae connected in one paganal association thus marked themselves off from the civitates liberae which became numerous under Augustus.

How far Rome in the organization of her territory and in her system of exploitation was a direct inheritor of the Carthaginian system is a debatable question. Under the Carthaginian system we can distinguish three modes of exploitation.[65] Near Carthage were rich men's estates with gardens and villas, which were probably worked for the most part by slave labor, since the owner dwelling in Carthage could spend considerable time there to oversee. Farther off were large estates or territorial units where Libyan tenants paid rent or a tribute in kind and lived in semi-independent villages. This form of exploitation was developed most intensely in the period between the second and the third Punic

[64] *C.*, 68.

[65] For an account of Carthaginian agriculture, see Gsell, *Hist. anc.*, IV, pp. 1-75. The Roman interest in the agricultural treatises of the Carthaginian Mago does not seem to have been applied immediately to African soil. Translations were made and later Roman writers such as Varro and Columella selected what they wished from Mago's 28 books. The forty or so quotations which have come down to us indicate that he dealt with almost every branch of agriculture. The fact, mentioned by Columella, I, 1, 6, that Mago's precepts were not always successful when applied practically in Italy shows that his treatise was based primarily on African conditions. How far it was intended as a manual for capitalistic farmers we cannot decide since the Roman writers who used him selected passages from him primarily with the capitalistic system in view.

wars when Carthage was driven to make the best possible use of limited resources, but had always been characteristic. Her arrangements regarding grazing lands and with the people of the more mountainous regions are unknown. Rome however seems at first to have set herself to destroy Carthage and everything Carthaginian, and had removed into slavery or had driven away the major portion of the population. The native communes were legally non-existent. For a while the land lay fallow. When development came in Africa the land upon which Carthage had built up a prosperous agriculture in cereals, grapes, olives, fruit and cattle was turned almost exclusively to the production of cereals for the Roman market [66] while the territories of the free cities, productive throughout, doubtless followed the same economic trend. In the course of time the natural conditions under which Carthage had built up her system tended to impose parallel developments upon the Roman exploiters and their indigenous laborers and tenants. It must also be remembered that the market which Rome provided for African products was a stimulus to production such as Carthage can hardly ever have supplied and that the demand of the Roman market was primarily for cereals and secondarily and later for oil.[67] In view of the

[66] See Cagnat, L'Annone d'Afrique, *Mém. Acad. Inscr.*, 1916, pp. 247-77.

[67] Plut., *Caes.*, 55, Caesar's boast re African grain and oil; *Bell. Afr.*, 97, 3, the oil exacted from Leptis Magna; cf. Juv., *Sat.*, V, 90-91; Gsell, *Riv. della Tripolitania*, 1924-5, p. 41 ff., on the oil from Leptis.

continuance of these demands we must attribute the tendency apparent in the empire to a cultivation of fruits and olives in the Bagradas valley to a deterioration of the soil, resultant upon a continuous cultivation of cereals and a lack of soiling crops. At the moment the presence of the market, and the availability of so much public land merely stimulated the investor while the natural exigencies of distance and of marketing helped to determine the form of the exploitation. In the region immediately west and southwest of Tunis as far as Sicilibba no important Roman sites have been found. Here grew up probably the slave-worked estates of rich landlords who could live first in Utica, later in Carthage and come out to their villas, and whose merchandizing could be done in the capital; while farther off grew up the tenant-worked estates of the middle Bagradas region. To one who has seen estates such as that of Bir Kassa, or the villas of Mohammedia today, the situation seems not without its modern counterpart.

From the point of view of Africa the Jugurthine war is important because it resulted in another advancement of the Roman occupation and established, though slightly, a Roman contact with the hitherto untouched hinterland. The genius of Masinissa had established a measure of real authority over the shifting and fickle Numidian tribesmen and their shadowy chieftains from the Tripolitanian coast to the Mulucha river.[68] Under Punic influence he had developed at Cirta a measure of civilized life supported by the fertile agricultural land near the town and by its contact with the sea at the ports of Rusicade and of Chullu.[69] Within the kingdom were other prosperous cities such as Sicca [70] and Vaga [71] and royal dwelling places, either of the Numidian king or of his vassal princes, such as Zama Regia,[72] Bulla Regia,[73] or Capsa.[74] Most of these cities were in territory once occupied and developed by Carthage.[75] Cities like Cirta,[76] Vaga,[77] and probably other towns such as Sicca gave opportunity for the residence and

[68] On the political and social development of the indigenous people, see Gsell, *Hist. anc.*, V and VI, especially V, pp. 27-81, 121-167, and 232-82. The vicissitudes in the careers both of Masinissa and of Jugurtha show how shadowy their sovereignty really was, and how dependent upon continued personal popularity and success. We may note the numerous royal capitals, probably originally tribal centers, such as Cirta, Zama Regia, Bulla Regia, and Capsa, the frequent repartitions of territory within the royal house, such as among the heirs of Masinissa and those of Micipsa, the insurgence of royal claimants such Iarbas and Arabio, the presence of vassal princes such as the Masinissa who held the territory of Cirta under Juba I or the Mastanesosus whom Cicero mentions (*In Vat.*, 5, 12), and the disorganized conditions among the tribes themselves, the Numidae, Nattabutes, Musulamii, and Cinithii as we find them in Roman times as evidence of the weakness and disunion of Numidia.

[69] Gsell, *op. cit.*, III, p. 304 ff., discusses Masinissa's policy.

[70] Sallust, *Jug.*, 56, 4.

[71] *Id.*, 29, 4; 47, 1.

[72] *Id.*, 56, 1; *Bell. Afr.*, 91; 92; 97.

[73] Orosius, V, 21, 14.

[74] Sallust, *Jug.*, 89; 91; 92.

[75] See Gsell, *op. cit.*, II, pp. 93-111; Sallust, *Jug.*, 16, 5: the eastern portion of Numidia had a greater urban development.

[76] Sallust, *Jug.*, 21 (togatorum!); 26.

[77] *Id.*, 47.

activity of *Italici* who came up from the port of Utica to Vaga and inland from Rusicade to Cirta. These were probably not Roman citizens but for the most part merchants and money-lenders from southern Italy,[78] attracted by the commercial advantages of the newly developing portions of Numidia.

The marches of Metellus and of Marius over waterless regions infested with snakes and scorpions to Thala [79] and to Capsa [80] were purely for strategic reasons but echoes of Marius' entry into Gaetulia were still to be heard in 46 B. C.[81] The most important result of the war was the annexation of the

[78] Especially before the extension of the Roman franchise in 89 B. C. See Parvan, *Die Nationalität der römischen Kaufleute.* Few Romans were engaged in foreign mercantile pursuits at this time: Frank, *Amer. Hist. Rev.*, 1912-3, p. 233 ff.; Hatzfeld, *Les trafiquants italiens dans l'Orient hellénistique.* The proportion of Roman citizens active in Numidia and in Africa was probably higher than in Delos since business opportunities dealt more purely with land and with the royal (*Bell. Afr.*, 97) and provincial revenues. There was an association of Italians in Carthage before the third Punic war, App., *Pun.*, 92, probably commercial and south Italian Greek. Greek influences had considerable strength at Carthage: Gsell, *op. cit.*, VI, pp. 117-8; IV, pp. 192-3.

[79] Sallust, *Jug.*, 75.

[80] *Id.*, 89-91. Capsa was a strategic site, the only important stopping-place on the road from southern Algeria to the region of the Syrtes. Its capture and destruction was a move to cut off half of Jugurtha's hinterland.

[81] *Bell. Afr.*, 32, 3; 35, 4; 56, 4: *eiusque beneficio agris finibusque donati, post Sullae victoriam sub Hiempsalis regis erant dati potestatem.* What lands are referred to is unknown: see Frank, *A. J. P.*, 1926, p. 170; Gsell, *op. cit.*, V, p. 266, n. 2. Whether free or nominally subject to the authority of the Numidian kings, there was no real difference in the condition or loyalty of the Gaetulians.

region of the middle Bagradas and the settlement there of veterans on lots of 100 *iugera* each probably assigned *viritim, iure Quiritium,* as to the colonists of the original province.[82] The new provincial boundary probably ran from Thabraca southward passing east of Bulla Regia, crossed the Bagradas east of Souk el Arba and skirted the edge of the territory of Sicca along the Oued Tessaa. It turned east along the slopes south of the Oued Arkou to join the previous frontier.[83]

The direct evidence for the Marian colonization consists of a passage of Aurelius Victor [84] and of the appearance in the third century A. D. of the cognomen Mariana in the official titles of Thibaris [85] and of Uchi Maius.[86] Subsidiary arguments have been found in the early appearance of *pagi* of Ro-

[82] Aur. Vict., *De Vir. Illust.,* 73; Cic., *Pro Balbo,* 48; App., *Bell. Civ.,* I, 29. Colonies as such were not led out under the Appuleian law which was abrogated, Cic., *De Leg.,* 2, 14.

[83] Since the insurgent Numidian prince Iarbas was slain at his capital, Bulla Regia, by Pompey in 80 B. C., the town was then outside of the Roman province, Orosius, V, 21, 14. So also was Zama Regia to the south, *Bell. Afr.,* 91. On the site of this town, see Gsell, *op. cit.,* III, pp. 255-8. On the other hand the estate of Cicero's friend, Lamia, Cic., *Ad Fam.,* XII, 29, appears to have been within the jurisdiction of Cornificius who was governor of Africa Vetus in 43 B. C. If, as is probable, this estate is to be identified with the Saltus Lamianus of the dominial inscriptions, *C.,* 25943, III, l. 7; 26416, II, l. 4, it indicates that this area was annexed to the Roman province previous to 46 B. C. Cf. note 114 below.

[84] *De Vir. Illust.,* 73.

[85] *C.,* 26181.

[86] *C.,* 15450, 15454, 15455, 26270, 26275, 26281.

man citizens in this area beside civitates [87] of Punic and of Libyan speech, organization, and worships; [88] in the fact that all of these pagi and civitates when developed into Roman municipalities belonged to the same tribe, the Arniensis, which is also the tribe of Carthage,[89] and that in their worships [90] and in the selection of patrons [91] and of magistri [92] a close con-

[87] Thignica, *C.*, 15212 = 1419; Numluli, *C.*, 26121, 26125; Avensensis, *C.*, 26157; Thibaris, *C.*, 26176 (civi?] tas), 26179; Thugga, *C.*, 26517; *I. L. A.*, 558; *C.*, 26615, 26597, and passim; see *C.*, p. 2615; Agbia, *C.*, 1548; Uchi Maius and the Civitas Bencennensis ?, *C.*, 15447.

[88] Some of the civitates, e. g., Thugga, were towns of some importance under the Carthaginian régime, Gsell, *op. cit.*, II, pp. 95, 110, and 301. The Punic deities were generally worshipped, Caelestis and Saturn at Thugga, see Carton, *Dougga,* pp. 51 and 92 ff., and the Cereres at Vaga, Carcopino, *Rev. hist.*, mai-juin, 1928. The suffetes of the bilingual inscription of Thugga do not seem to be the ordinary Punic municipal officials, Gsell, *op. cit.*, V, pp. 133-4, but in the first century A. D. the regular Punic form appeared, *C.*, 26517. The indigenous influences also continued, Carton, *op. cit.*, p. 108 ff.; Gsell, *op. cit.*, V, p. 264 ff.; VI, p. 251 ff. Other Libyan inscriptions were found at Thugga and throughout the region, Carton, *Découvertes en Tunisie,* p. 320 ff.; Chabot, *Jour. asiat.*, 1921, I, pp. 81-2. Other towns of the region, such as Thimida Bure, Thigibba Bure, Thubursicum Bure, seem to have been tribal villages of the Burenses; *cf.* C., 15335, where Buresis is probably an ethnicon.

[89] See ch. II, n. 78.

[90] *C.*, 26239, at Uchi Maius, a dedication to Karthagini Aug.

[91] Thibaris, *C.*, 26185; Uchi Maius, *C.*, 26276; Thugga, *C.*, 26609 = 1494, 26475 (42 A. D.), 26470, 15520, 26517, 26615, 26624; *I. L. A.*, 520 (42 A. D.), 558; Agbia, *C.*, 1548, 27420.

[92] Thibaris, *C.*, 26185; Uchi Maius, *C.*, 26250, 26252. Magistri of these pagi are surprisingly rare. Many individuals native to these pagi held municipal offices and priesthoods at Carthage: Thignica, *C.*, 1413d = 15205; Numluli, *C.*, 26121; Uchi Maius, *C.*, 26276; Thugga, *C.*, 26484, 26482, 26604, 26605, 26606, 26607, 26609, 26610; Agbia, *C.*, 1548, 27420. The payment at Uchi Maius of the summa honoraria for the priesthood of the Cereres at Carthage also indicates a very close relation, *C.*, 26255. See ch. II, n. 85 ff. and text, and ch. VI, n. 282 and text.

nection with Carthage is evident during the first and second centuries A. D. Since the incident which produced these results must be of early occurrence, and since Julius Caesar and Augustus [93] have left no trace of a regular survey and settlement here we are forced to accept the theory of a Marian colonization.

This area had been brought under cultivation by the Carthaginians [94] and had been seized and further developed by Masinissa,[95] but had been greatly disturbed and partially depopulated by the passage of combatants during the war with Jugurtha.[96] As Masinissa had probably assumed ownership of the land which had previously been the property of Carthaginian landlords or had been public land of Carthage, it is likely that much of the area was royal domain in the time of Jugurtha.[97] Upon the annexation of the territory it thus quite naturally became public land of Rome and available for colonization or sale. We may assume that the best land in the region was given to the Marian veterans—precisely where the pagi of Roman citizens are known for later times—in the valley of the Khalled between Dj. Gorra and Dj. ech Cheid, along the Oued Arkou and the Oued Tessaa about the southern and western

[93] Uchi Maius and Vaga are listed among the Augustan oppida civium Romanorum, Pliny, *H. N.*, V, 29; see ch. II, nn. 207, 209, and text.

[94] Gsell, *op. cit.*, II, p. 102; IV, p. 10 ff.

[95] Gsell, *op. cit.*, III, p. 313 ff.

[96] Sallust, *Jug.*, 46 ff.; 54, 6; 69, 2-4.

[97] Gsell, *op. cit.*, V, p. 191; pp. 209-10.

slopes of Dj. Gorra and around to the north in the plain between Dj. Gorra and the Bagradas river toward Souk el Arba and Souk el Khmis.[98] Whether the Marian settlement extended into less favored portions of the area or not here it took root and flourished; while the native communities which were left on the slopes about Djebel Gorra probably supplied the laborers and the tenants necessary to cultivate the large allotments of 100 *iugera*. For purposes of administration both the organizations of the settlers, and those of the natives were probably termed *pagi;*[99] the former as the natural cantonal organization of Romans who thus selecting as a corporate entity a patron attached themselves to the governmental officials in Utica, the latter as quasi-organizations of stipendiary people. With the gift of local autonomy during or shortly after the time of Augustus the native *pagi* with few exceptions became *civitates*, or free towns,[100] the local organization of which they may have kept, though unofficially, all along from Punic times, while the Roman *pagi* which had no object in changing remained as they were.

The remaining portions of this area whether in large part assigned to Marian settlers or not seem

98 See the *At. arch. Tun.*, folios Zaouiet Medienn, Béja, Souk el Khmis, Oued Zerga, Souk el Arba, Teboursouk.

99 On the analogy of the pagi of the province of 146 B. C. Town organizations were not recognized until the time of Augustus. Could the Pagus Assalitanus, *I. L. A.*, 501; *At. arch. Tun.*, Teboursouk, 218, have been too unimportant to assume the title of civitas later on?

100 See ch. II, n. 212 ff., and text.

to have had a quite different history.[101] For these developed into the region of the great imperial estates. North of the Bagradas river the level land by the river broadens to westward from the Oued Zerga to Souk-el-Khmis and is quite fertile; to northward and also included in the Burunitan saltus rises a country quite hilly, rough, and forbidding for agricultural purposes except in an occasional valley and in the fertile area about Vaga.[102] Southward about Djebel Zeldou, near Hr. Mettich, and Ain el Djemala is another hilly region varying in altitude from 500 to 1500 feet above sea-level which was the center of the saltus region. Although none of the double communities characteristic of the area of Marian colonization occur north of the Bagradas river or in the district about Djebel Zeldou the mention of *coloni* who were Roman citizens[103] in the saltus inscriptions proves that portions at least of this land were originally assigned,[104] while the mention of *subseciva*[105] proves that portions were left unassigned either to Romans or to natives. The valleys, lower slopes, and upper plateaus are quite arable, and as the area had but recently been put under cultivation and the effects

[101] On the peculiar history of this region, see Frank, *A. J. P.*, 1926, pp. 55-73.

[102] Vaga, destroyed in the war with Jugurtha, Sallust, *Jug.*, 69; cf. Strabo, XVII, 3, 12.

[103] *C.*, 10570, I, l. 14.

[104] Note the phrase, *centuriis elocatis*, *C.*, 25943, II, ll. 9-10; 26416, II, ll. 1-2; cf. Frank, *A. J. P.*, 1926, pp. 61-2.

[105] *C.*, 25902, I, ll. 7-8.

of erosion were not yet apparent, the region seemed in all probability much more inviting to soldiers who had toiled on Sabine or Ligurian hillsides than it seems to us today. The indigenous character which Sustri retained[106] was probably due to its situation in the roughest part. Since the *subseciva* had not been occupied until the Lex Manciana permitted occupation we can hardly estimate how far the estates grew up from the purchase or lease of land which had been unassigned to natives or colonists. They probably arose largely from the purchase of the land assigned to colonists who failed and sold, and either moved away or remained as tenants where previously they had been owners; while many doubtless had suffered death or loss when Pompey vanquished the Marians in 80 B. C.[107] The evidence for the presence of imperial estates, however, comes chiefly from the more broken and hilly sections of the area.[108] But as evidence of such estates has also been found in the valley of the Khalled east of Thubursicum Bure[109] and well to the southeast on the slopes

[106] Carton, *Découv. en Tunisie*, p. 320, a Libyan inscription.

[107] See n. 116 below.

[108] For the sites involved see *At. arch. Tun.*, Oued Zerga, 118 (Henchir Mettich); 104 (Sustri); Souk el Khmis (Burunitan saltus); Teboursouk, 37 (Ain el Djemala); 112 (Ain el Wassel). The areas included in the estates probably extended considerably farther than this would indicate since inscriptional evidence is less likely to survive in the more cultivable regions. Allowance must also be made for the territories of the communities in the region. Thugga in particular had a very considerable territory, *C.*, 25988; *At. arch. Tun.*, Teboursouk, 215.

[109] *I. L. A.*, 503.

of Djebel ech Cheid [110] it is probable there were other imperial estates in the more prosperous region about Thugga, where the *conductores* had an association,[111] but the evidence for them has disappeared. It is notable, however, that the private estates which remained in this area belong to families which made Africa their home.[112] The process of absorption began soon after the colonization. For one estate, the Saltus Lamianus,[113] was probably in the hands of the Lamia family, the ancestors of Horace's friend, by 62 B. C.[114] During the first century A. D. these estates came into the emperor's possession by confiscation.[115]

It was natural that Marian sympathizers should find a stronghold in Africa. Pompey's whirlwind campaign of forty days crushed the Marians and ended in the death at his capital, Bulla Regia, of their ally, the Numidian prince Iarbas.[116] A process

[110] *C.*, 25988.

[111] *I. L. A.*, 568; Carcopino, *Rev. ét. anc.*, 1922, p. 13 ff.

[112] Pullaieni, *At. arch. Tun.*, Souk el Arba, 64; *C.*, 26615, 26267, 26415, 26419 and numerous epitaphs in the region of indigenous people who probably drew their names from service in the family; Volusiani, *At. arch. Tun.*, Teboursouk, 68; *C.*, 25990.

[113] *C.*, 25943, II, 12; III, 7; 26416, II, 4; III, 5.

[114] See note 54 above; also n. 83. Cic., *Ad Fam.*, XII, 29. Lamia had procuratores, liberti, and a familia. On the names of the various imperial estates, see Carcopino, *Mél. éc.*, 1906, p. 433 ff. The family of Caelius Rufus had estates in Africa previous to 63 B. C., Cic., *Pro Cael.*, 73; of a Julius Calidus also, Nepos, *Atticus*, 12, 4; see Alois Früchtl, *Die Geldgeschäfte bei Cicero.*

[115] Pliny, *H. N.*, XVIII, 35.

[116] Plutarch, *Pompey*, 8-12; Orosius, V, 21. Certain bodies of Gaetulians who had been given lands by Marius were placed once

of confiscations from the land of the Gracchans and Marians who had opposed him or who had been killed may have hastened considerably the accumulation into large estates, while a diminution in the numbers and the importance of the progeny of these early colonists may help to account for the strong Pompeian leaning of the province in 46 B. C. Otherwise the general organization remained unchanged and the natural economic tendencies continued. During the next thirty years the rich exports of African grain made her wealth and fertility famous.[117] The activity of the *conventus* of Roman citizens, mostly *negotiatores* and of the commercial people, Roman and Italian, within the province, and in the kingdom of Numidia, is characteristic of the period.

The *conventus civium Romanorum* found in Africa both in Republican and imperial times varied widely in the pursuits of their members. Associations of non-Roman Italic merchants had sprung up even previous to the Third Punic war;[118] and were active in the commercial penetration of Numidia as well as of the Proconsular province before the Jugurthine

more under the authority of the Numidian king, *Bell. Afr.*, 56, 4; cf. n. 81. Pompey rewarded with Roman citizenship certain citizens of Utica, Cic., *Pro Balbo,* 51, where the Marian propraetor, Hadrianus, had been burned, Livy, *Epit.*, 86; Cic., *In Verr.*, II, 1, 70; Val. Max., IX, 10, 2; Orosius, V, 20.

[117] See nn. 66 and 67 above.

[118] App., *Pun.*, 92; cf. n. 78.

war.[119] Such associations can hardly have included many Roman citizens among their numbers before 89 B. C. Roman citizens, knights, money-lenders and tax farmers came in increasing numbers especially to Utica where the business of the province centered most.[120] In 46 B. C. the *conventus* of Utica consisted *ex variis generibus,* and was composed of traders and money-lenders.[121] Some of its members were knights,[122] perhaps also some of the senatorial order who fled from Caesar were included. The *conventus* of Hadrumetum[123] and of Thapsus[124] were probably similar. From the time of Gaius Gracchus these Romans had come to the coast ports and settled there to carry on business. Being individually of a superior legal status to the people among whom they lived they naturally gathered

119 Sallust, *Jug.*, 47, 1 (Vaga); 26, 3; 21, 2 (Cirta). There was probably a larger proportion of Romans trafficking in Africa than elsewhere, since African business consisted mostly in investments in land, in the handling of the vectigalia, and of the exported produce. The revenues of the Numidian king probably also figured, *Bell. Afr.*, 97; cf. 43: *stipendiariis Gaetulis Numidisque.*

120 Sallust, *Jug.*, 64, 5-6.

121 Caesar, *Bell. Civ.*, II, 36; Plutarch, *Cato Min.*, 59, 2. The three hundred seem to have been Cato's selection from the larger body of the conventus, Plutarch, *l. c.;* App., *Bell. Civ.*, II, 397. Caesar, *Bell. Afr.*, 90, mentions the *Romanos negotiatores,* and those who among the three hundred had contributed to Varus and to Scipio, as if they were two separate bodies, while (*id.*, 88) the three hundred had made the war contribution. At any rate the fine was assessed on the three hundred and paid collectively, *id.*, 90, 4. The phrase, *id.*, 36, *negotiatoribus Italicis,* may indicate a distinction between Italic and Roman members of the various conventus.

122 *Bell. Afr.*, 68, 4.

123 *Bell. Afr.*, 97, 2.

124 *ib.*

together to form local associations probably of an unofficial character for the performance of cult and the protection of business interests.[125] With the granting of Roman rights and organization to provincial towns the reason for their existence disappeared, but they continued on among many of the native towns within the province during the empire, where their aggressive devotion to the imperial cults marks them as especially active centers of Roman influence.[126] Such organizations were a characteristic feature of the Republican exploitation of Africa.

The Bellum Africanum provides us with some further information regarding the development of the province by 46 B. C. Inland from the Sahel of

[125] On the general subject of the Conventus, see Kornemann, *De Civibus Romanis in Provinciis Consistentibus,* and his article Conventus in *Pauly-Wissowa.* His view has been corrected by Hatzfeld, *Les trafiquants italiens.* See also Parvan, *Die Nationalität der römischen Kaufleute;* Schmidt, *Die römischen Ritter von den Gracchen bis zum Tode Ciceros;* Früchtl, *Die Geldgeschäfte bei Cicero.*

[126] Thinissut, *I. L. A.,* 306; *Augusto deo | cives Romani | qui Thinissut | negotiantur;* Masculula, *C.,* 15775: *Divo Augusto | sacrum | conventus |· civium Romanor(um) | et Numidarum qui | Mascululae habitant:* Numidae are anomalously included; Tipasa of Numidia, *I. L. Al.,* 1985 (Hadrian): *cultores Larum et Imaginum Augusti;* Vicus Haterianus, *C.,* 23125 (Hadrian): *cives Romani qui vico Hateriano morantur.* The organization at Aubuzza in the territory of Sicca Veneria was probably a pagus of Roman citizens, *C.,* 16367: *Genio coloniae Juliae Veneriae Chirtae Novae . . . . cives Romani qui*] *Aubuzza consistunt paganicum pecunia sua a solo* [*resti*]*tuer*-[*unt*]; cf. at Sigus, *C.,* 5695: *cultores qui Sigus consistunt,* a dedication to Victoria Augusta. Note the free application of the verb *consisto* to other associations as in *I. L. Al.,* 3992: *conductores qui in regione Hipponiensi consistent* (sic).

Sousse there was no settled life. The raids of the Gaetulians came as far north as the latitude of Hadrumetum (Sousse) so that the villas within the Roman province had to be kept in a state of defence.[127] The mention of numerous towns and villas show that the early prosperity of the district had continued undisturbed.[128] In the region from Enfida southward to Thysdrus the general attempt to raise cereal crops is certain; the absence of the available man power, however, on military service had made a harvest impossible in 46 B. C.[129] The presence of 75,000 bushels of grain at Thysdrus is explained by the fact that this was a center of concentration for a considerable area.[130] The villas near Aggar had large quantities of barley, oil, wine, and figs, but, as we should expect, little wheat.[131] The olive must have been generally cultivated both here and southward. Leptis Magna was fined a yearly tribute of 3,000,000 pounds of oil.[132] In the northern part of the prov-

[127] *Bell. Afr.*, 67, 2; 65, 1.

[128] Aggar, *Bell. Afr.*, 67, 1; 76, 3; 79, 2. Zeta, 68, 1; 68, 4; 74, 1. Ruspina, 6, 6; 9, 1; et alibi. Thysdrus, 36, 2; 76, 2; 86, 5; 93, 1; 97, 4. Sarsura, 75, 3; 76, 1. Tegea, 78, 1. Thabena (Thaenae, Gsell, *Hist. anc.*, V, p. 247, n. 6), 77, 1 and 2. Vaga (Vagense aliud ?, Pliny, *H. N.*, V, 30), 74, 1. Usseta, 89, 1. Uzitta, 41, 1; 58, 3; et alibi. Parada, 87, 1, farther north is probably Feradi Maius, *At. arch. Tun.*, Enfida, 34; Poinssot, *C. R. Ac.*, 1927, p. 62; *Année epig.*, 1927, no. 26. Villas are mentioned *Bell. Afr.*, 67, 2; 65, 1; and passim.

[129] *Bell. Afr.*, 20, 4. The *aratores* in this passage are cultivators, in 36, 2, probably renters of land.

[130] *Bell. Afr.*, 36, 2: 300,000 modia of wheat.

[131] *Bell. Afr.*, 67, 2. Thysdrus was mulcted but a small amount of grain, *id.*, 97, 4.

[132] *Bell. Afr.*, 97, 2; Gsell, *Riv. della Trip.*, 1924-5, p. 41 ff.

ince we may assume that similar prosperous conditions arose during the previous thirty years of comparative peace, while the presence of villas on the road from Thapsus to Zama Regia [133] and of a large estate near the latter town owned by a Numidian named Gaius Julius Masinissa [134] indicates a similar development in the contiguous portions of Numidia. On the Cape Bon peninsula Clupea [135] and Neapolis [136] had risen from their ruins. The Bagradas and the Miliana valleys probably presented an appearance similar to the Sahel of Sousse with native villages near farms and villas, but due to the Gracchan and Marian settlements with an admixture of Italic folk. Here cereals were the main crop upon which the reputation of Africa was based.

The social strata may be defined with reasonable clearness. At the top the propraetor or proconsul as the case might be, and his staff were non-permanent residents. The Roman landowners, senatorial or equestrian, were sometimes permanent residents of the coast towns.[137] The money-lenders and the business men who handled the produce were partly of this class, partly below it. Their financial strength is shown by the huge fines they paid to

[133] *Bell. Afr.*, 91, 1.

[134] Vitruvius, VIII, 3, 24-5; Gsell, *Hist. anc.*, V, pp. 208, and 269, n. 6.

[135] *Bell. Afr.*, 2, 6; 3, 1.

[136] *Bell. Afr.*, 2, 6.

[137] It is evident that the three hundred of Utica were almost all regular residents, Plutarch, *Cato Min.*, 59, 2.

Caesar.[138] Whether the *negotiatores Italici* at Thysdrus [139] were different we cannot say. In the regions of the middle and lower Bagradas valley were the descendants of the original colonists mostly of Italic stock. Along with these and far outnumbering them were the stipendiary people still in their hill-top villages with paganal organizations or supplying tenants and laborers for the colonists and large landowners. Of these the majority were Punicized, but the Libyan substratum persistently maintained itself especially in the more mountainous and border regions of the province.[140]

In general Roman policy toward Africa may be described as one of exploitation; but with qualification, for it was not a systematic policy of state exploitation. Amid the turmoil of party strife which characterized the period after the Gracchi no consistent policy was possible. The colonization which the Gracchans and Marians had favored was displeasing to their senatorial opponents and the colonists who came were allowed no official recognition as municipal entities and were probably weakened in influence by the rise of landed estates and by the upheavals of the civil wars. A stipendium was exacted from the indigenous people not as grievous as the tribute of one-fourth which Carthage had demanded.[141]

[138] *Bell Afr.*, 90, 4; 97.
[139] *Bell. Afr.*, 36.
[140] Gsell, *Hist. anc.*, V, p. 261 ff.
[141] Polybius, I, 72, 2; Gsell, *Hist. anc.*, II, p. 303.

The course of development may be summed up as follows. After a period of neglect the Gracchan colonization drew the attention of Roman investors to the possibilities of the province. With the liquidation of the Gracchan legislation the senatorial victors while continuing to discharge their legal and moral obligations refused to develop the province directly by further settlement, but turned the exploitation of the province as far as possible over to members of their own and of the equestrian order. The result of this policy was the formation of the large estates, which were characteristic of the whole period of the Roman occupation, some owned by senatorial or equestrian landlords, some by colonists who had maintained themselves on their generous allotments. On these sprang up a population of tenants, practically all indigenous but including a few Roman citizens in their number. The soil, part of which was comparatively recently broken, part of which had lain fallow, produced abundantly and the foundations of a prosperous life were laid.

The life of the towns, on the other hand received no such stimulus. The chief town Carthage had been destroyed and was not permitted to revive. The seven free cities, especially Utica, now the chief city of the province, prospered considerably since they were necessarily the bases of export, collection, and distribution, and received an influx of Roman business men among their population. With the exception of these the indigenous towns and villages received no recognition as municipal units. The country however was well repopulated as the levies of 46 B. C. reveal [142] and in the towns and villages the indigenous forms of communal organization doubtless maintained their existence. Despite the selfish rule of the republic and the confusion of the civil wars, the sea-board, and the Bagradas and the Miliana valleys were already developing along characteristic lines. With the reestablishment of peace and the inception of a more liberal policy toward the indigenous people this portion of Africa came to an early bloom. It remained for the empire as the successor to the Numidian kings to develop the hinterland of Numidia.[143]

[142] *Bell. Afr.*, 19; 1, 4; 20, 2; 48, 1; App., *Bell. Civ.*, II, 401. Many were not Africans, but cf. *Bell. Afr.*, 20, 4; Cagnat, *Armée rom.*,[2] intro., pp. xiii-xiv.

[143] See Toutain, *Mél. Cagnat*, pp. 319-25.

CHAPTER II

The Times of Caesar and Augustus in Africa

After his victory Caesar annexed the adjacent portions of Juba's kingdom, organizing them as the province of Africa Nova.[1] The rest was divided into two portions, one, probably coterminous with the later Federation of Cirta, was given to Sittius;[2] the other west of the Ampsaga (El Kebir) river to the king of Mauretania.[3] With the annexation of Numidia Rome inherited the Numidian king's claim to suzerainty over the tribes to the south but for the present this claim was not effectively pressed. The practical boundary extended southwest from the previous one[4] to include the territory of Sicca

[1] *Bell. Afr.*, 97, 1: *ex regnoque provincia facta.* Cirta in Juba's kingdom, *Bell. Afr.*, 25, 3; *oppidum opulentissimum eius regni,* and under the control of Juba's vassal Masinissa, App., *Bell. Civ.*, IV, 252-3, was given to Sittius with its surrounding territory. Caesar's account is incomplete. In 50 B. C. Curio probably acting as Caesar's agent had as tribune proposed the annexation of Juba's kingdom. Caesar was perhaps even then looking for land on which to settle soldiers, *Bell. Civ.*, II, 25, 5.

[2] App., *Bell. Civ.*, IV, 233; see Gsell, *At. arch. Alg.*, f. 27, 126, and p. 10, col. 1. Conditions remained unsettled. Sittius was soon after slain by Arabio, the son of Masinissa, who joined the Caesarian governor of Africa Nova, Sextius, against Cornificius, the senatorial governor of Africa Vetus, who fell in the subsequent engagement. See App., *Bell. Civ.*, IV, 233 ff.; Cic., *Ad Att.*, XV, 17, 1; Dio Cass., XLVIII, 21; Pallu de Lessert, *Fastes des provinces africaines,* pp. 53-62.

[3] App., *Bell. Civ.*, IV, 233.

[4] See ch. I, n. 14.

Veneria, and passed westward near Madauros [5] along the edge of the territory of the Musulamii to Gadiaufala (Ksar Sbehi) where an ancient fort remains.[6] A number of forts signaled in the Itinerary of Antonine and the Tabula of Peutinger probably following a line southwest of Gadiaufala and south of Tigisi, and westward along the broken line of hills toward Ain Mlila seems to mark the early southern line of defence of the Cirtensian territory.[7] After arranging the financial affairs of the new province, Caesar set Sallust in charge and returned to Rome.[8]

The interpretation of the Caesarian and Augustan development in Africa depends almost entirely on data drawn from two sources: Pliny's description of Africa and Numidia in Book V of the Natural

[5] The boundary of the new province followed the nominal boundary between Numidia and Gaetulia; Madauros was *semi-numida, semi-gaetula,* Apul., *Apol.,* 24; note *Bell. Afr.,* 25, 3: Sittius and Bocchus, having captured Cirta, immediately attacked two Gaetulian towns, otherwise unknown, but probably not far distant.

[6] Gsell, *At. arch. Alg.,* f. 18, 159.

[7] Ad Centenarium, *Tab. Peut.,* between Gadiaufala and Tigisi, *At. arch. Alg.,* f. 17, 340. On the meaning of centenarium, see Gauckler, *Mél. Perrot,* pp. 125-31. Turris Caesaris, *Itin. Ant.,* ed. Parthey and Pinder, p. 14, 15 miles from Sigus. See Gsell, *At. arch. Alg.,* f. 18, 180; 17, 126, p. 11, col. 1; 335, route 5; 462; 513; Tissot, *Géog. comp.,* II, pp. 427 and 430. These forts became unnecessary when the Musulamii were pacified and southern Algeria was occupied by the legion. Cagnat, *Armée romaine,*[2] intro., p. xix, ascribes the well-known castella and pagi of Cirta to the Sittian system of defence. These were rather indigenous centers previously existent, see Gsell, *Hist. anc.,* V, p. 275.

[8] *Bell. Afr.,* 97 and 98; Dio Cass., XLIII, 9, 2; App., *Bell. Civ.,* II, 415.

History,[9] and on the evidence of the inscriptions. The inscriptional evidence shows that Pliny's account is incomplete, while at many other points the two traditions appear contradictory. Of nineteen undoubted or possible colonies with the cognomen of Julia, six Augustan colonies appear in Pliny in their proper category,[10] six appear under the uncertain title of oppida civium Romanorum; of these one, Utica, received favors both from Caesar and from Augustus,[11] one is conjectural,[12] one is clearly Augustan,[13] and three belong to the class either of Caesarian or Augustan foundations;[14] five are designated in Pliny as oppida libera; of which four are certainly coloniae Juliae,[15] and one is uncertain;[16] two appear in Pliny as oppida without designation.[17]

[9] Pliny's account draws on two main sources: a Periplus or Chorography with insertions from Polybius, Agrippa, the reports of the expedition in 19 B. C. under Balbus against the Garamantes, and from Callimachus; and a Formula Provinciae Africae giving in some form the legal status of various African towns. Both sources are of Augustan date, and appear, unlike the account of Mauretania, to have been uncorrected by later information. See Detlefsen, *Geographie Afrikas bei Plinius und Mela.*

[10] Carthage, Cirta, Maxula, Thuburbo, Uthina, Sicca Veneria.

[11] Caes., *Bell. Civ.*, II, 36; *Bell. Afr.*, 87, 2; Dio Cassius, XLIX, 16, 1.

[12] Tibidrumense ?, Col. J]ul. Thub. (Menzel el Gorchi), *C.*, 14452; *At. arch. Tun.*, Zaouiet Medienn, 123; cf. Ptolemy, IV, 3, 7, ed. Müller, p. 644.

[13] Simitthu.

[14] Thuburnica, Thabraca, Assuras.

[15] Curubis, Neapolis, Clupea, Thysdrus (cf. *C. I. L.*, VI, 3884, 5, 4; XII, 686; Pliny, *N. H.*, VII, 37).

[16] Hadrumetum, see *C.*, p. 2319 (C. I. H. on tiles); Cagnat, *Rev. epig.*, 1913, p. 4 ff.

[17] Hippo Diarrhytus and Carpis. There is no evidence that Thuraria was a Julian colony, cf. *C.*, 25372, and *Tab. Peut.*

Conversely, of Pliny's fifteen oppida civium Romanorum, four appear in the inscriptions as Caesarian or Augustan foundations,[18] one is doubtful,[19] one is an Augustan colony,[20] one is an Augustan municipium,[21] three remained civitates of natives until the second and third centuries A. D.,[22] one was a pagus of Roman citizens until the time of Alexander Severus,[23] four are unknown to epigraphy.[24] Of his thirty (?)[25] oppida libera, four belong to the old group of the seven civitates liberae et immunes, probably since their resistance to Caesar no longer immunes;[26] five are Julian colonies;[27] many are unknown to epigraphy; four are cited as native centers in the Bellum Africanum but without evidence as to their status,[28] three of these were near Thapsus, one, Zama, in Numidia; three more appear in inscriptions later as native civitates;[29] another, Materense, is known from the modern name Mateur. The mention of Tunis shows that it had revived;[30] Canopitanum was probably

[18] Thabraca, Assuras, Thuburnica, Thunusuda.

[19] Tibidrumense, n. 12.

[20] Simitthu.

[21] Utica.

[22] Tibiga (Thibica), Chiniava, Vaga.

[23] Uchi Maius.

[24] Abutucense, Aboriense, Canopicum, Uchi Minus.

[25] 26 towns are designated by Pliny as oppida libera, 4 as oppida; 6 more are mentioned by name only. In the Tripolitaine, only since 46 B. C. under the Roman power, 1 is termed a civitas, 4 oppida.

[26] Leptis, Acholla, Thapsus, Hadrumetum.

[27] Clupea, Curubis, Neapolis, Thysdrus, Hadrumetum (see n. 16).

[28] Aggar, Ruspina, Zama, Vaga (Vagense aliud).

[29] Avitta, Thisica, Thagaste.

[30] Cf. ch. I, n. 3.

near Thuburbo Maius.[31] Theudalis is listed as oppidum immune; Chullu and Rusicade of the four colonies of Cirta are mentioned merely as oppida; so also Carpis, Missua, and Hippo Diarrhytus; while six, Hippo Regius,[32] Thaenae, Aras, Macomades, Tacape, and Sabrata are left without designation.[33] Uzalis one of the former civitates liberae et immunes is termed oppidum Latinum and Castra Cornelia, oppidum stipendiarium. In the Tripolitaine,[34] Oea was a civitas, and Leptis Magna,[35] Neapolis,[36] Taphra,[37] and Habrotonum,[38] though termed oppida, were, since they were old Punic towns recently annexed, probably also autonomous at this time.

Two important attempts have been made to solve the discrepancies between the two traditions especially with regard to the Julian colonies, and thus to interpret the underlying principles of the Caesarian

[31] *I. L. A.*, 246.

[32] An Augustan municipium, *I. L. Al.*, 109.

[33] Thaenae, the Thabena of Bell. Afr., 77, 2, and other towns of Juba's kingdom annexed in 46 B. C. probably kept whatever previous organization they had. Thaenae had the right to coin money in the time of Augustus, Müller, *Num. de l'Afr.*, II, p. 40.

[34] At the time of Pliny's sources, the province of Cyrenaica seems to begin at the lesser Syrtis, *H. N.*, V, 25 and 38; cf. 28. Since Leptis Magna was the base of action against the Garamantes in the war with Tacfarinas, see Tac., *Ann.*, III, 74; ch. III, n. 19, and under the command of Blaesus, the region was probably by then incorporated in the African province.

[35] Leptis Magna, an ally of Rome since 111 B. C., Sall., *Jug.*, 77, had kept her own municipal constitution throughout.

[36] A Greek term for Leptis, inadvertently used by Pliny, Strabo, XVII, 3, 18.

[37] Taphra = Gaphara ? Periplus of Scylax, 110, p. 86.

[38] Sabrata, Strabo, XVII, 3, 18. On these three Punic sites, see Gsell, *Hist. anc.*, II, p. 121 ff.

and Augustan developments in Africa.[39] Kornemann's theory may be stated as follows: Caesar attributed a large area to his new foundation, Carthage, and many of the localities within this area shared with Carthage colonial rights. Augustus broke up this federation and revoked the rights given these communities by Caesar's liberal policy, but later during the first and second centuries A. D., when these communities, now independent, regained their rights, they remembered their former status under Caesar and added to their titles the cognomen Julia. These propositions all require qualification. Kornemann's theory rests in part on the assumption that the documents Pliny used were a full and complete account of the legal status of the various communities within the province. This need not be so, and besides, Pliny's known inexactitude elsewhere would make such an assumption unsafe. We must be chary of basing an argument on his omissions even with the discovery of an approximate principle of omission. It is unlikely, moreover, that Augustus would demote Julian colonies properly founded.

Barthel's interpretation is quite different. Pliny's document, an official formula of the province, contained an account only of towns with the legal status of which Augustus himself had something to do. As a result, Caesarian foundations remained unmen-

[39] Kornemann, *Philologus,* 1901, p. 402 ff.: Die caesarische Kolonie Karthago und die Einführung römischer Gemeindeordnung in Afrika; summarized in his article Colonia in *Pauly-Wissowa,* Bd. IV, 533-5; Barthel, *Zur Geschichte der römischen Städten in Afrika,* Greifswald, 1904; see also Toutain, *Les cités romaines dans la Tunisie,* p. 321 ff.

tioned.[40] Where oppida libera are mentioned in Pliny but the epigraphical evidence favors a Julian colony, there was on the same site a free town, given its autonomy by Augustus and administratively separate from the Julian colony.[41] The coinage,[42] certain late fasti,[43] and a passage of Tertullian[44] prove the existence of this condition in Carthage itself. Coins indicate it also for Hippo Diarrhytus.[45] Since the publication of Barthel's thesis proof of just such a

[40] Barthel concludes that the Augustan document which Pliny used, *H. N.*, III, 46, for Italy distinguished by naming their status Augustan foundations only from the fact that pre-Augustan foundations are not so distinguished. The names of later foundations were probably added out of Pliny's personal knowledge. The omission of the Caesarian Coloniae Juliae is therefore not an indication of their non-existence but of a similar condition in the Augustan document as referring to Africa, *op. cit.*, p. 33. One may add that possibly some of Pliny's sins of omission are due to the fact that having mentioned coast towns such as Hippo Diarrhytus from the Chorography without mention of their status, he did not repeat their names from the Formula. We may suppose also that the elevation of Hippo Regius to municipal and of Simitthu to colonial rank occurred within the time of Augustus but later than Pliny's sources.

[41] Barthel, *op. cit.*, pp. 20 and 32.

[42] Müller, *Num. de l'Afr.*, II, nos. 319 and 320.

[43] Mommsen, *Chronica Minora,* I, p. 217, Consularia Constantinopolitania (28 B. C.).

[44] *De Pallio,* 1. The union of the two Carthaginian communities previous to the preparation of the documents Pliny used precluded the mention of the free town in Pliny.

[45] Müller, *op. cit.*, II, p. 167 ff.; nos. 374, 375, 379. Dessau, *Klio,* 1908, p. 457 ff., has shown that the evidence for the existence of Hippo Libera until the time of Clodius Albinus is untrustworthy. Kubitschek, *Wien. Akad.*, 1916, Zur Gesch. von Städten d. rom. Kaiserr., p. 97 ff. says that there are no valid parallels for such forms of double community, and that the title "libera" refers to a past stage in the development of a town. Thuburbo Maius, see note 46, is a certain instance.

double community has come to light at Thuburbo Maius.[46] Barthel's theory as we shall see does not completely explain away our difficulties with Pliny's oppida civium Romanorum [47] but the assumption of the double community seems the least objectionable explanation of these Coloniae Juliae.

The Coloniae Juliae fall into three classes: those which are termed oppida or oppida libera in Pliny; those termed oppida civium Romanorum; the Augustan colonies. The first class was composed of Caesarian foundations.[48] A passage of Dio Cassius tells us that Caesar, before leaving Africa, "got rid of the older men among his soldiers for fear that they might mutiny again." [49] In the settlement of these men Caesar gave attention to the needs of defence, especially against such landings as he had made. For Pompeians were still at large. He scattered, therefore, detachments of veterans at various vulnerable points along the coast. In 49 B. C. Curio had landed near Clupea.[50] The fortifications of Clupea, and of several other forts near the sea had forced Caesar to go southward and land near Hadrumetum.[51] When, therefore, inscriptional evidence informs us that Curubis was fortified by the Pompeians in 47 B. C.,[52] and was fortified again after

[46] *C.*, 848; *I. L. A.*, 235, 240.

[47] See n. 187 ff. and text.

[48] The second and third classes are discussed under the Augustan development.

[49] XLIII, 14, 1.

[50] Caes., *Bell. Civ.*, II, 23

[51] *Bell. Afr.*, 2, 6; 3, 1.

[52] *C. I. L.*, I,[2] 780.

Caesar's victory in 45 B. C.,[53] that in the same year it had a duovir,[54] who was like the officials in several other Caesarian colonies including Carthage,[55] a freedman,[56] and that it later termed itself Colonia Julia,[57] the conclusion is obvious. Detachments were probably also settled at other coast towns, Clupea,[58] Carpis,[59] Hippo Diarrhytus,[60] perhaps also at Hadrumetum,[61] and a detachment at Thysdrus[62] to ward off Gaetulian raids. The division of the soldiers of a single military unit between Carpis and Hippo Diarrhytus would explain the epithet *consanguinei*.[63] Whether Caesar placed any detachments at inland points, we do not know. It is possible that the Roman towns of Thuburnica[64] and perhaps Thuburbo Maius[65] were thus settled.

[53] *C. I. L.*, I,[2] 788.

[54] *C. I. L.*, I,[2] 788.

[55] *C. I. L.*, X, 6104.

[56] On freedmen in Caesarian colonies, see Hübner, *C. I. L.*, II, p. 191; and suppl., p. 851.

[57] *C.*, 24100.

[58] A duovir, *C. I. L.*, X, 6104.

[59] *C.*, 25417. Some building at Carpis in 43 B. C., *C.*, 24106.

[60] *C.*, 25417.

[61] See n. 16.

[62] See n. 15.

[63] *C.*, 25417. Since these settlements antedated the refounding of Carthage they could not well have been attributed to her.

[64] Thuburnica, *At. arch. Tun.*, Ghardimaou, 7, was an old indigenous center well Punicized, Gsell, *Hist. anc.*, V, p. 263, overlooking valley land which had probably been Numidian royal domain and was now public land of Rome. This town has been identified by Ritterling, *Pauly-Wissowa-Kroll*, art., Legio, as an Augustan foundation, on the basis of an inscription, *C.*, 14697: *meiles Leg. V*, who was twice duovir. Note that the fifth legion was in Africa with Caesar, *Bell. Afr.*, 28, 2; 47, 6; and that it was necessary to settle detachments of soldiers in this region to defend it from the hillmen's raids, which were still dangerous in the time of Nero in this area, *C.*, 14603.

[65] See n. 134.

Caesar as the heritor of the Gracchan and the Marian policies, refounded Carthage, or left orders for the refounding among his memoranda.[66] The colony was led out in 44 B. C. after Caesar's death.[67] Caesar most probably had the commercial advantages of the site in mind, and wished to reduce the numbers of the plebs urbana at Rome but there were soldiers also among the new colonists.[68] Whether there was an extensive confiscation of land for the benefit of the colony or not cannot be said. For the new colonists would be available lands of Caesar's opponents who had borne arms against him and remained unforgiven.[69] The territory once added to Utica was perhaps returned to Carthage and to Hippo Diarrhytus. The sale of all property which belonged to those who had served under Juba and Petreius,[70] and the large fines levied on the conventus of Utica,[71] and on the conventus and townsmen of Hadrumetum and of Thapsus [72] must have resulted in

[66] App., *Pun.*, 136, where as Gsell points out, *Rev. hist.*, nov., 1927, the accounts of the Caesarian and of the Augustan foundations have become confused; Strabo, XVII, 3, 15; Plutarch, *Caesar,* 57; Paus., II, 1, 2; Dio Cass., XLIII, 50. Discussions of value will be found in Gsell, *l. c.; Pauly-Wissowa,* art., Karthago; Audollent, *Carthage* romaine, p. 42 ff.; Barthel, *op. cit.,* p. 16 ff.

[67] App., *Pun.,* 136; Solinus, 27, 11; Dio Cass., XLIII, 50. Probably not by Octavian despite Appian, *l. c.;* see Gsell, *Rev. hist.,* nov., 1927, p. 228; Carcopino, *Rev. hist.,* mai-juin, 1928, p. 2, n. 2, opposes this dating.

[68] Strabo, XVII, 3, 15.

[69] *Bell. Afr.,* 97, 1.

[70] *Bell. Afr.,* 97, 2.

[71] *Bell. Afr.,* 90, 4 and 5.

[72] *Bell. Afr.,* 97, 2. The presence of many of the proscribed who had fled to Africa, many of them presumably to their estates, in the

considerable exchange, if not actual confiscation, of property at this time. It is suggested also that certain people of the neighborhood who were added to the colony were probably the descendants of the Gracchan colonists.[73] The early years of the colony were quite unfortunate,[74] and after the re-establishment of peace Augustus reinforced it with a fresh deduction of veterans, probably the 3000 veterans of Appian's account.[75] Punic people flocked back to their ancient capital, as the cults show,[76] and were responsible for the resurgence of a brilliant commercial life. Augustus allowed them in 28 B. C. an autonomous government under their own suffetes and even granted them the right to coin money. Within a few years the free town and the colony had united.[77] Carthage at once became the chief city of the province and within a century and a half the third city of the Roman empire.

---

army of Cornificius and of Laelius indicates that here as elsewhere the chief confiscations occurred under the Second Triumvirate; App., *Bell. Civ.,* IV, 241.

[73] App., *Pun.,* 136; Gsell, *l. c.*

[74] Tertullian, *De Pallio,* 1: *Post Gracchi obscena omina et Lepidi violentia ludibria, post trinas Pompei aras et longas Caesaris moras, ubi moenia Statilius Taurus imposuit, sollemnia Sentius Saturninus enarravit, cum concordia iuvat, toga oblata est.* On Lepidus, see also Dio Cass., LII, 43.

[75] App., *Pun.,* 136; Dio Cass., LII, 43.

[76] In general see Toutain, *Les cultes paiens,* III, ch. I; Audollent, *op. cit.,* p. 367 ff.; on Tellus see Gsell, *Rev. hist.,* nov., 1927, p. 229; on Tellus and the Cereres, Carcopino, *Rev. hist.,* mai-juin, 1928, pp. 4-5.

[77] Barthel, *op. cit.,* p. 17 ff.; Tertullian, *De Pallio,* 1; Gsell's discussion, *l. c.;* and nn. 42-4 above.

The theory that a considerable territory was for a while at least attributed to Carthage has the following general considerations in its favor: the extension of the tribe of Carthage, the Arniensis, over a considerable area of the province both coastal and inland;[78] the worship of Carthage in the area of the middle Bagradas valley;[79] the fact that the pagi of Roman citizens in the same area chose their patrons and their rare magistri from among prominent citizens of Carthage;[80] the extension of the worship of the Cereres, the priests of which date their era either from the building of the temple of Ceres in Carthage or from the founding of the colony itself.[81] None of these considerations offers positive proof. The Quirine tribe occurs with disturbing frequency in the ter-

[78] The following towns are known to have belonged to the Arniensis tribe: Neapolis, *C.*, 971; Curubis, *C.*, 980; Bisica, *C.*, 12298; Mun. Aur. Comm. (Hr. bou Cha), *C.*, 825 ?; Thuburbo Maius, *C.*, 842, 854; *I. L. A.*, 237; Thibiuca?, *C.*, 14291; Thignica, *C.*, 15090, 15097, 15216; Thubursicum Bure, *C.*, 1441; Numluli, *C.*, 15380; Thimida Bure, *C.*, 1470, 15430; Thibaris, *C.*, 15445, 26199; Uchi Maius, *C.*, 15462, 26295; Thugga, *C.*, 1525, 15545, 26598; note the presence of individuals of other tribes, *C.*, p. 2615, n. 4; Aunobari, *C.*, 15566; Agbia, *C.*, 1548; Vaga, *C.*, 14392, also the Fabia, *C.*, 1224; the commune at Ghardimaou, *C.*, 14731; Thabraca, *C.*, 17337; at Thuburnica many tribes including the Arniensis occur, *C.*, 14687, 14705. The Arniensis tribe also appears in the Pagus Suttuensis, *C.*, 15484.

[79] *C.*, 26239; Merlin et Poinssot, *Notes et Documents,* II, Les inscriptions d'Uchi Maius, p. 25 ff. Cf. the dedications to the genius of the colony of Cirta, *C.*, 6042; 18752 (?); 5693.

[80] See ch. I, nn. 91 and 92.

[81] Gsell suggests that their era is not the era of Carthage but of their temple, *Rev. hist.*, nov., 1927. In any case it began before 39 B. C., *C.*, 26255; *I. L. A.*, 390, on which see Villefosse, *C. R. Ac.*, 1910, p. 135; cf. Carcopino, *Rev. hist.*, mai-juin, 1928, p. 2.

ritory near Carthage.[82] The Arniensis however is predominant among the inhabitants of the various centers of the area of the Marian colonization.[83] On the extension of the worship of the Cereres no argument can be based. They were the Roman form of the cult of Demeter and Core which the Carthaginians had borrowed from Sicily long before and were worshipped quite widely in Africa.[84] The second and third points hold good only for the middle Bagradas area.

The local rural associations which the Marian settlers had probably formed for purposes of cult and for the management of local affairs, even if they did not possess any legal validity, provided a convenient

[82] The Quirine tribe occurs in Utica, *C.*, 1328; Hippo Diarrhytus, *C.*, 14334 (cf. Villefosse, *Bull. des antiq.*, 1893, p. 243; Papiria); Thuburbo Minus, *C.*, 1175; Bulla Regia, *C.*, 25544; Simitthu, *C.*, 14631; Masculula, *C.*, 27505; Lares, *C.*, 16322, and Fabia, *C.*, 16327; Sicca Veneria, *C.*, 27636, and its territory passim; Cirta and its territory passim; Hippo Regius, *I. L. Al.*, 10, 1378; Madauros, *I. L. Al.*, 2194, 2202. Two Augustan foundations, Uthina, *C.*, 3067, and Assuras, *C.*, 1814, 1821, were inscribed in the Horatian tribe. See Kubitschek, *Imperium Romanum Tributim Descriptum.*

[83] Note that Gabinius Datus and Gabinius Bassus who were prominent both among the conductores and in the municipal life of the region of Thugga were of the Quirine tribe. The family was probably of indigenous origin, since Gabinia Felicula was the name of the mother of a suffete of the civitas in 48 B. C. See *C.*, 26517, 26470, 26467, 26459-62; *I. L. A.*, 568, 569; Carcopino, *Rev. ét. anc.*, 1922, p. 30 ff., after Poinssot.

[84] Gsell, *Hist. anc.*, IV, pp. 267 and 346 ff.; Audollent, *Mél. Cagnat*, p. 360 ff., where occurrences of the cult are listed. Carcopino, *Rév. hist.*, mai-juin, 1928, p. 1 ff., has shown that the Cereres when turned from Punic to Latin appear as a combination of Tellus and of Ceres and were a fertility cult popular and persistently and widely worshipped throughout Africa from before the fall of Carthage.

organization through which to choose patrons to look after their interests with the governmental officials in Utica. From Appian we learn that with the refounding of Carthage people were added to the colony from the neighborhood.[85] Although these pagi were not in the immediate vicinity of Carthage it is probable that these people were thus included as full citizens of the new town at the beginning. Such a condition would explain the rare appearance in these pagi of the magister, the usual chief official of a pagus.[86] It would explain also the frequent occurrence of natives of these pagi as citizens, and often priests and high officials of Carthage,[87] and the comparative rarity of the praefectus iure dicundo, the official who regularly represented the larger center in attached or outlying communities.[88] The few praefecti who are found were perhaps appointed to meet special exigencies. Like all private organizations these pagi could contract the patronate relation but the grant of the right of receiving legacies to the pagus of Thugga by Marcus Aurelius [89] proves that they were not considered juristic persons until that time. Because of their distance from Carthage they retained their neighborhood feeling. As they grew in

[85] App., *Pun.*, 136.

[86] Thibaris, *C.*, 26185, a decurion of Carthage; Uchi Maius, *C.*, 26250 (177 A. D.); 26252, to Faustina Augusta. One is undated; two belong to the later part of the second century A. D.

[87] Ch. I, n. 92.

[88] Thibaris, *C.*, 26185; Uchi Maius, *C.*, 26244 (time of Antoninus Pius?); Thugga, *C.*, 26615 (c. 130 A. D.); *I. L. A.*, 520 (42 A. D.).

[89] *C.*, 26528b (168 A. D.); see Poinssot, *C. R. Ac.*, 1911, p. 496 ff.

prosperity and as they assimilated themselves to the Punic and Libyan people in the free towns beside them the attachment to Carthage weakened. Many of them coalesced with the free towns and became Roman municipalities in the time of the Severi.[90] In origin and character they were therefore quite different from the pagi of Cirta.[91]

The famous inscription of Phileros [92] suggests the possibility of a different type of attribution. This freedman of Marcus Caelius, perhaps of Marcus Caelius Rufus who owned lands in Africa,[93] was aide-de-camp of Titus Sextius who was governor of Africa Nova in 43 B. C. and captured Africa Vetus from Cornificius and Laelius, becoming again governor in 41-0 B. C.[94] Phileros became aedile of the colony of Carthage probably about 40 B. C. He next became praefectus iure dicundo for the letting of the quinquennial vectigalia in the 83 castella. As prefect he was apparently a city official, and perhaps a substitute to do the duties of a regular colonial official the duovir quinquennalis whose appointment would

[90] See ch. VI, n. 213 ff. and text, re double communities.

[91] See n. 145 ff. and text; ch. VI, n. 297 ff. and text.

[92] *C. I. L.*, X, 6104: *M(arcus) Caelius M(arci) l(ibertus) Phileros accens(us) T(iti) Sexti imp(eratoris) in Africa, Carthag(ine) aed(ilis), praef(ectus) i(ure) d(icundo) vectig(alibus) quinq(uennalibus) locand(is) in castell(is) LXXXIII, aedem Tell(uris) s(ua) p(ecunia) fec(it), IIvir Clupeae bis, Formis Augustalis . . . .*

[93] Cic., *Pro Cael.*, 73. Phileros became Augustalis at Formiae; could the reading of *Pro Cael.*, 5, be *praesenti prae* (a dittography) *Formiani* and Formiae be the native town of Caelius Rufus? Praetutiani however has respectable Ms. authority.

[94] Pallu de Lessert, *Fastes*, pp. 53-8; 61-2; 309.

be due by 39 B. C. at least. It is possible that Lepidus who had charge of Africa from 40 to 36 B. C.[95] was honored by the colony with the position of duovir quinquennalis and delegated his functions to Phileros who ranks the position next to his aedileship. At this time also he built the temple of Tellus at Carthage.

The problem presented by the inscription centers about the meaning of the word castellum and involves the relationship of the castella to Carthage and of both to the quinquennial vectigalia. There are two possible meanings of the word. First the castellum was a little fort or fortified site in which the population of a country canton gathered together for purposes of security. Such hill-top villages were numerous in Africa in the period previous to the Roman occupation[96] and the sites of many ancient African towns show that they originated as indigenous refuges.[97] Such probably were most of the numerous " cities " which invaders such as Agathocles[98] and Regulus[99] found in Carthaginian territory, three hundred of which still remained in the restricted territory of 149 B. C.[100] Livy speaks of the seventy oppida castellaque which Masinissa seized from Carthage in 174-3 B. C.[101] and Appian of the fifty πόλεις

[95] *ib.*, p. 62.
[96] Gsell, *Hist. anc.*, V, pp. 240-4; II, pp. 104-6.
[97] Toutain, *Les cités*, p. 46 ff.
[98] Diodorus, XX, 17, 6.
[99] App., *Pun.*, 3.
[100] Strabo, XVII, 3, 15.
[101] Livy, XLII, 23.

which he seized soon afterwards,[102] evidently the same types of foundation, in the district about Thugga. Sallust speaks of the castella in the same region.[103] Appian also in describing the exploits of the Punic cavalry under Himilco Phameas, and the looting expeditions of the Romans in Carthaginian territory in 149 B. C. mentions the *πύργους καὶ φρούρια,* numerous in the land, to which the Libyans fled for refuge.[104] In the second place, since the Carthaginian territory had been developed by Punic landlords,[105] probably from the first under a system of tenantry we can not exclude the possibility that these *πύργοι* were the central villas of estates, fortified as was necessary in that country against the ever-present danger of raids. The *πύργοι* of the Persian landlords of the Pergamene land,[106] or certain farm villas in Egypt[107] and in Palestine[108] are interesting parallels.

Institutions corresponding to these two meanings of the word castellum appeared in Africa under the Roman régime. The indigenous people continued to dwell in their hill villages in the center of the territory assigned to them.[109] The whole was a pagus

102 App., *Pun.*, 68.

103 Sallust, *Jug.*, 54, 6; 87, 1.

104 App., *Pun.*, 101.

105 Cf. Gsell, *Hist. anc.*, IV, pp. 9-11; 46-8. The culture of cereals was largely carried on through the indigenous people, but rural slaves also were numerous under Carthage.

106 *Anatolian Studies presented to Sir William Ramsay,* p. 359 ff. (Rostovtzeff).

107 Preisigke, *Hermes,* 1919, p. 423 ff.

108 E. Meyer, *Hermes,* 1920, p. 100.

109 Note Pliny, *H. N.*, V, 1: *castella ferme inhabitant.*

and the center was a castellum.[110] It was not until Augustus, probably after his grant of " freedom " to Carthage in 28 B. C.,[111] began to grant autonomy to the native villages that an indigenous municipal life was officially recognized in Africa. On the other hand there had been a great development of estates from the time of the Gracchi on. Although the civil wars and the confiscations had caused a great deal of disturbance and some of the lands in 40 B. C. had not yet passed to new owners or to incoming colonists the tendency to estates still continued and the former centers remained. Protection against raiders was necessary in almost all parts of the province until the middle of the first century A. D.[112] It is probable that the tower and defensive works so often to be seen in the African farm mosaics were frequent in the villas themselves.

An inscription of Uchi Maius may perhaps be restored thus: [113] *M C]ae[l(ius) Ph]ileros castellum divisit inter colonos et Uchitanos termin(um)que constituit.* Should this identification be true the castellum mentioned would be a territorial unit, and perhaps one of the 83 castella. The Uchitani may be the descendants of the original Marian colonists or

[110] See ch. I, nn. 55-7 and text.

[111] See nn. 41-4 and text.

[112] Cf. *Bell. Afr.*, 67, 2; 65, 1; *C.*, 14603.

[113] *C.*, 26274; see Merlin et Poinssot, *Notes et documents*, II, p. 65 ff., Les inscriptions d'Uchi Maius, where a reference to a water tower or to the division of land necessitated by the Severan colonial deduction under Caesonius Lucullus, *C.*, 26262 is supposed. Such a division would also require the clear restoration of stones marking off previous divisions of land.

they may be indigenous, more probably the former since no indigenous civitas of the name of Uchi is known and the relation of Uchi Maius to the civitas Bencennensis is unknown.[114] It is possible that land had been confiscated here, that incoming settlers were taking it up and that Phileros made a division between land of the new settlers[115] which may have been subject to vectigal[116] and the descendants of the old settlers on land that was tribute-free. Further evidence is necessary to any valid conclusion.

With certain exceptions such as land granted to colonists in Quiritary right, all provincial land was subject to stipendium or vectigal. The right to collect the vectigalia was let for five-year periods[117] to mancipes[118] who seem to have been local officials for unitary areas. The mancipes of an inscription of Rome[119] of the time of Augustus were mancup(es) stipend(iorum) ex Africa. The stipendiary people in Africa had paid a set tribute per capita and a tax on their land;[120] the payment however must necessarily have been made in kind and was probably collected and administered by mancipes for unitary areas such as their pagi were. When the indigenous villages were granted their autonomy and became civitates the local council became responsible

[114] *C.*, 15447.

[115] See below n. 204 ff. and text.

[116] i. e., if ager privatus vectigalisque had been confiscated.

[117] *Corp. Agrim.*, ed. Thulin, p. 79.

[118] *Corp. Agrim.*, *l. c.*; cf. *C. I. L.* VI, 31713; Rostovtzeff, *Gesch. d. Staatspacht,* p. 416.

[119] *C. I. L.*, VI, 31713.

[120] See ch. I, n. 43.

for the payment of the tribute.[121] On the other hand, many of the private estates were composed of ager privatus vectigalisque and contracts had also to be made for the collection of payments from them. It is hardly likely that the associations of conductores who may during the empire have handled the produce of private estates as well as of the imperial domains [122] were as yet active in Africa. In any case the local contracts for the collection of the vectigalia may possibly deal with either class of land.

The mancipes of the inscription cited [123] made their dedication to the provincial quaestor. The stipendiary pagi before the refounding of Carthage did the same.[124] Phileros however appears to have been an official of the colony. We have seen that the descendants of the Gracchan and the Marian colonists were probably included in the newly-founded city.[125] It is probable that the Caesarian organization of Carthage followed the lines of the Gracchan plan in some measure, and perhaps with some remembrance of the Caesarian organization of Gaul [126] made the new city the administrative head and financially responsible for a considerable area of the province. Phileros as prefect, perhaps doing the duty of the

[121] Apul., *Apol.*, 101, 17; Abbott and Johnson, *Munic. Admin.*, p. 132.

[122] *I. L. A.*, 568; *I. L. Al.*, 285, 3992; Carcopino, *Rev. ét. anc.*, 1922, p. 28.

[123] *C. I. L.*, VI, 31713.

[124] *I. L. A.*, 422.

[125] See nn. 85-7 and text.

[126] Hirschfeld, *Kleine Schriften*, Die Organization der drei Gallien durch Augustus; Kornemann, *Philol.*, 1901, p. 425.

quinquennalis, had the task of letting the contracts, valid for five years, for the local collection of the revenues in these centers whichever their character within the jurisdiction of Carthage to the persons who laid the assessments in their turn upon particular individuals and particular plots of land. The fact that he later moved to Clupea and was twice duovir there does not pertain to the problem. This town as we have seen [127] was a previous Caesarian foundation.

The liberal grant of local autonomy under Augustus broke up much of this attribution. Whatever the relation of the pagus of Thugga to Carthage the civitas of Thugga, as Barthel has pointed out, once it became a civitas could no longer be involved in the attribution.[128] The collection of the vectigalia from the stipendiary land appears to have returned under the Augustan reorganization to the supervision of the provincial quaestor.[129] That however a system of grouping non-autonomous communities under a prefect continued is indicated by an inscription of Gsar bou Fatha [130] which mentions a prefect of the 62 c(astella?) in 158 A. D.

Whatever developments Caesar may have intended in Africa the evidence of a far-reaching policy is not to hand. His organization of Numidia and

[127] See n. 58 and text.

[128] *Op. cit.*, p. 43.

[129] *C.*, VI, 31713.

[130] *C.*, 23599 (158 A. D.); cf. *C.*, 622. Several communities of this region appear in inscriptions as civitates shortly after the date of this inscription.

the settlement of detachments of soldiers seem to have been inspired by his desire to reward his allies and by his regard for the defensive needs of the province. The refounding of Carthage was of course epochal both in its political and its commercial results. The inclusion of a large area in the territory of Carthage was bound in view of the previous development of the Bagradas valley to be merely a temporary condition. A more liberal policy is hinted in the admission of freedmen to important municipal positions. Caesar did not have time to put any definite scheme for the development of Africa into operation, if indeed he shaped one. The chief changes of the period seem to have happened spontaneously and in the time of Augustus.

The traditions of Pliny and of the inscriptions agree regarding the six Augustan colonies. The deduction to Carthage in 29 B. C.[131] was probably contemporaneous with the deduction of the veteran settlements in the Miliana valley. Pliny mentions the regular colonies of Maxula,[132] Uthina,[133] and Thuburbo,[134] but omits the paganal settlements of vet-

[131] See n. 75.

[132] *At. arch. Tun.*, La Goulette, 2; *C.*, 12253.

[133] *At. arch. Tun.*, Oudna, 48.

[134] *At. arch. Tun.*, Zaghouan, 67. Since Thuburbo Maius occupied a site near the indigenous area of the central massif of Tunisia, and suitable for the defence of the Miliana valley, was of the Arniensis tribe (see n. 78), and had the double organization which grew up in many Caesarian Julian colonies (n. 46), while Thuburbo Minus, like the majority of the Augustan foundations was of the Quirine tribe (n. 82), was evidently a veteran colony of the eighth (*I. L. A.*, 414) as Uthina of the thirteenth legion (*C.*, p. 2427), and should, judging by

erans at Medeli [135] and at Sutunurca.[136] The Miliana valley thus appears as a special area of Augustan colonization. This valley which includes some of the most fertile land in Tunisia,[137] was probably developed quite early by the Carthaginians. Three points of peculiarity warrant a special interpretation of conditions in this valley during the Roman period. At Hr. Avin in the plain by the Miliana about 4 km. north of Uthina was found a trilingual dedication, Greek, Latin and Punic, the last portion in old Punic letters in the year of the suffetes Abd Melqart and Adonibaal.[138] Near by and also on the plain, on land where we should expect to find Roman proprietors and colonists appears the native community of Thimida Regia; [139] similarly in the region between Dj. Oust and Thuburbo Maius are found on the plain near the river the sites of Giufi (Bir Mecherga)[140] and of Gor (Hr. Draa el Gamra),[141] both native civitates. The Augustan veterans were settled in pagi

its site, be an early foundation, it is possible that Thuburbo Maius was a Caesarian, and Thuburbo Minus an Augustan foundation. We may note that Forum Julii, also a colonia octavanorum was a foundation of Octavian in 30 B. C., Pliny, *N. H.*, III, 35; Mela, II, 77. Pliny however merely gives the name Thuburbo. Thuburbo Maius is known as a Julian colony (*C.*, 848), and the Miliana valley was an area of Augustan colonization.

135 *At. arch. Tun.*, Oudna, 22; *C.*, 885.

136 *At. arch. Tun.*, Oudna, 75; *I. L. A.*, 301.

137 The vineyards of the plain of Mornag are famous today.

138 *At. arch. Tun.*, Oudna, 43; *C.*, 24030 (91 B. C.); see ch. I, n. 56.

139 *At. arch. Tun.*, Oudna, 42; *C.*, 883: cf. Poinssot, *C. R. Ac.*, 1907, p. 470, n. 2; Gsell, *Hist. anc.*, V, pp. 265-6.

140 *At. arch. Tun.*, Oudna, 172.

141 *At. arch. Tun.*, Zaghouan, 22.

in the central portion of the lower Miliana valley, northwest of Dj. Oust; and one of these pagi, Sutunurca is found to have had on the same site a native civitas.[142] A native civitas also shared the site of the regularly constituted colony of Thuburbo Maius, and continued administratively separate for almost two centuries.[143]

Traces of the Gracchan survey have been found on the plain of Mornag. This area near the mouth of the Miliana was a most probable site for the villas and estates of the class of people on whom the vicissitudes of the civil wars, the proscriptions, and the confiscations bore most hardly. Hence land was easily available for the colony of Maxula. The assumption that land in this valley was confiscated and re-sold or distributed successively by Pompey, Caesar, and the Triumvirate does not explain the evident presence of a commune of Punic form in the plain and under its own magistrates during the early part of the first century B. C., or the presence of three other communes Punic or indigenous in the valley near it. It may be conjectured that a portion of this area was land granted to the Punic deserters

[142] *C.*, 24004. Note at Hr. el Khandak, Mun. A[ugus]t Abbir, *I. L. A.*, 296; cf., Pliny, *N. H.*, V, 30: Abziritanum. From the analogy of the cognomina the pagus Minervius near Hippo Diarrhytus, *C.*, 25423, was probably similar to the pagus Mercurialis of Medeli, and the pagus Fortunalis of Suturnurca, but its magister was of the Papiria, Trajan's tribe.

[143] The division of the portions of the town is clear in its plan with the capitol at one end and the temple of the Baalat at the other. See Merlin, *Notes et documents,* VII, Le forum de Thuburbo Maius; *C.*, 848; *I. L. A.*, 235, 244, 281.

of 146 B. C. When we recall the generous treatment accorded to the seven free cities we need not find the grant of such good land given under a similar right to the deserters so surprising. The settlement of small detachments of soldiers in pagi in conjunction with indigenous civitates, in an area where sufficient good valley land could have been found for colonies like Uthina and Thuburbo is evidence of a desire on the part of Augustus to disturb conditions as little as possible. He seems rather to have used what land was otherwise available or to have purchased restricted amounts of land in this special area.[144] At any rate it seems certain that there was in this area a section of peregrine land subject to special conditions. Thuburbo Maius marks the southern limit of the Augustan colonization.

Cirta presents a unique situation. Sittius was treacherously slain by Arabio, son of the Masinissa whom he had despoiled.[145] The latter assisted Sextius against Cornificius and Laelius [146] but later perished himself in the confusion of the civil wars.[147] For the next few years the exact position of Numidia seems obscure.[148] It is probable that it was administered along with the old province since the whole was according to Dio Cassius created a senatorial

144 *Mon. Ancyr.*, 16, attests the purchase of land for veteran settlements.

145 App., *Bell. Civ.*, IV, 234; Cic., *Ad Att.*, XV, 17, 1.

146 App., *Bell. Civ.*, IV, 240 ff.

147 Dio Cass., XLVIII, 22-3.

148 On the period immediately after 46 B. C. in Numidia, see Pallu de Lessert, *Fastes*, pp. 48 ff.; 307 ff.; Barthel, *op. cit.*, pp. 12-5; Gsell, *At. arch. Alg.*, f. 17, 126, p. 10.

province in 27 B. C. Dio's accuracy has been questioned on the strength of two other passages which indicate that Juba II reigned in his father's kingdom.[149] There is no proof that Juba II ever was king in Cirta.[150] It is certain that in 25 B. C. Augustus made him king of all the territory from the Ampsaga river westward. He thus became the ruler of his father's kingdom with the exception of the provincial land, and of the territories of the deceased kings of Mauretania, Bocchus and Bogud.[151] Cirta became a Roman colony but is found a century later to have a peculiar organization: a contribution or federation with Cirta of three other important towns of colonial rank, and a large attributed territory with castella and pagi territorially and administratively distinct. This organization seems to have had its origin in the condition of Cirta first as head of a Numidian principality, and later as the possession of Sittius, who settled his followers on the best lands of the area.

The appearance of duoviri in Cirta instead of the triumviri who usually administered the contribution, on two inscriptions for which an early dating[152] is favored, and the mention of Chullu and of Rusicade in Pliny merely as oppida[153] inclines one to the view

[149] Dio Cass., LI, 15; LIII, 26; cf. LIII, 12, 4.

[150] Pallu de Lessert, *op. cit.*, p. 311; cf. De la Blanchère, *De rege Juba regis Jubae filio,* p. 20 ff.; Barthel, *op. cit.*, pp. 12-5.

[151] Strabo, XVII, 3, 7; cf. Dio Cass., LIII, 26; XLVIII, 45; XLIX, 43.

[152] *C.*, 7117, and perhaps 7110; cf. 7099: duomvir vicensumari.

[153] Pliny, *H. N.*, V, 22.

that the contribution in the form in which we find it may not have been original with the founding of the colony. The cognomina, Veneria Rusicade,[154] Minervia Chullu,[155] and Sarnensis Mileu,[156] are not usual for imperial or even for Augustan foundations[157] unless paganal,[158] while the last one refers particularly to Sittius who was a native of Nuceria[159] near the river Sarnus in Campania. It is probable that Cirta exercised authority over all alike at first but that the importance of these three towns,[160] and the presence of numerous Sittians now Roman citizens and of other Romans gave them a status superior to other smaller, more rural and indigenous pagi which soon modified the organization of the whole. Being largely African they remained in the attachment which their local historical background favored but shared in the administration. By the time of Trajan a central board of triumviri for the four colonies sat at Cirta,[161] while praefecti iure dicundo who held this office after their triumvirate

[154] *C.*, 7960.

[155] *C.*, 6710.

[156] *C.*, 6710.

[157] See Mommsen, *C.*, p. 618, on the Cirtensian federation; more fully in *Hermes,* 1866, p. 47 ff.

[158] Cf. the pagi of n. 142 ff.

[159] Sallust, *Cat.*, 21, 5; where the Sarnus had a special cult, as Venus at Pompeii and Minerva at Surrentum. See Peterson, *The Cults of Campania,* pp. 295, and 307.

[160] Rusicade and Chullu had been Punic trading-posts, Chullu with a dye industry, and probably were ports for the region of Cirta under the Numidian kingdoms and during Roman times. See *At. arch. Alg.*, f. 8, 29 (Chullu); 196 (Rusicade); f. 17, 59 (Mileu).

[161] *C.*, 7069; and p. 618; Gsell, *At. arch. Alg.*, f. 17, 126, p. 11, col. 2.

administered the affairs of the particular colonies.[162] Whether Cirta's official title Colonia Julia Juvenalis Honoris et Virtutis Cirta [163] is due to the devotion of Sittius and his freebooters to this cult or to some favor from Vespasian or to some other reason is unknown.

The pagi of Cirta seem to follow territorial divisions that existed in the time of the indigenous kingdoms.[164] The names are indigenous; [165] the sites correspond to the indigenous fortified refuges or castella,[166] common everywhere in the land; about them the indigenous remains are more frequent,[167] and the indigenous worships retained greater strength.[168] The pagus is the territorial designation for the area of which the castellum was the center. Thibilis, an important pagus and the center of a considerable area,[169] had a strong easily defended site.[170] Similarly

162 Gsell, *l. c.*, p. 12, col. 1.

163 *C.*, 7041, 7071, and a coin representing Honos and Virtus, cf. *C.*, p. 1849.

164 Gsell, *Hist. anc.*, V, p. 275.

165 See Gsell, *At. arch. Alg.*, f. 17, p. 12, col. 2: Caldis, Tiddis, Celtianis, Thibilis, Tigisi, Gadiaufala, Saddar, Sila, Sigus, Subzuar, Arsacal, Elephantum, Mastar, Uzelis, Phua, and others the ancient names of which are unknown, e. g., Ksar Mahidjiba, f. 17, 172 (Castellum Fabatianum ?).

166 All but two, Celtianis, *At. arch. Alg.*, f. 8, 91, and Saddar, f. 17, 276, are on easily defended sites.

167 Gsell, *Hist. anc.*, V, p. 275.

168 Notably the worship carried on by the people of Phua in the grotto of ez Zemma, *At. arch. Alg.*, f. 17, 109, and by the people of Thibilis to Bacax in the grotto of Dj. Taya, f. 9, 109; see Toutain, *Cultes païens*, III, pp. 47-9.

169 Gsell and Joly, *Khamissa, Mdaourouch, Announa*, iii, Announa, p. 11 ff.

170 *At. arch. Alg.*, f. 18, 107.

the centers of other large pagi such as Sila[171] and Sigus[172] occupy strong positions. While in general referred to as the pagi Cirtenses,[173] some even large pagi such as Sigus are mentioned as castella.[174] Their magistri however are magistri of the pagi. The local autonomous unit however appears under the term res publica castelli or simply res publica.[175] How far Sittians were originally included in the pagi is uncertain.[176] The appearance of boundary stones at various points throughout the Cirtensian area marking off the ager publicus of Cirta from the ager acceptus of citizens of Cirta may be explained by the Sittian assignations.[177] The pagi for the most part remained rural and indigenous in character. Thibilis the most important still paid official worship to the god Bacax in the grotto of Dj. Taya through her magistri in the third century A. D.[178] and only two of them, Thibilis and Tigisi, ever achieved municipal rank.[179] The indigenous character of the pagi

171 *At. arch. Alg.*, f. 17, 333; the territory of Sila extended northward to Khroub, f. 17, 167; *C.*, 10295.

172 *At. arch. Alg.*, f. 17, 335.

173 Cf. Tacitus, *Ann.*, III, 74.

174 *C.*, 19121; cf. 5683, 19114; cf. at Phua, *mag. pag.*, *C.*, 6267 ff.; *mag. castelli Phuensium*, *C.*, 19252, 19278, 6298.

175 There is no occurrence of the term res publica pagi; res publica castelli: Subzuar, *C.*, 19216; Mastar, 6356; Celtianis, 19693; res publica: Sigus, 5693, 19131; Sila, 10295, 19198; Saddar, 5934; Arsacal, 6048; Phua, 6267, 6307, 10326; Uzelis, 6341; Tiddis, 6702.

176 They were settled throughout the region, App., *Bell. Civ.*, IV, 233, and the name occurs in almost all the pagi, the exceptions being Tiddis and Tigisi, but Julii are in general more numerous.

177 See ch. III, n. 134.

178 *C.*, 18828 ff.; 5504 ff.

179 See ch. IV, n. 137.

and the fact that the Sittians were themselves mostly Africans with some Spaniards and a few Italian exiles [180] helps to explain why despite the undoubted degree of Romanization that was achieved in Cirta they and their descendants clung so long to the tribal territorial form of government about Cirta which they had inherited instead of passing quickly to the independent Roman municipal forms.

The old Punico-Numidian center of Sicca Veneria Nova Cirta,[181] also an Augustan foundation,[182] was the center of a large territory which included several castella and perhaps a Roman pagus.[183] Sometime within a few years after the annexation of Africa Nova the town was given colonial status by Augustus but the whole complex as in the case of Cirta was probably left undisturbed. The probable attachment of a considerable territory including villages and pagi to the Punic foundations of Hippo Regius [184] and Thabraca [185] seems despite the favor in which Hippo is said to have been held by the kings of Nu-

[180] App., *Bell. Civ.*, IV, 231; Dio Cass., XLIII, 3, 1.

[181] Gsell, *Hist. anc.*, V, p. 266: II, p. 96; III, p. 101-2.

[182] *C.*, 27568.

[183] At Nebeur, *C.*, 15726; Ucubi, *C.*, 15667; both of which occupy strong positions guarding roads which lead to Sicca; Aubuzza, *At. arch. Tun.*, Ksour, 35; *C.*, 16367. It is possible that the castellum of Tituli was in the territory of Sicca, *C.*, 27828.

[184] Gsell, *Hist. anc.*, II, p. 149, ff.; V, p. 248; *At. arch. Alg.*, f. 9, 59; see *I. L. Al.*, intro. p. 9, on the territory of Hippo; also nos. 134 (*At. arch. Alg.*, f. 2, 10), and 109 (f. 10, 1).

[185] Gsell, *Hist. anc.*, II, p. 148-9; *I. L. Al.*, 109. For the pagus Trisipensis, *C.*, 25485; *At. arch. Tun.*, Zaouiet Medienn, 3, and the pagus Mas . . . . rensium, *C.*, 17327; *At. arch. Tun.*, La Calle, 7.

midia[186] to be due to the tendency, natural in a land such as Africa where the watersheds are natural units, to run territorial boundaries along a height of land. It is noticeable that large territorial attributions of these types are clearly proven and possessed a degree of permanence only in territories once under the sway of the Numidian kings. Augustus made no attempt to change unduly such organizations as were existent or to force Roman municipal forms upon regions where the inhabitants were unready or unwilling to accept them.

The oppida civium Romanorum of Pliny appear in the inscriptions under several categories. For those which are termed coloniae Juliae we must suppose the attainment of municipal rights in Augustus' own day. But the term oppidum civium Romanorum may be non-technical and also designate recognized paganal and conventual organizations of Roman citizens. Utica which had probably been granted the Latin right by Caesar,[187] received full municipal status from Octavian in 36 B. C.[188] Simitthu, situated near the famous quarries of Numidian marble also received municipal status but did not become a colony until after 27 B. C.[189] Thabraca seemed unimportant to Pliny's source except for

[186] As signified by the name Hippo Regius, *Bell. Afr.*, 96, 1; cf. Silius Italicus, III, 259: *antiquis dilectus regibus Hippo.*

[187] Caesar, *Bell. Civ.*, II, 36; *Bell. Afr.*, 87, 3; cf. E. Meyer, *Cäsars Monarchie,* p. 490, n. 2.

[188] Dio Cass., XLIX, 16.

[189] *C.*, 14612: *Colonia Julia Augusta Numidica Simitthu.*

marble and wild beasts,[190] but some organization of Roman citizens was recognized there. The foundation of the colonia V(irtutis?) P(ietatis?)[191] analogous to Honoris et Virtutis Cirta was probably while early later than Pliny's sources. Hippo Regius was also an Augustan municipium either omitted by or posterior to Pliny's sources.

The discussion of the development of Thuburnica and of Assuras and the reconciliation of the rest of Pliny's oppida civium Romanorum with the inscriptional evidence involves the question of the agricultural immigration to Africa.[192] Some 170,000 people in Italy had been rendered homeless to provide land for the soldiers of the Second Triumvirate. Africa had already gained in Rome and Italy a reputation for fertility. It was but natural that many of the dispossessed who were agricultural people should come to Africa to make new homes for themselves.[193] Once they arrived several possibilities were open to them. Within the old province the proscription had

190 Pliny, *H. N.*, V, 22; cf. Juv., *Sat.*, X, 193-5. The quarries of Simitthu were little used in Carthaginian days, Gsell, *Hist. anc.*, IV, p. 50, but according to Pliny, *H. N.*, XXXVI, 49, Numidian marble began to be used in Rome by 78 B. C. There was probably little exploitation of the quarries before the commencement of the Augustan building program. The term officina regia, *C.*, 14578-9, 14583, may keep up the memory of the use of the quarry under the Numidian kings, Gsell, *op. cit.*, V, p. 212. The passage over the hills from Simitthu by Ain Drahim to Thabraca, though old, must have been difficult. The earliest recorded road was built under Hadrian in 129 A. D., *C.*, 22199.

191 *I. L. Al.*, 109.

192 Frank, *Class. Rev.*, 1926, p. 15; Rostovtzeff, *Gesch. d. Kol.*, p. 319 ff.; for an opposing view, see Heitland, *J. R. S.*, 1918, p. 34 ff.

193 Note Vergil, *Ecl.*, I, 64: *At nos hinc alii sitientes ibimus Afros.*

rendered available a considerable amount of land which had previously belonged to members of the equestrian and senatorial orders.[194] The civil wars had caused the ruin of several towns and a very considerable displacement of people. In the newly annexed portions of Numidia were two areas of valley land, probably once domain land of the Numidian kings,[195] which were available for settlement, ready of access, and probably partially developed. The first lies in the Bagradas valley beyond the Marian centers between Souk el Arba and Ghardimaou. Caesar had probably placed a small detachment of soldiers at Thuburnica;[196] perhaps, although it is unlikely, also at Masculula just into the hills to the south of the river valley.[197] This area near the quarries of Simitthu now became one of Roman settlement. Thuburnica with a good strip of land between it and the river which flows from the southwest at this point soon attracted additional settlement and was probably given municipal status by Augustus. Thunusuda to the south of the river near Hr. Sidi Meskine owed its foundation and status to the same development.[198] Masculula remained a little conven-

[194] Note the proscribed who fought with Cornificius and Laelius against Sextius, App., *Bell. Civ.*, IV, 241.

[195] Gsell, *Hist. anc.*, V, pp. 208-9; note also the presence of an estate near Zama, Vitruvius, VIII, 3, 24-5; Gsell, *l. c.*

[196] See n. 64; and *C.*, 14697.

[197] See ch. I, n. 126; cf. at Sua, *C.*, 25850.

[198] An inscription from the military cemetery at Ammaedara marks Thunusuda as the patria of a soldier who probably died before 75 A. D., *Ann. epig.*, 1927, n. 38. The soldier was of the Pollia tribe which occurs also at Thuburnica, *C.*, 14697, 14718; *I. L. A.*, 471, 479.

tus which anomalously associated some of the indigenous people about it in its organization.

The second area lies in the line of valleys and plains which extend southwest of Thugga and Sidi bou Rouis toward the head-waters of the Oued Tessaa. Hemmed in at first by Dj. Maiza and Dj. Massouge the valley opens into the plain of Sers and beyond after a low rise into the Plaine des Zouarines. To the west lies Dj. Lorbeus and the territory of Sicca; to the east, the hills of the central massif toward Mactar. On a rise to the south of the Plaine du Sers is the site of Colonia Julia Assuras.[199] The settlement may owe its origin to the need of defence against indigenous marauders [200] such as the nomadic Musulamii but it must have been the coming of settlers at a comparatively early date that induced Octavian to give it municipal status. The occurrence of a boundary stone of the Cellenses Numidae [201] in the middle of the Plaine des Zouarines marks either an indigenous assignment or sets a probable limit to Roman settlement.[202] Mustis situated near the Ro-

---

Thunusuda became a colony later, *C.*, 22193, 22194. There was also a commune at Ghardimaou at the head of the valley, *C.*, 14727: a flamen of Augustus in 52 A. D.

199 *At. arch. Tun.*, Ksour, 80; *C.*, 1798.

200 See *C.*, 16456 (3-6 A. D.); and n. 203.

201 *C.*, 16352.

202 Lares on the western slope of Dj. Lorbeus, *At. arch. Tun.*, Ksour, 70, was an indigenous town on the edge of the territory of Sicca. The pagus Veneriensis on the low ridge between the plaine du Sers and the plaine des Zouarines (*At. arch. Tun.*, Ksour, 77) may be similar to the Augustan pagi at Medeli and at Suturnurca (see n. 142), but some of its worships were Punic, *C.*, 27763, and the cognomen Veneriensis may refer to Sicca Veneria (see n. 183); cf. Poinssot, *C. R. Ac.*, 1913, p. 424; Toutain, *Les cultes païens*, III, p. 72.

man line of penetration and in possession of a considerable territory upon the plain of el Ghorfa was probably one of the foundations of the early period.[203]

Within the limits of the old province Pliny's oppida civium Romanorum, so far as we can discover their location, seem to possess a different character. Thibica (Hr. Bir Magra) appears in the inscription as a native civitas under suffetes in the time of Antoninus Pius.[204] There was found however slightly west at the Vicus Haterianus a dedication to Hadrian by a small body of Roman citizens who stayed

[203] Mustis, *At. arch. Tun.*, Jama, 3, is the only municipality of the Cornelia tribe in Africa, *C.*, 15576, 27438, individuals belonging to which appear at Thuburnica, *C.*, 14698, 14703, and at Ellez, *At. arch. Tun.*, Mactar, 121; *C.*, 16456. One limit of its territory was set at Dj. bou Kohil in the time Antoninus Pius, *C.*, 27459. The extent of the occurrence of the Cornelia tribe over the plain of el Ghorfa makes probable the attribution or connection with Mustis of several centers, such as Hr. el Oust, *At. arch. Tun.*, Jama, 28; res publica, 188 A. D., *C.*, 16417, and from its ruins a town of some importance; Hr. bou Aouia, *At. arch. Tun.*, Jama, 15; *C.*, 16405; Hr. Tetuai, *C.*, 16406; *At. arch. Tun.*, Jama, 16; and the fundus of Hr. Sidi Khalifa, *At. arch. Tun.*, Jama, 17; *C.*, 16411; while a praefectus iure dicundo pro duoviro also appears, *C.*, 15585. Although there is no datable evidence that Mustis had the Roman municipal organization before 164 A. D., *C.*, 15576, it probably belongs to the earlier period of settlement. The inscription of Ellez, *C.*, 16456, 3-6 A. D., when Passienus Rufus was proconsul of Africa, Pallu de Lessert, *Fastes,* p. 86, was set up, by a Roman citizen enrolled in the Cornelia tribe and his wife, the fathers of both of whom had been Roman citizens, to the Juno of Livia Augusta on being saved from some peril. Since these people were living on frontier lands, and we know that Passienus Rufus gained the ornaments of a triumph for victories over the natives, Vell. Pat., II, 116; Cagnat, *Armée romaine,*[2] p. 8, they were probably colonists of Italic stock saved from a frontier raid.

[204] Thibica, not Thigibba, I take as nearest to Pliny's text, Tibigense: *H. N.*, V, 29. The "ineffabilia nomina" of the African towns have played havoc with Pliny's text. See *At. arch. Tun.*, Bou Arada, 124; *C.*, 12228.

there.[205] It is probable that Pliny's notice refers to the recognition of such an organization at Thibica. The cognomen *peregrinorum* in the case of Chiniava probably implies an additional non-peregrine organization there [206] which would be the successor to the organization referred to by Pliny. Vaga was called Colonia Septimia Vaga after the deduction of 209 A. D. and for a slight period previously.[207] We find however a temple of Tellus built there by a Roman citizen in 2 A. D.[208] Uchi Maius although known to epigraphy only as a pagus of Roman citizens until the time of Septimius Severus perhaps attracted other Romans to the neighborhood.[209] With the exception of Thibidrumense which if the identification with Col. J]ul. Thub. is correct is a settlement of Roman colonists in a small area of valley land toward the mountains northwest of Vaga,[210] the rest of the Plinian oppida civium Romanorum are unknown to epigraphy.

205 *At. arch. Tun.*, Bou Arada, 112; *C.*, 23125. The towns southwest and west of Thuburbo Maius are clearly in a strongly indigenous area which developed mostly in the time of Hadrian. Italic settlement probably ended with the hills and salt lakes north and west of Avitta Bibba, *At. arch. Tun.*, Bou Arada, 51. It was in the less valuable area near Hr. Snobbeur, *At. arch. Tun.*, Bou Arada, 64; *C.*, 23956, the inscription re the depredations of the flocks and herds was found.

206 *At. arch. Tun.*, Mateur, 226; *C.*, 25450. This town just north of the ridges which flank the Bagradas valley is also in an area predominantly indigenous, near the Civ. Vaz., Uccula, and Aulodes.

207 *At. arch. Tun.*, Béja, 128; *C.*, 14394 (197 A. D.); 1222 (209 A. D.).

208 *C.*, 14392; note building also at Choud el Batel, *At. arch. Tun.*, Medjez el Bab, 79; *C.*, 25844, in the time of Tiberius.

209 See nn. 113-6 and text.

210 *At. arch. Tun.*, Zaouiet Medienn, 123; *C.*, 14452.

To explain the situations revealed above we must suppose that during the period of the evictions scattered groups of people came to Africa from Italy and settled in various towns and villages throughout the province. Some securing land or a business opening located and formed associations which received some recognition as municipal, conventual, or paganal organizations;[211] others, more poverty-stricken, became tenants. Many went on to the unoccupied lands farther west and built up important areas of Italic settlement. The fact that the Augustan veteran settlements of 29 B. C. were confined largely to the single area of the Miliana valley where Punic people seem to have enjoyed special privileges and where land may have been purchased for the settlements infers a sufficient immigration and occupation in Africa before 29 B. C. to compensate for the wastage of the civil wars. A huge immigration, such as was at first supposed, we have no warrant to assume.

Pliny's list of oppida libera is evidence of a new development due to Augustus in the municipal life of the province: the grant of local autonomy to indigenous communities. The free cities which were on the same sites as the Caesarian colonies but administratively separate from them have already been discussed.[212] The seven original civitates liberae et

[211] Such was probably the only organization officially recognized in these places during the earlier part of the Augustan period, since Pliny records no oppida libera and oppida civium Romanorum upon the same sites.

[212] Nn. 48-65 and text.

immunes apparently lost their position during the vicissitudes of the civil wars. To Theudalis alone was the privilege of immunity reconfirmed by Augustus.[213] Four however were given or continued to keep their autonomy.[214] One achieved the Latin right.[215] The towns of Ruspina, Aggar, and Vaga, mentioned as oppida in the Bellum Africanum[216] appear as free towns in Pliny's list. There appear also Avitta Bibba[217] in the area west of Thuburbo Maius; Thisica[218] near Mateur which itself was the free town, Materense;[219] Thagaste near the head-waters of the Bagradas river;[220] and Tunes on the site of the modern city. The important Numidian cities of Zama Regia[221] and of Bulla Regia shared the same privilege. Many other names exemplify the process but the sites are as yet unknown. It is significant for our appreciation of the attitude of Augustus to note that these towns were all in portions of the province which Carthage had once firmly occupied or strongly influenced. The Punic coast cities and

[213] Pliny, *H. N.*, V, 23.

[214] See n. 26. Hadrumetum, Leptis, and Thysdrus are quoted by Pliny, *H. N.*, V, 25, from the Chorography; Acholla from the Formula, *H. N.*, V, 30; cf. n. 9; Detlefsen, *op. cit.;* and n. 40.

[215] Uzalis, Pliny, *l. c.*, 29.

[216] Ch. I, n. 128.

[217] *At. arch. Tun.*, Bou Arada, 51; *C.*, 797.

[218] *At. arch. Tun.*, Mateur, 79; *I. L. A.*, 432.

[219] *At. arch. Tun.*, Mateur, 8.

[220] *At. arch. Alg.*, f. 18, 340.

[221] On the site of Zama Regia, see Gsell, *Hist. anc.*, III, pp. 255-8; V, pp. 268-9; on the town see also *C.*, 23601; *C. I. L.*, VI, 1686; Vitruvius, VIII, 3, 24-5; ch. IV, nn. 149 and 151; Gsell, *Hist. Anc.*, V, p. 262.

perhaps some of the inland towns had had municipal institutions under the Carthaginian régime. Where they had not had municipal institutions the coming of Punic people had fostered them. Now under Augustus their normal form of local government was officially recognized. Various towns not mentioned in Pliny's list were now or soon afterwards granted local autonomy. Such was probably the case of Thugga, which we find as a civitas of Punic constitution in the time of Claudius.[222] During the time of Tiberius Apisa Maius [223] on the edge of the central massif and southwest of Thuburbo Maius was a civitas of Punic constitution and Siagu [224] in the Cape Bon peninsula near Neapolis. The development of the pagus of Gurza near Hadrumetum to a civitas [225] in the first century A. D. illustrates the same process. The principle which governed the relation of the authorities to these towns was the same throughout. All were communities which had long had commercial life, a somewhat developed community life, and civilizing contacts, and were already prepared for local self-government. The pagi Assalitanus [226]

[222] *C.*, 26517 (48 A. D.); note *C.*, 26580, the friendship of the Thuggenses with Passienus Rufus, proconsul 3-6 A. D.

[223] *At. arch. Tun.*, Bou Arada, 111; *C. I. L.*, V, 4921.

[224] *At. arch. Tun.*, Hammamet, 4; *C. I. L.*, V, 4922. The towns of Thimiliga and of Themetra have not yet been located, *C. I. L.*, V, 4919, 4920.

[225] *At. arch. Tun.*, Sousse, 2; *C.*, 68, 69. Civitas probably does not possess in this instance the usual technical sense. Cf. the oppidum stipendiarium, Castra Cornelia, Pliny, *H. N.*, V, 29.

[226] *At. arch. Tun.*, Teboursouk, 218; see Poinssot, *C. R. Ac.*, 1920, p. 288; *I. L. A.*, 501.

and Thac(iensis)[227] were perhaps native pagi too unimportant to develop. Castella appear to have been grouped under prefects perhaps under some form of attribution (see n. 130).

The period of Augustus in Africa despite the confusion of the civil wars is clearly one of considerable development. The refounding of Carthage gave the province a capital, and greatly benefited its commercial life. Veteran settlements were made in the form of colonial or paganal foundations as convenient and seem to have been planned to disturb conditions as little as possible. During the period of the civil wars and of the confiscations a certain amount of unorganized settlement had come to Africa mostly to newly opened areas in Africa Nova while some of it stopped in the old province and formed associations of Roman citizens in various centers there. The coast towns long developed and prosperous were given local autonomy and many other inland towns, mostly in developed areas of the old province shared in the same gift. On the other hand the great areas attached to Cirta and to Sicca Veneria which had as yet been little touched by the Carthaginian and the Roman love for local self-government were left unchanged. Augustus wisely recognized African conditions for what they were. While his grant of local autonomy to the various indigenous centers is the mark of a more understanding and liberal policy than the comparative neglect of the previous times

[227] *At. arch. Tun.*, Teboursouk, 195; *C.*, 27416.

it was not a step in a deliberate policy of urbanization, but a recognition of the stage of development which they had reached. While the exploitation, if we may so call it, of the province still continued to depend largely upon private enterprise there is this evidence of a policy desirous of securing prosperity and peace for all sorts and conditions of people within the province.

CHAPTER III

The First Century A. D. in Africa

The first century after Christ in Africa was characterized by two processes: the extension of effective Roman sovereignty among the nomadic peoples of the interior; and by a process of development and of consolidation in both the older and the newer portions of the province, which varied according to the conditions of the various regions.

At first no measures were taken to make good Rome's claim to suzerainty over the hinterland beyond Caesar's acceptance of the nominal attachment of the Gaetulian " clientes C. Marii "[1] and the probable settlement of detachments of soldiers at the frontier towns to prevent raids. With the final establishment of peace Augustus undertook a definite assay of all the resources of the empire. This necessitated in Africa even in outlying portions a certain degree of definition and organization of all land in which the treasury could claim an interest, and therefore necessarily entailed some attempt to settle or limit the native ranges in such a way as to make an inventory possible.[2] Further, and more important, scattered notices of disaffection in southern

[1] *Bell. Afr.*, 35, 4; 56, 4.

[2] The Augustan inventory of the provinces did not necessitate a complete survey, e. g., there was no talk of a survey in Judaea along with the registration of the inhabitants.

Tunis and Algeria, all the way east from Juba's kingdom to the Tripolitaine indicate how necessary it was to protect the southern frontier and to secure some settlement with the marauding tribes beyond.[3] The expedition of Balbus in 20 B. C. far into the Tripolitanian hinterland,[4] the triumphs accorded to Sempronius Atratinus,[5] to Passienus Rufus,[6] and to Cossus,[7] who received the surname Gaetulicus, and the honors which rewarded Juba's aid[8] show that Roman arms had penetrated far by 6 A. D., but as these were victories over scattered bands of natives for whom guerrilla warfare was the national sport the results were quite indecisive.[9]

The milestones set by Asprenas in 14 A. D.[10] found on the road from Tacape to Capsa show what the Roman method really was. This road was evidently a strategic military highway from the winter camp of the legion to Tacape by way of Capsa. The winter camp was situated at or a little north of Ammaedara.[11] We learn from Tacitus[12] that until 18 or 19 A. D. the soldiers of the legion were scattered

[3] Cagnat, *Armée romaine,*[2] p. 1 ff.

[4] Pliny, *H. N.*, V, 34-8.

[5] *C. I. L.*, I,[2] p. 50.

[6] Vell. Pat., II, 116; *C.*, 16456.

[7] Orosius, VI, 21; Vell. Pat., II, 116; Florus, IV, 12, 40.

[8] Müller, *Num. de l'Afr. anc.*, III, no. 70 (coin of Juba); De la Blanchère, *De rege Juba,* p. 27.

[9] Gsell, *Hist. anc.*, V, p. 136 ff.

[10] *C.*, 10018, 10023: *viam ex cast(ris) hibernis Tacapes muniendam curavit.* See Toutain, *Mém. soc. ant. Fr.*, 1905, p. 152 ff.

[11] Where the permanent camp was established during the war with Tacfarinas, De Pachtère, *C. R. Ac.*, 1916, p. 273 ff.

[12] Tac., *Ann.*, III, 74.

during the inactive season in the cities of the province. They probably came out to camp when the winter migration northward of the indigenous tribesmen began.[13] By means of this road the Roman authorities drew a cordon about a large portion of southern Tunisia with the intention of stopping the migrations and apparently with little understanding of the herdsman's need of wide seasonal ranges in that region of scanty rainfall. Often in the same person as the soldier came the surveyor,[14]

[13] Seasonal ranges were necessary in that region of scanty rainfall. It was the habit of the indigenous people to retire southward into the mountains in the summer and advance northward into the steppes and plains in the winter, Gsell, *Hist. anc.*, V, p. 176-7.

[14] See Toutain, *Mém. Acad.*, 1907, Le cadastre de l'Afrique romaine; Schulten, *Bull. du com.*, 1902, p. 129 ff., L'arpentage romaine en Tunisie; but especially Barthel, *Bonn. Jahrb.*, 1911, p. 39 ff.; cf. also Schulten, *Arch. Anz.*, 1912, p. 395. The survey was almost certainly begun in the time of Augustus. In 30 A. D. it was being carried on by the Leg. III Aug. under the proconsul Vibius Marsus, *C.*, 22786. It advanced in some measure with the Roman advance into the province and was completed by the limitation of the southern tribes under Trajan. The theory of a survey planned as province-wide and centering near Ammaedara as outlined in Barthel's thorough and brilliant study of Roman Limitation in Africa (l. c.) is open to the following objections: 1. The conditions of the interior and the southern part of Tunisia as described by Mela, I. 42; Strabo, XVII, 3, 15 and 19; and Tac., *Ann.*, III, 74; II, 52; make the demand for a full survey of this desert country seem unlikely before the time of Trajan. It is probable rather that a military road was laid out and some boundaries were marked to aid in policing the district. A forma would be drawn so far as such operations went, *C.*, 22787. Any later continuations of course accorded with the original lines. 2. No evidence of such a survey has come to light in the northern and western portions of the province but only in the far south and inland from Sfax. 3. Town plans near the supposed center of the survey and probably later in date were not in accord with it, e. g., Ammaedara, Barthel, *op. cit.*, p. 100; Sufetula, see the plan in *Notes et documents*, V, Forum et églises de Sufetula (Merlin).

not as yet to go through all the country with the groma, and prepare it for settlement but to mark off certain necessary areas and boundaries along the road, and to complete the inventory of the province. We must not suppose that pressure of immigration into Africa had rendered the government land hungry;[15] for the immigration was not enormous, and it was almost a century after the civil wars before there was sufficient development in the southern regions to tempt settlement.

Like the Indians and the half-breeds in the Canadian northwest, the tribesmen rebelled, and were finally pacified only after seven years of guerrilla warfare.[16] The back-bone of the native resistance was the strong tribe of the Musulamii under their leader Tacfarinas, whose territories lay directly along the main pathway of Roman penetration.[17] Other tribes involved were the Cinithii near Gigthis,[18] and the Garamantes [19] south of Leptis Magna. The Moorish tribes to the west were also roused.[20] In Numidia the insurgents besieged the town of Thubursicum Numidarum.[21] The pagi Cirtenses re-

[15] Cf. Rostovtzeff, *Soc. and Ec. Hist.*, pp. 281-2.

[16] Tac., *Ann.*, II, 52; III, 20-1, 74; IV, 23-5; Cagnat, *Armée romaine,*[2] p. 9 ff.; Toutain, *Les cités*, p. 17; Cantarelli, *Atene e Roma*, 1901, p. 3 ff.

[17] Toutain, *Mém. soc. ant. Fr.*, LVII, p. 270 ff.; Gsell, *Mél. éc.*, 1899, pp. 47-8; Carton, *Les Musulamii.*

[18] Tac., *Ann.*, II, 52.

[19] Tac., *Ann.*, III, 74. The participation of the Garamantes in the war makes De Pachtère's suggestion that Leptiminus is the Leptis of the Tacitean account unlikely, *C. R. Ac.*, 1916, p. 273.

[20] Tac., *Ann.*, II, 52; IV, 23.

[21] *ib.*, IV, 24.

quired defence,[22] and Ptolemy, Juba's successor, aided in the final engagement in the west at Auzea.[23] The Musulamii who occupied a large territory from Madauros southward to a point beyond Theveste, and eastward at least as far as the later Saltus Beguensis were probably not at this time confined to their later limits,[24] but a considerable part of their best land now or soon afterwards became public land or capable of passing into private ownership,[25] The legionary camp was placed at Ammaedara,[26] a town which the legion first laid out,[27] on land which wedged into and partially divided the Musulamian territory. The Cinithii whose territory lay close to the coast of the lesser Syrtis were either attributed to Gigthis or under Roman government developed Gigthis as a center.[28] The Garamantes remained quiescent until 70 A. D. when they appeared once more ready to raid in the Tripolitaine.[29] The Musunii Regiani, a small interior tribe, were left in their territory near the forts of Thelepte and of Cillium.[30] There was as yet

[22] *ib.*, III, 74.

[23] *ib.*, IV, 25.

[24] On the Trajanic limits see Gsell. *I. L. Al.*, p. 267; *At. arch. Alg.*, f. 18, 519; Carton, *C. R. Ac.*, 1923, p. 71.

[25] See n. 55 ff. and text.

[26] Until the time of Vespasian, De Pachtère, *C. R. Ac.*, 1916, p. 273 ff.

[27] *Corp. Agrim.*, ed. Thulin, p. 144.

[28] *C.*, 22729, and ch. IV, n. 17.

[29] Tac., *Hist.*, IV, 49 and 50.

[30] *At. arch. Tun.*, Kasrin, 136; *I. L. A.*, 102, 103. Whether the Sabarbares which were probably pacified at this time were attached to Cirta or not is uncertain. See Gsell, *At. arch. Alg.*, f. 17, 214; Cagnat, *Mél.* Boissier, p. 99.

no consistent mode of organization. Some tribes were conquered and left to a reduced territory; others merely driven back into the desert. Others perhaps attributed to some urban center if such were near but the general absence of towns made such a policy almost impossible. The aim of the Roman administration was to secure order and safety in whatever way was feasible.

From the time of Caligula on the newly pacified regions which depended on the legion for security were under the authority of the legate of the legion;[31] and the affairs of particular tribes which had not been attributed were administered by a military prefect, whose duties probably corresponded somewhat to those of a British resident or of a French chef des bureaux arabes.[32] The office seems to have been held conjointly with a military command in the case of Calpurnius Fabatus,[33] a Roman knight who was at once prefect of the 7th Lusitanian cohort and of the " six Gaetulian tribes which are in Numidia "; somewhat later a prefect of the Musulamii appears to have been either previously or contemporaneously duovir of Ammaedara.[34] The tribe of the Numidae,

[31] Africa had been abnormal in that it was a senatorial province with a military command. See Pallu de Lessert, *Fastes*, pp. 118 ff. and 312. On the relation of the legate and the proconsul until the constitution of the province of Numidia under Septimius Severus, see Schulten, *Das römische Afrika*, p. 98, n. 29; Cagnat, *Armée romaine*,[2] p. 26 ff.

[32] Cagnat, *op. cit.*, p. 263.

[33] *C. I. L.*, V, 5267; Tac., *Ann.*, XVI, 8; cf. Schulten, *Rh. Mus.*, 1895, p. 511.

[34] *I. L. Al.*, 285; 3992.

which were probably not among the six Gaetulian tribes, also had their prefect, in one case a Roman knight whom we know to have been procurator of Corsica in the time of Vespasian.[35] The prefect of the tribe of the Salassi in the territory of Cirta was probably not a military officer at all since Cirta was not under the supervision of the legate at this time.[36] Apart from this general military supervision the tribesmen were probably permitted to keep their own forms of organization.[37]

We are told [38] that in the course of the war against Tacfarinas, Blaesus, the Roman commander, ceased the practice of withdrawing the soldiers to the old province when the fighting season was over but spread them out in small bands in forts on the edge of the theatre of war to keep the tribesmen in check.[39] As the native life was naturally nomadic these forts were probably necessary to peace and order for a considerable period and many of them became permanent settlements and centers of Roman influence. It is likely that they were placed near the few avail-

[35] *Ann. epig.*, 1896, no. 10 (70 A. D.); Cagnat, *op. cit.*, p. 37, n. 2; *C. I. L.*, X, 8038. On the Cinithii, see ch. IV, n. 17.

[36] *At. arch. Alg.*, f. 8, 139; *C.*, 19923.

[37] Cf. princeps = chief at Thubursicum Numidarum, *I. L. Al.*, 1297, 1341; at Calama, *I. L. Al.*, 233, 290; the tribe of Misictri in the region of Hippo Regius, *I. L. Al.*, 138; 156; 174; the survival of clan organization among the Musunii Regianii, *I. L. A.*, 107; cf. *I. L. Al.*, 3869; and among the Musulamii, *I. L. Al.*, 2836, 2853, 3144; see Pliny, *H. N.*, V, 17; Gsell, *Hist. anc.*, V, p. 54.

[38] Tac., *Ann.*, III, 74.

[39] A system which was throughout characteristic of the African Limes, Cagnat, *op. cit.*, p. 523 ff.

able springs, and that an attempt was made to use the land about them for sustenance. Such is the probable origin of Sufes,[40] situated near the fringe of the Punic settlement about Mactar. Centers such as Cilma,[41] Sufetula,[42] Cillium,[43] Thelepte,[44] Gemellae [45] on the military road to Capsa, [46] and Thiges [47] beyond Capsa near the Chott el Djerid originated in this way.[48] The natives now compelled to give up their nomadic habit of life were forced to use their land in a more intensive way. Some doubtless attached themselves to these fort-settlements and all found there in some measure an example of agri-

40 *C.*, 11427; 11418, a dedication to Augustus? The name, like that of Sufetula, is Punic. It was perhaps a frontier fort on the edge of the area of Punic infiltration about Mactar. Many of these had probably been indigenous castella.

41 Modern Djilma.

42 *C.*, 23216: Ca]es Ves[pasianus. As in other towns which were advanced in status by Vespasian the citizens were of the Quirine tribe: *C.*, 11345; 11349; 23226; *I. L. A.*, 137; 138; 139.

43 At first a fort dependent on Thelepte, *C.*, 211, 216; cf. Toutain, *Les cités.*, pp. 316-7.

44 See Toutain, *l. c.;* It gained municipal rights from Trajan, being inscribed in the Papiria tribe, *C.*, 211. Its territory included Cillium, and extended westward perhaps to Soumat el Kheneg, *At. arch. Alg.*, f. 40, 99 where land was at least administered from Thelepte, *I. L. Al.*, 3834.

45 Vicus, *Tab. Peut.;* there was a pottery industry there, Toutain, *op. cit.*, p. 261 ff.

46 The old tribal center of the Capsitani, Pliny, *H. N.*, V, 30; cf. *C.*, p. 2349.

47 *C.*, 23166 (97 A. D.). The civitas is non-technical in meaning or perhaps like the civitas Nybgeniorum really a tribal territory, *C.*, 23165 (83 A. D.).

48 Thala near Ammaedara was a praesidium, Tac., *Ann.*, III, 21; see n. 55. Cf. the military station at Bir Oum Ali, *At. arch. Alg.*, f. 40, 106; *I. L. Al.*, p. 372, and 3841-4.

culture, particularly as veterans like Flavius of Cillium,[49] on completion of their term of service took up favored bits of land near these posts.

The development of southern Tunisia arose as a result of two main causes; the restriction of the native tribes compelled them to change their way of life and to make their territories more productive; the castella of soldiers provided some centers of settled life and an example of the means of using the soil. The Roman government wanted the indigenous peoples fixed within reasonably definite limits, settled, producing, and tax-paying. That accomplished, the slow outworking of economic forces through two or three generations did the rest.[50]

The regions involved differ considerably in character. Between Althiburos, Theveste, Sufes, and in general the northern slopes of the central massif cereals can usually be cultivated in the valleys, plains, and lower slopes, while the higher slopes provide grazing. Rainfall though not always certain is reasonably assured. Consequently the basic conditions for a settled life were soon attainable. To the south beyond the high ridges of Dj. Chambi and Dj. Semmama the amount of precipitation is considerably less. As cereal crops were quite uncertain, agriculture necessarily became largely arboriculture.

[49] *C.*, 211.

[50] The Basutos of South Africa may be cited as a modern parallel since limitation of territory and the multiplication of the native stock is compelling the natives to give up their communal pastoral life and turn to agriculture and private ownership.

Subsoil moisture, the result of a seepage from the hills is available for the deep roots of the olive all along the southern edge of the central massif in the plateau which extends in an arc of a circle from Djilma to Thelepte. Eastward toward Triaga and southward toward Capsa conditions are still less favorable and it still remains to be seen if the methods of cultivation in use at Sfax will bring the culture of the olive there. No Roman sites are known in this region except the stopping-places mentioned in the Itineraries.

It was natural, therefore, that development came more quickly in the northern portion and that it was different in character in the two regions. By the time of Vespasian the tribesmen were not only well settled but were providing cohorts of auxiliaries for the Roman army.[51] The legionary camp was then moved on to Theveste to protect the occupied territory from the hillmen of the Aurès mountains and the nomads of the western plains.[52] The town which had grown up about the camp and was composed mainly of veterans was given colonial status.[53] With the pacification of the country and signs of development, Punic influences began to be increasingly felt.[54]

[51] Cohors Musulamiorum, Cagnat, *op. cit.*, p. 245; *C.*, 4879; recruits from the Numidae, *Ann. epig.*, 1896, no. 10.

[52] De Pachtère, *C. R. Ac.*, 1916, p. 273 ff.; cf. Cagnat, *op. cit.*, p. 428 ff.; *I. L. Al.*, 3098.

[53] Colonia Flavia Augusta Emerita Ammaedara, *C.*, 308.

[54] Althiburos and Mactar were strongly Punicized centers to the north and east, Gsell, *Hist. anc.*, II, p. 196; V, p. 267; *C.*, 27774. The

The presence of at least three classes of land in this region apart from the land still in the possession of the natives brings up the question of the principle which the Romans followed in the alienation of this land. The territory of Ammaedara itself was quite extensive;[55] near by was an imperial estate, the Saltus Massipianus;[56] east of that the estate of the senator, Lucius Africanus, the Saltus Beguensis;[57] near Kalaat es Senam was found a stone marking the boundary between the estate of Valeria Atticilla and the Musulamii;[58] all on territory which must once have belonged to the Musulamii. Whether Rome at

---

extension of Punic influences into the newly pacified country is in part due to the presence of soldiers recruited in other parts of Africa. No doubt the merchants now came in greater numbers. The extension of the cult of Saturn, and the occurrence of place names such as Sufes and Sufetula and family names like Saturninus are evidences of a Punic infiltration.

[55] One frontier bordered the territory of the Musulamii at Khanguet Nasseur, 14 Km. northeast of Theveste, *I. L. Al.*, 2939 bis (116 A. D.) where was also the limit of an imperial domain. Whether *I. L. A.*, 180: *int(er) col(onos) et soc(ios) Tal(enses)* marks a limit between the land of Ammaedara and land granted to a private association or between two categories of land within the territory of Ammaedara is unknown; see *Mél. éc.*, 1912, p. 205. Thala although not the Thala of Sall., *Jug.*, 76, see Gsell, *op. cit.*, V, pp. 276-8, appears from the remains about it to have been a strongly indigenous center, and remained as a castellum with seniores, *I. L. A.*, 195. Any advantages of position it may originally have had were neutralized by the foundation of Ammaedara with superior status and a large territory. Two epitaphs of people inscribed in the Quirine tribe indicate that the territory of Ammaedara extended southward into the plain of Foussana, *C.*, 295, 296. See Piganiol and Saint-Laurent, *Mél. éc.*, 1912, pp. 69 ff.

[56] *C.*, 587 (Marcus Aurelius). See *At. arch. Tun.*, Thala.

[57] *C.*, 11451, 23246.

[58] Carton, *C. R. Ac.*, 1923, p. 71.

this time took the attitude that all conquered land was public land of the Roman people, and that its disposal was completely at the discretion of the governing authority is a debatable question.[59] The principle followed in this case seems to be that the nomadic tribesmen were held to be ranging far more territory than they were putting to any profitable use; therefore with their settlement considerable areas of their best land were alienated. The logical conclusion of such a principle would involve the acceptance of a policy reserving a definite amount of land for the tribes as soon as they had been compressed into a sufficiently small space; such a policy as in fact Trajan followed. Some of the land of the Musulamii was probably held for the support of the legion and with the departure of the legion Ammaedara fell heir to it.[60] Whether the imperial estate, the Saltus Massipianus, is the result of an original occupation of a portion of tribal territory or a later confiscation of it as a private estate we cannot know. The Saltus Beguensis in 138 A. D. was still stated to be in the territory of the Musulamii although it was far outside of the Trajanic boundaries. The explanation is probably that the estate was acquired at a time when land had been alienated from the tribesmen and sold or granted to a private owner,

[59] The full assumption of the theory of "dominium in solo provinciali" seems to have been delayed until the second century A. D., Frank, *J. R. S.*, 1927.

[60] See ch. IV, on the legionary territory about Lambaesis; *C.*, 4322.

that the land purchased or granted was specified in the bill as " in the territory of the Musulamii " and that the resolution of the senate regarding market-days spoke in terms of the original title.

With the signs of possible development, Roman investors had bought up considerable tracts of this untilled land, keeping the native population there to work what they had previously ranged. The castella and vici, really indigenous villages found on both senatorial and imperial estates,[61] originated in the necessity of points of defence in a previously unsettled country, and in the natural clustering of the people about springs. A certain degree of community life grew up. We find magistri on the Saltus Massipianus,[62] where the coloni erected buildings at their own expense.[63] The pagus at Sidi Mohammed ech Chaffai west of Thala where the cultores Iovis Opt. Max. erected a paganicum at their own expense was probably in the territory of Ammaedara.[64] For the rest we can hardly estimate how far native territories in this region were thus alienated. Thala remained a native center of some importance.[65]

[61] *Corp. Agrim.*, ed. Thulin, p. 45. Many agricultural and other ruins attest the character of the ancient settlements here. At Bordj el Arbi, *C.*, 587, was the center of the Saltus Massipianus, but there was also near by the Fundus Ver.., *C.*, 11735, *At. arch. Tun.*, Thala, 40, and Mutia, Thala, 52. Casae was the central vicus for the Saltus Beguensis. Note also the vicus at Ain Maja, 28 Km. east of Thala, *I. L. A.*, 198.

[62] *I. L. A.*, 194.

[63] *C.*, 587.

[64] *C.*, 23326.

[65] See n. 55.

The development of the southern area came somewhat later owing to the more gradual discovery of the means of conserving a sufficient supply of water [66] and to the slower growth of the olive. While there is some possibility that Sufetula was the center at some time of a region for the collection of revenues [67] there is no evidence of the amassing of large imperial and private estates. The mode of putting the land in use was necessarily different; the returns on an investment were necessarily much slower. Just as today therefore the process could much better be carried on by the permanent inhabitants in their own small areas. In some favored spots soldiers who had been campaigning there, or had been stationed in the castella took up land on securing their discharge. A good instance of the process is the case of Cillium.[68] Flavius Secundus, a soldier probably of Vespasian's time, on his discharge took up land at Cillium by one of the rare springs of the region. As Cillium was attached to Thelepte the settlement must have been quite small and so Flavius could find sufficient moisture to water his garden and boast that he was the first man in all that region to grow grapes. There never was a sufficient natural supply for vineyards and olives were the chief prod-

[66] On some of the Roman modes of catching and conserving moisture in this region see *Enquête sur les install. hyd. rom.*, I, p. 331 ff.; II, p. 3 ff.

[67] *C.*, 23219, 23226 (patrimonial officials); 23222-5 which may mark the boundary between the public land of Sufetula and a private estate. On the region of Hadrumetum see ch. V, n. 51 ff. and text.

[68] *C.*, 211; cf. 211-6 from the tomb of the Flavii.

uct. Punic families came into the settlement which grew to some importance and a mingling of the stocks began. One Saturninus, son of Masac, espoused Flavia Fortunata, doubtless a descendant of the original Flavius.[69]

We may suppose that Sufetula developed first. It belonged to the Quirine tribe usual among Vespasianic foundations [70] and was the patria of legionary soldiers at Lambaesis in the second century A. D.[71] Thelepte, the citizens of which were enrolled in the Papirian tribe, received its status from Trajan.[72] Like Ammaedara, it had an extensive territory including Cillium to the north and extending westward beyond Bir Oum Ali.[73] How soon Cillium became a separate municipium is unknown. It is mentioned as the patria of a legionary soldier at Lambaesis who entered service in 173 A. D.[74] The Musunii Regiani remained on their own territory on the plain between Cillium and Thelepte, keeping hidden under Roman terms much of their clan and tribal organization.[75] The numerous ruins of oil presses and of agricultural exploitations in all this area show the character of the settlement and prove how successful was the adaptation to the basic economic conditions of the

69 *C.*, 11312.

70 See n. 42.

71 *C.*, 2567, 1, 29.

72 Toutain, *Les cités,* p. 318.

73 *C.*, 211, 212; *I. L. Al.*, 3834; *At. arch. Alg.*, f. 40, 99.

74 *Mél. éc.*, 1891, p. 315, 11. 4 and 22; cf. *C.*, 2568, 1. 46. These soldiers were Julii.

75 See n. 37.

area.[76] The development of municipal life was the work of the succeeding century.

The extension of the Roman occupation to the westward followed a system similar to that in southern Tunis. The military center, the camp, was moved on to Theveste. But the fact that the Trajanic limit of the Musulamian territory was at Ain Kemallel [77] more than half-way on the road from Theveste to Mascula shows how far the forts and stationes had to be sent out at an earlier date. It was necessary also to watch the passes of the Aurès mountains, and to guard against the incursions of the unsubdued tribes to the west about the Chott el Hodna. Such is the probable origin of Vazaivi,[78] Mascula,[79] and the nearby Aquae Flavianae, from which has come to light a dedication of 76 A. D.[80] We may note that the Flavians began to establish regular communications

[76] See *At. arch. Tun.*, Sbeitla, Kasrin, Feriana. The development of the Bahiret el Arneb, south of Theveste and west of the territory of Thelepte though later may be discussed here. The ruins prove a considerable culture of the olive probably under conditions similar to those about Cillium and Thelepte, see Gsell, *At. arch. Alg.*, f. 40; and *I. L. Al.*, p. 351; but there is evidence of large senatorial estates such as existed about Ammaedara. See *I. L. Al.*, 3625, 3636, a senatorial estate containing the villages of Thesecthi and Vesat., and 3634, a senatorial estate. These probably grew up during the second century after the development of Sufetula, Cillium and Thelepte had revealed the most profitable mode of exploitation. Cf. *C. I. L.*, VI, 2108, one of these senators was an Arval brother in 231-9 A. D.

[77] *At. arch. Alg.*, f. 28, 163; *I. L. Al.*, 2988, 2989: Musulamii and imperial property; note also 2978: Musulamii and Tisibennenses.

[78] *C.*, 17626; *At. arch. Alg.*, f. 39, 49.

[79] *C.*, 2251; 17673; *At. arch. Alg.*, f. 28, 138.

[80] *C.*, 17725; *At. arch. Alg.*, f. 28, 137. On these sites see Gsell and Graillot, *Mél. éc.*, 1893, p. 492 ff.

between these regions and the long occupied regions to the north[81] but the effective occupation and development of the country west of Theveste was the work of the second century.

Another Flavian foundation perhaps contemporraneous with the elevation of Ammaedara was the colonization of the old native town of Madauros[82] with a settlement of veterans. While there was probably little military necessity for such an act by the time of Vespasian, the site of the colony must have been selected for strategic purposes.[83] For slightly to the south was the territory of the Musulamii; only a short distance to the northwest the territory of the Numidae about Thubursicum; and while the towns and villages of Thagora, Naraggara, Civitas Popthensis, and Masculula were a short distance to the northeast, portions of the country were none too well developed and hillmen were still carrying on dangerous raids on the valleys in 65 A. D.[84] The territory of Madauros, fertile probably in both cereals and olives, though none of the latter may be seen there today, was never extensive, nor did it, as the size of its ruined forum and theatre show, ever have a very large population.[85]

[81] Theveste-Hippo road, *I. L. Al.*, 3885, 76 A. D.

[82] See Gsell and Joly, *Khamissa, Mdaourouch, Announa*, ii, Mdaourouch, p. 8 ff.; *I. L. Al.*, 2070, 2064 bis, 2152; Apul., *Apol.*, 24.

[83] Or, as Gsell suggests, *op. cit.*, p. 10, also as a Roman settlement to check a strongly indigenous area.

[84] *C.*, 14603; on the region see *At. arch. Alg.*, ff. 18 and 19.

[85] Gsell and Joly, *op. cit.*, p. 16 ff.; cf. Apul., *Apol.*, 24: *splendidissima colonia.*

Madauros was at the frontier of Numidia and of Gaetulia;[86] to the south conditions favored a pastoral nomadic life; to the north a region of well-watered hills and fertile valleys invited agricultural settled existence wherever the broken country permitted. Within the latter area were towns such as Thagaste and Calama which had been under Punic influences.[87] But the major portion of the region was composed of indigenous tribal or clan territories. At the head-waters of the Bagradas was the tribe of the Numidae;[88] over the height of land toward the Oued Cherf were the Nattabutes.[89] A pagus may refer to a similar but small aggregation about Thagaste;[90] we may note also areas under magistri at Koudiat Setih[91] and at Hammam Zaid;[92] Libyc inscriptions are frequent in all the region; some Punic ones are found.[93] The pacification and development of these tribal territories was well begun in the first century A. D.

The Numidae appear to have joined the Gaetulian tribes in the attack upon Thubursicum in 24 A. D.[94] We find them in Vespasian's time supplying auxil-

[86] Apul., *Apol.*, 24.

[87] See *I. L. Al.*, pp. 20, and 81; nos. 233 and 290; Thagaste was a free town from Augustan days, Pliny, *H. N.*, V, 30, but always small.

[88] Gsell and Joly, *op. cit.*, i, Khamissa, p. 11 ff.

[89] *At. arch. Alg.*, f. 18, 135 and 200; *I. L. Al.*, pp. 57 and 60; cf. n. 100 ff. and text.

[90] *I. L. Al.*, 883.

[91] *At. arch. Alg.*, f. 18, 282; *I. L. Al.*, p. 88 and nos. 950-2.

[92] *At. arch. Alg.*, f. 18, 352; *I. L. Al.*, p. 87, and no. 928.

[93] See *I. L. Al.*, introductions; *At. arch. Alg.* passim; Gsell, *Hist anc.*, V, pp. 263 and 270.

[94] Tac., *Ann.*, IV, 24.

iary troops to the army and supervised, like the Musulamii who also were supplying auxiliary cohorts at that time,[95] by a military prefect.[96] By 100 A. D. their chief town became a civitas [97] and received municipal status shortly afterwards.[98] The comparatively short time required for their development was directly due to the superior economic advantages of their territory. Whether the tribe became an entity apart from its municipal center, or whether the territory of the municipium coincided with the previous tribal territory is uncertain.[99] The probable development of two centers in the case of the Nattabutes at Oum Krekèche [100] and at Guelaa bou Atfane,[101] the latter of which may have been connected with some other area [102] would point to a division in the organization of this tribe. The two centers are too close together to admit of a theory of resettlement for one or the other. It is probable that the natural development of the native villages produced this result. Roman policy tended to treat the local entity according to the local conditions, and to secure peace and order with as little disturbance as possible to the natural order of development.

We have evidence of imperial estates near Ca-

[95] *I. L. Al.*, 1335.

[96] *Ann. epig.*, 1896, n. 10.

[97] *I. L. Al.*, 1244.

[98] *I. L. Al.*, 1239; Gsell and Joly, *op. cit.*, p. 11 ff.

[99] See ch. IV, n. 22 and text.

[100] *At. arch. Alg.*, f. 18, 135; *C.*, 4826; ch. IV, n. 23 ff. and text.

[101] *At. arch. Alg.*, f. 18, 200; *I. L. Al.*, 561.

[102] A praefectus iure dicundo, *I. L. Al.*, 572.

lama, belonging to Claudius,[103] Nero,[104] and Domitian.[105] Their origin we can hardly determine. They were probably private holdings since confiscated, but may go back even to Numidian royal domain land. There is evidence also of an imperial estate in the first century A. D. at Hr. el Hammam.[106] One at Aioun el Maker belonged to a prominent citizen of Thagaste.[107]

Hippo Regius [108] and Thabraca [109] were dowered with extensive territories from early times but excepting the plain close to Hippo and the river valley at Thabraca the country was difficult and hilly, although well-watered and, where cultivable, fertile.[110] The region particularly in the hills northwest to northeast of Thagaste, southeast of Hippo Regius and south of La Calle remained strongly indigenous in character with some admixture of Punic in-

[103] *I. L. Al.*, 323.

[104] *I. L. Al.*, 324.

[105] *I. L. Al.*, 325.

[106] *At. arch. Alg.*, f. 18, 208; *I. L. Al.*, 758, 759, 863.

[107] *At. arch. Alg.*, f. 18, 326; *I. L. Al.*, 881, 982.

[108] *At. arch. Alg.*, f. 9, 59; see Holmes Van Mater Dennis 3d, *Hippo Regius from Earliest Times until the Vandal Invasion*, Princeton, 1925. Cf. ch. II, n. 184. The territory of Hippo extended from the Oued Ouider, *Atlas*, f. 2, 10 where it adjoined the Cirtensian territory, *I. L. Al.*, 134, eastward to Blandan, *Atlas*, f. 10, 1 and the territory of Thabraca, *I. L. Al.*, 109, and southward till it touched the territory of Calama near the hill of Fedjoudje, *Atlas*, f. 9, 86; *I. L. Al.*, 132. The castellum Fussala, St. Aug., *Letters*, 209, which bordered upon the territory of Hippo was forty miles away probably southeastward. There were many villages about the town in the plain, Gsell, *Atlas*, f. 9, 59.

[109] See ch. II, n. 185.

[110] Rivière et Lecq, *Traité pratique d'agriculture*, p. 22.

fluence.[111] As the terrain favored grazing rather than agriculture there was little municipal development. We have the mention of two pagi probably dependent on Thabraca,[112] and of a civitas of the first century A. D., Thullium, bordering on the territory of Hippo Regius.[113] The region is particularly rich in Libyc inscriptions.[114] Evidence of many estates both imperial [115] and private,[116] some belonging to local grandees of Hippo,[117] are found within the territory of the city. The evidence for these estates has come however from sites in the plain of Hippo or near the main roads. Little evidence of estates in the broken hinterland of the territory of Hippo has yet been found. The date of the formation of these estates is uncertain. The procurator of the praedia and the saltus of the region of Hippo mentioned in an inscription of Hippo [118] and in one of Calama [119] dates probably from the time of Trajan or of Hadrian but as economic conditions favored a somewhat earlier development on these lines we may assume it. The care of the imperial estates of the region of Hippo was not too engrossing to exclude that of the region of Theveste by the same procura-

111 Gsell, *Hist. anc.*, V, p. 263; *At. arch. Alg.*, ff. 9 and 10 passim; *I. L. Al.*, pp. 15, 87, 94.

112 See ch. II, n. 185.

113 *At. arch. Alg.*, f. 9, 242; *I. L. Al.*, 137.

114 See Gsell, *At. arch. Alg.*, ff. 9, 10, 18, 19; *I. L. Al.*, 11. cc.

115 *I. L. Al.*, 89, 93, 131; *At. arch. Alg.*, f. 9, 60, 71, 80.

116 *I. L. Al.*, 97, 102, 127; *At. arch. Alg.*, f. 9, 193, 185, 216.

117 *I. L. Al.*, 95 and 96, 132; *At. arch. Alg.*, f. 9, 193, 81.

118 *I. L. Al.*, 3992.

119 *I. L. Al.*, 285.

tor.[120] The town of Hippo was an Augustan municipium [121] but is mentioned in Ptolemy [122] and in the Itinerary of Antonine [123] as a colony. Since Vespasian was the one who realized the importance of the town sufficiently to build roads connecting it with Carthage [124] and Theveste [125] it probably owed its advancement to him.

There is almost no datable evidence from the Cirtensian territory during the first century. The pagi Cirtenses required protection during the war with Tacfarinas.[126] The people of the three federated colonies,[127] and the citizens in Cirta and in the various pagi built up a brilliant and prosperous life which centered particularly about the city of Cirta itself. From the latter part of the century on we find natives of Cirta important in administrative positions and in the literary life of the empire.[128] Native tribes within the area seem to have been administered by prefects probably non-military in character.[129] It is probable that the Sabarbares to the southwest were not included within the Cirtensian territory,

[120] *I. L. Al.*, 3992, 285; see ch. V, n. 46 ff. and text.

[121] *I. L. Al.*, 109.

[122] IV, 3, 2, p. 615, ed. Müller: the title colonia should be joined to Hippo not Aphrodisium.

[123] Ed. Parthey and Pinder, p. 8.

[124] *C.*, 10116, 76 A. D.

[125] *C.*, 10119, 76. A. D.

[126] Tac., *Ann.*, III, 74.

[127] *C.*, 7069; see ch. II, n. 152 ff. and text.

[128] Gsell, *At. arch. Alg.*, f. 17, 126, p. 13; Lully, *De Senatorum Romanorum Patria*, p. 243 ff.

[129] *C.*, 19923.

but the question is uncertain.[130] Within the area appear as elsewhere large senatorial estates, but these for the most part occur noticeably in portions clearly apart from those taken up by the various classes of land of Cirta or of its pagi. Such was the Saltus Bagatensis east of Cirta and north of Dj. Oum Settas,[131] and the estates of Arrius Pacatus and of his wife, Antonia Saturnina, in the plain to the southwest of Cirta.[132] The estate, at Tiddis, of Lollius Urbicus, who seems to have belonged to a local Cirtensian family probably also was acquired during the first century A. D.[133] Evidence for the presence of proprietors within the municipal territories is

130 See n. 30; *C.*, 10335, 8270; Gsell, *At. arch. Alg.*, f. 17, 201, 214; f. 16, 468, 472, 473.

131 *At. arch. Alg.*, f. 17, 158: a large estate with several agricultural establishments in the area partly of good, partly of broken land east of a portion of the public land of Cirta, *Atlas,* f. 17, 134, and west of the territory of Thibilis. The owner was M. Pacceius Victor Rufinus, *Rec. de Constantine,* 1901, pp. 190-3; cf. Tac., *Hist.*, IV, 41: a Pacceius Africanus was a senator in the times of Nero and Vespasian.

132 *At. arch. Alg.*, f. 17, 237, of Arrius Pacatus; *C.*, 8241, 7032; cf. 7031, the Pacatian bath at Cirta. *At. arch. Alg.*, f. 17, 386, of Arria Saturnina his wife, *C.*, 8280; cf. 7032. As in the case of the estate of Lucius Africanus, the Saltus Beguensis, market days were held at the vicus of the estate; cf. also near by *Atlas,* f. 17, 384: *nundinas Emadaucapens(es) immunes.* As Antonia Saturnina was a connection by marriage in the same generation as the parents of Antoninus Pius and daughter of the Lucius Antonius Saturninus who was proclaimed emperor at Mayence in 88 A. D. the estate dated at least from Flavian times and was probably acquired under conditions similar to the Saltus Beguensis from the former range of a pacified tribe, perhaps the near-by Sabarbares.

133 *C.*, 6706. The date of the inscription from the saltus of Caelia Maxima is unknown, *At. arch. Alg.*, f. 17, 66; *C.*, 19328.

found in the agri accepti of Cirta,[134] and in the agri divisi of Sigus.[135]

In the original province the first century A. D. was for the most part a period of quietness, peace, and prosperity. The development of the interior enriched the coastal cities where the products were exported. Toutain has justly remarked[136] that in Africa the road system was not built as a net about particular centers but was a means of joining the interior to the sea at as many points as possible. Naturally Carthage profited most, but the cities of the eastern coast, the Emporiae, were quite prosperous also. Settlers old and new, native population, and owners of estates worked to one end, the production of food for Rome.[137] The importance of the African grain supply probably entered into the calculations of Macer and of Valerius Festus[138] during the troubles of 68-70 A. D. Having Africa they thought to control the situation.

[134] Ager publicus of Cirta: *At. arch. Alg.*, f. 17, 59; *C.*, 7089 = 8211 = 19433; *Atlas*, 140; *Ann. epig.*, 1908, 246; *Atlas*, 167; *C.*, 7087, 7084 = 19431, 7085 = 19432, 7088; *Atlas*, 261 ?; *C.*, 8268; *Atlas*, 331; *C.*, 7090; *Atlas*, 307; *C.*, 19104; *Atlas*, 340; *C.*, 18768. Ager Acceptus of Cirta: *Atlas*, 66; *C.*, 19329; *Atlas*, 331; *C.*, 7090; *Atlas*, 167; *C.*, as above; *Atlas*, 463; *Rec. de Const.*, 1904, p. 34; *Atlas*, 340; *C.*, as above.

[135] *At. arch. Alg.*, f. 17, 335; *C.*, 19132-4. The division was made by P. Cassius Secundus, Hadrian's legate.

[136] *Les cités*, p. 143.

[137] Cagnat, L'annone d'Afrique, *Mém. Acad.*, 1916, p. 247 ff. In estimating the contribution of the Roman market to African prosperity the amount of produce sent as tribute and as rental on imperial land must be taken into account. For commercial development note the offices at Ostia of various African cities, Calza, *Bull. Comm.*, 1915, p. 75; *Guida di Ostia*, p. 106.

[138] Pallu de Lessert, *Fastes*, pp. 318 and 321 ff.

How soon the tendency apparent in the saltus inscriptions toward a certain cultivation of grapes, olives, and fruits began we do not know.[139] The Romans wished grain from Africa but the hot summer climate of the Bagradas valley does not permit a proper rotation of crops for soiling purposes or the extensive use of ordinary soiling crops. Consequently there must have been a tendency to other crops as a continued cultivation of cereals gradually exhausted the soil. The prohibition of Domitian probably checked the planting of vines, but the extension of olive culture continued.[140]

A certain extension of Roman influence to the less accessible parts of the province and a certain degree of assimilation and of Romanization within the older portions may be noted. The imperial cults spread into the mountains of central Tunisia. At Mograwa[141] there was found a dedication to Rome and Tiberius; at Chusira there were flamens in 70 A. D.[142] In the more developed areas as also at Cirta the better families of African origin took to themselves the forms of the names and in some measure of the institutions of the dominant Romans.[143] At Gurza in 12 B. C. the officials had Punic names. In 68 A. D. the officials, still Punic, used the Roman form of

[139] In the saltus inscriptions production of cereals, also of olives and of figs is assumed. Grape-vines might be planted to replace old vineyards, *C.*, 25902, Hr. Mettich, II, 1. 25.

[140] Rostovtzeff, *Soc. and Ec. Hist.*, pp. 189 and 545, n. 11.

[141] Ancient name unknown, *C.*, 11912.

[142] *C.*, 698.

[143] On the onomastic, see Toutain, *Les cités*, p. 167 ff.

name but incorrectly.[144] In 48 A. D. the civitas of Thugga was governed by suffetes with Punic or Libyan names.[145] Later names in the town have the Roman form. The process of assimilation was in general too gradual to have been the result of official pressure and never penetrated far down among the lower classes.[146]

Another movement comparatively small in itself gives a significant indication of the conditions within the province. During the surveys of the provincial land certain small patches called subseciva of steeply sloping, rough land, or land otherwise considered unfit for occupation had been left outside of the regular survey and had often been left unassigned.[147] Consequently the title to much of these subseciva remained with the state. It is probable that there were none of these left unassigned in the original province of 146 B. C. after all the agrarian legislation, but a certain amount was left in the Marian area.[148] Throughout the century or so before Vespasian owners of adjoining estates and municipalities with territories adjoining such areas encouraged their tenants, or possessores, following an old and usually safe precedent to enclose them and put them to what-

[144] *C.*, 68 and 69.

[145] *C.*, 26517, and the inscriptions of the Gabinian family; cf. at Cillium, *C.*, 11308, 11310, 11312. As Latin was the official language its public use need imply no great degree of Romanization. Its improper use however is significant.

[146] Toutain, *Les cités*, pp. 195-6; cf. *Cultes païens*, III, p. 96 ff.

[147] *Corp. Agrim.*, ed. Thulin, p. 41.

[148] Inscription of Hr. Mettich, *C.*, 25902, I, l. 8.

ever productive use was possible.[149] Such a process is evidence of the closer settlement and the greater pressure for land, which resulted from the continued period of prosperity.

A tendency became apparent toward centralization and consolidation particularly striking in the case of the public land. The personal control of all revenues encouraged by the Augustan system [150] began the movement which the Claudian bureaus carried on. The distinction between land the revenues of which went to the public chest and that of which the revenues were part of the emperor's private fortune [151] tended to disappear as the emperor's personal control extended to each and as he at times drew on his private fortune to meet public demands. In Africa probably the greatest single step toward a centralization of the large estates was the confiscation by Nero of large areas of land held by senatorial land-owners.[152] These additions and the confusion of the years 68-70 A. D. doubtless made necessary a reorganization, but there is evidence that in Africa at

[149] *Corp. Agrim.*, l. c.; the law of Mancia reveals how one proprietor leased such land to his tenants, *C.*, 25902; cf. Frank, *A. J. P.*, 1926, p. 166.

[150] Gardthausen, *Augustus*, I, pp. 607-8; Frank, *Rom. Hist.*, pp. 358-60; Hirschfeld, *Kais. Verwb.*, p. 125 ff.; Dessau, *Gesch. d. Kaiserzeit*, I, p. 190 ff.

[151] e. g., perhaps the estate of Claudius at Calama, *I. L. Al.*, 323; on sources of imperial private fortunes see Hirschfeld, *Kl. Schr.*, p. 516 ff.

[152] Pliny, *H. N.*, XVIII, 35 exaggerates but represents the general process. See Rostovtzeff, *Gesch. Kol.*, p. 320.

least Vespasian made little change in the usages already in force in particular estates.[153]

Vespasian's attitude was also shown in his attempt to reclaim the subseciva and to sell them for the benefit of the treasury. From various parts of the empire he gained not a little money for the treasury in this way, but finally in view of the protestations of Italian land-owners he desisted without giving up his claim. Domitian by edict gave up his claim to these lands in Italy, but nothing is said about the provinces.[154] The provisions of the Trajanic procurators in the inscription of Hr. Mettich show how the practical difficulties of the question were met while the laws of Hadrian removed the legal question.[155] The resurvey of the fossa regia of 146 B. C.

[153] The Lex Manciana, most probably a private regulation, see Frank, *A. J. P.*, 1926, p. 156; cf. Rostovtzeff, *op. cit.*, p. 321 ff. for an opposing view, was still used as a basis of agreement on one saltus by the coloni and the Trajanic procurators, and only later and in part extended in application to other saltus. We find that the estate of Lamia was managed by a procurator in 43 B. C., Cic., *Ad Fam.*, XII, 29, 2, but vilici are found on imperial property in the first century A. D., *I. L. Al.*, 323; C., 12314. Note also a procurator of Augustus in the Byzacene, Pliny, *H. N.*, XVIII, 95. The sweeping confiscations under Nero doubtless compelled a reorganization and extension of the system of administration of the imperial estates, probably under Vespasian; see ch. V, n. 8 ff. and text.

[154] *Corp. Agrim.*, ed. Thulin, p. 41.

[155] The Trajanic procurators in the Hr. Mettich inscription, using the terminology of Mancia's rule confirmed in heritable possession the occupation of the subseciva, title to which Vespasian's activity had rendered uncertain; the law of Hadrian which legalized the occupation and granted full possession on set terms of all rough or uncultivated land within the imperial estates put an end to the question, Frank, *A. J. P.*, 1926, p. 166; cf. ch. V, n. 64 ff. and text.

was doubtless connected with this activity. Marking as it did the boundary of the old province where the economic life had been built up under the provisions of the Lex Agraria of 111 B. C., and the Marian settlement to the west, and the indigenous regions to the south, it defined areas containing different categories of land of which Vespasian's policy had made a re-definition necessary.[156]

In spite therefore of the comparatively scanty information we possess regarding the development of Africa during the first century A. D. the main outlines are reasonably clear. It was a century of conquest, expansion, and pioneer development in the newer parts of the province; of consolidation and of assimilation in the old. The Roman legion pushed its outposts southward in the interests of peace and security compelling the nomadic tribesmen to settle on limited territories and to live in peace. Wherever the economic basis of urban life could be found, native centers developed, or legionary forts provided centers about which settlements could gather. Agricultural development began at once where conditions were favorable, and extended as better adaptations to the soil and climate were discovered. Blocks of land alienated from the tribal ranges became large private or imperial estates, or as in the case of Ammaedara were given to veteran settlements. In such

[156] See ch. I, n. 14. There were probably no subseciva in the province of 146 B. C. since the Agrarian law of 111 B. C. had provided for all classes of land.

foundations however as Ammaedara, Madauros, and Theveste we must not see an attempt to Romanize the country or an imperial policy of urbanization. These towns were composed largely of veterans from towns possessing the Roman municipal form, and were already fitted by tradition and training for urban life. After their term of service in the army they were settled on sites where they could best watch the indigenous tribesmen.

The ready market which Rome provided for African products brought prosperity to the sea-port towns and to the developed inland regions. The natural increase of population and the rise in the value of productive land probably tended to increase the area of cultivation. Owners of estates encouraged their tenants to bring uncultivated and unassigned land into use; municipalities also developed the subseciva within or adjoining their territories. In the areas of Roman settlement we may assume a degree of assimilation; Latin, the official language and that of the dominant stock began to be adopted by the more ambitious or prominent indigenous families, and the presence everywhere of the priests of the imperial cult was not without its influence. It was the combined effect of the prosperous development of the economic resources of the province and of the natural assimilation of the diverse elements of the population that made the municipal development of the second century A. D. possible.

The Roman government however took little part in fostering this development beyond maintaining the peace and order which ensured the yearly tribute and the supply of grain for the capital. The Neronian confiscations though important in their results can hardly be attributed to a governmental policy. The extension and organization of the imperial cults [157] seems to have been aided by governmental action as well as by the isolated conventus of Roman citizens. Such action was rather motivated by the desire to impress the symbols of Roman authority.

[157] See ch. I, n. 126. Vespasian may have reorganized the provincial cult and have established the office of the sacerdos provinciae, Hirschfeld, *Zur Gesch. d. röm Kaisercult.*, p. 841; Toutain believes the era of the sacerdos provinciae is a provincial era dating from the disturbances of 70 A. D., *Cultes paiens,* I, p. 80. The omnipresent flamen perpetuus in the provincial towns was connected with the imperial cults, Abbott and Johnson, *op. cit.*, p. 64. Note *C.*, 26517 where the post of flamen divi Augusti is the highest honor in the indigenous civitas of Thugga.

CHAPTER IV

The Second Century in Africa

Trajan's first task was the settlement of the southern border. To meet the incursions of the tribesmen of the western plains near the Chott el Hodna, and of the Aurès mountains, and to close the gateways of the desert, the practice of stationing small detachments of soldiers out in forts was continued, while settlements of veterans were led to strategic points.[1] Timgad situated in the rolling country north of one of the passes of the Aurès was established in 100 A. D. as a veteran colony of some 2000 men.[2] Forts farther afield probably guarded the great road to the desert, the defile of El Kantara, the ancient Calceus Herculis. Westward from Capsa the line of forts was extended south of the Aurès mountains, through Negrine, Ad Badias, and Ad Maiores to Vescera completing by 106 A. D. the girdle of the mountain massif.[3] Soon stationes were placed within the mountain valleys themselves, but no organized attempt at conquest was made.[4] Eastward the fron-

[1] It is possible that even previous to Trajan's accession there were forts at Timgad, Verecunda, and Lambaesis, since the area known to have been pacified extended beyond Mascula: ch. III, nn. 79, 80.

[2] *C.*, 2355, 17841; *At. arch. Alg.*, fol. 27, 255.

[3] On the African Limes see Fabricius, *Pauly-Wissowa-Kroll,* art. Limes; Cagnat, *Armée romaine,* 2nd ed., p. 523 ff.; Gsell, *At. arch. Alg.*, indices for particular places; *C.*, 22348, 2478, 17971, and 23166.

[4] See n. 92; cf. Procopius, *Bell. Vand.*, IV, 13, 23-5: the Aurès remained a strongly indigenous region throughout.

tier with its forts was consolidated below the Chott el Fedjedj and passed south of Leptis Magna toward the Cyrenaica. There was little more war for a century in the proconsular province.

The extension and establishment of the frontier brought peace. It brought also the problem of developing the newly occupied territories. Under the Flavians posts had been established as far west as Mascula and Aquae Flavianae.[5] It is possible that under Trajan the legion stayed for a period at Mascula also.[6] West of Mascula the land had been uncultivated, the range of nomads who came to the plains with their herds in the winter and retired up into the mountains for the summer. These northern slopes of the Aurès receive the last drops of moisture from the northern winds and as they possessed a naturally fertile, unexploited soil provided the economic basis for a prosperous development. The veteran colony of Timgad, castella throughout the region such as Bagai probably was, and the later legionary camp at Lambaesis provided centers about which commercial and indigenous people gathered to build up prosperous towns.[7] The natives of the Aurès were checked; areas of the plain were set aside for the upkeep of the legion, probably not all worked or tenanted by native people since a vexillatio of the

[5] Ch. III, nn. 79, 80.

[6] Cagnat, *op. cit.*, p. 433.

[7] On the characteristics and the development of this region see Gsell, *At. arch. Alg.*, ff. 26, 27, 28 passim; Gsell and Graillot, *Mél. éc.*, 1893, p. 461 ff.; 1894, p. 17 ff.: Ruines romaines au nord de l'Aurès; and *id.*, 1894, p. 501 ff.: Ruines romaines au nord des monts de Batna.

legion itself was sent out to cut the hay at Casae.[8] The various towns as they grew up had territoria about them probably with native cultivators.[9] As in other parts of the province, there were formed large private estates, some senatorial, and also imperial domains. The infertile region about the salt lakes remained hardly touched by Roman influences.

Under Trajan first appears in Africa the evidence of a policy of reservations for the native tribes. Large amounts of territory had been alienated from the range of the Musulamii, and given with their resident population to form the territories of veteran colonies or of private and imperial estates.[10] This process now ceased; for the occupation of the territory to the west made it necessary either to assign a definite area to these natives or else to push the process of division and absorption to a conclusion. Trajan chose to adopt the logical conclusion of the earlier process—now that the best land had already been taken—and carried through a delimitation of tribal boundaries by his legates Minicius Natalis and

[8] *C.*, 4322; *At. arch. Alg.*, f. 27, 141.

[9] Diana, *At. arch. Alg.*, f. 27, 62, had an extensive territory, see n. 89; Timgad, Mascula and Bagai seem to have had smaller territories. The apparent presence of an indigenous substratum in the population throughout the area, but no communes of proven indigenous origin favors the theory that the native ranges were all thus divided and no reservations made except for larger tribes like the Musulamii and the Sabarbares, which had previously been settled. Trajan's treatment of this area points to a more definite theory of the ownership of occupied land than was held in the first century.

[10] Ch. III, nn. 55-8.

Acilius Strabo.[11] The Musulamii were thus hemmed in on the poorer land. For the bare hills south of Madauros, and the equally bare and often salty plains about Meskiana, and along the Oued Chabro can hardly have supported a very prosperous life. In the course of time the tribesmen developed a center at Morsot but we do not know what rank it achieved.[12] It can never have been very imposing. Trajan was thus the first definitely to apply a system of reservations which assigned the tribe some land and enabled it to continue as a corporate entity. What degree of Romanization was achieved under these circumstances was purely the result of natural influences and contacts.

In southern Tunisia a similar process went on. In 30 A. D. Vibius Marsus[13] had already limited the northern boundary of the Nybgenii and marked off their territory from that of the Capsitani.[14] Under Trajan the boundaries of the Nybgenii were completely fixed on their northern and eastern sides,[15] while the south and west sides were probably defined by the Limes itself. The territory of Tacape extended inland to the eastern border[16] and they were thus re-

[11] Gsell, *I. L. Al.*, p. 267; Carton, *C. R. Ac.*, 1923, p. 71; also the Tisibennenses, west of Theveste, a small tribe otherwise unknown, *At. arch. Alg.*, f. 28, 269; *I. L. Al.*, 2978.

[12] *At. arch. Alg.*, f. 29, 66; *I. L. Al.*, p. 271.

[13] *C.*, 22786; Ptolemy, ed. Muller, IV, 3, 6; Cagnat, *C. R. Ac.*, 1909, p. 568 ff.

[14] Pliny, *H. N.*, V, 30: *non civitates tantum sed plerique nationes iure dici possunt; C.*, p. 2349.

[15] *C.*, 22786e, 22787, 22788f; Barthel, *Bonn. Jahrb.*, 1911, p. 87 ff.

[16] *C.*, 22787, 22788e.

strained to the inhospitable land about the Chott el Fedjedj. Their tribal center, Turris Tamalleni, owes its name and perhaps its origin to the establishment of a legionary fort.[17] The Sabarbares who had previously had the freedom of the plains southwest of Cirta about St. Arnaud were now definitely limited to a restricted territory about the Chott el Beida[18] while estates like those of Antonia Saturnina had grown up on parts of their former range.[19] The Col. Tutcensium within their territory was perhaps like Turris Tamalleni a tribal center.[20]

The appearance of Thubursicum in 100 A. D. as a civitas and shortly afterwards as a municipium re-

[17] There are several oases in the region but developed urban life was practically impossible. Turris Tamalleni became a municipium under Hadrian probably including as its territory the former tribal territory. A development in similar fashion from gens to municipium may be true of Gigthis and the Cinithii: 1. Gigthis is not known to be a Punic foundation, Gsell, *Hist. anc.*, II, p. 125; 2. It is unusual for a peregrine civitas to have a tribe attached to it. The Cinithii were subdued by 24 A. D., but Gigthis did not become a Roman municipium until after Hadrian, *C.*, 22707. 3. Cinithii were prominent in the town, *C.*, 22729; 4. Ptolemy places the Cinithii on the shore of the lesser Syrtis where Gigthis was, IV, 3, 6, ed. Muller, p. 641; 5. The mention of a praefectus gentis Cinithiorum, *C.*, 10500, military in character favors the view that they remained as an unattributed corporate entity, since the other military prefects of the first century are found only over tribes which remained unattributed and had not yet developed a tribal center, see ch. III, nn. 33-5. Against this view it may be urged that the words Cinithii and Cinithio, *C.*, 22729, pointedly distinguish Pacatus from the Gigthenses who were at that time the citizens of a Latin if not of a Roman town. On Gigthis see Constans, *Gigthis,* 1916.

[18] *At. arch. Alg.,* f. 16, 468, 472; f. 17, 214, 201, 246; *C.*, 8270, 10335; see ch. III, n. 130.

[19] *At. arch. Alg.,* f. 17, 386, 384; ch. III, n. 132.

[20] *C.*, 8270.

veals further the character of the process of municipal development. The tribe of the Numidae had been pacified and settled long since, was under a military prefect in the time of Vespasian, was situated near established towns, and by the end of the first century had doubtless developed a measure of prosperity.[21] Since the total territory of the gens was not large and the princeps of the tribe is found as a Roman citizen taking part in municipal life it seems probable that as at Turris Tamalleni, at Capsa, and probably at Gigthis the territory of the civitas or later of the municipium included all the territory of the tribe, and that the title of princeps continued on as an honorary dignity.[22] The process of development of the Nattabutes[23] is more obscure. An inscription of 209 A. D. at Oum Krekèche mentions the G[ens] or C[iv(itas)] Nattabutum;[24] later the municipium Nattabutum is mentioned.[25] Within the apparent territory of the tribe was the center of Guelaa Bou Atfane[26] which also developed first into a civitas[27]

[21] See ch. III, nn. 95-9.

[22] *I. L. Al.*, 1297, 1341; the latter who was not a Roman citizen perhaps dates from the period before the municipium; the former was a Roman citizen who held a flaminium within the municipium. It seems best to suppose that with the grant of municipal status the post of princeps continued as an honorary office. See Gsell and Joly, *op. cit.*, i, Khamissa, p. 15 ff.

[23] See ch. III, nn. 100-2.

[24] *C.*, 4826; *At. arch. Alg.*, f. 18, 135; Toutain, *Mél. Cagnat*, pp. 342-4.

[25] *Ann. epig.*, 1895, no. 82 (time of Valens); the interpretation of the R. P. C. (astelli ?) R., *Ann. epig.*, 1895, no. 83, and the R. P. C. R. C. M., *C.*, 22270, 22274, 22275, is unknown.

[26] *I. L. Al.*, 561: flaminium C. N. G.; *At. arch. Alg.*, f. 18, 200.

[27] *I. L. Al.*, 561.

then into a municipium.[28] A citizen is described as the flamen of the civitas of the Nattabutum and the incumbent of the principatus of his own civitas presumably that at Guelaa Bou Atfane.[29] As the loosely organized indigenous tribes easily broke up into clan or family divisions [30] we may suppose that the principatus of the civitas represented the position of chief of one of these smaller divisions now started on the path of municipal development.[31]

The mention of the Numidae brings up the question whether Rome followed in Africa the practice in use elsewhere of dividing tribes opposed to her and of resettling a portion of the population in another region. The appearance of the Cellenses Numidae [32] in the Plaine des Zouarines, of Numidae at Masculula,[33] of the tribe of the Numidae about Thubursicum, and the limitation in Hadrian's time of a Gens Numidarum southwest of Sitifis near Bordj Bou Arreridj [34] have led to the theory that this was a large tribe which once centered about Thubursicum but was divided and resettled. This is unlikely, since Numidae may well be a general term for many

[28] *I. L. Al.*, 571, 572, 573.

[29] *I. L. Al.*, 561.

[30] See ch. III, n. 37.

[31] On the various meanings of princeps in Africa as tribal chief and as magistrate in a quasi-commune, see Gsell and Joly, *op. cit.*, pp. 18-9. The meaning of the princeps at Calama, *I. L. Al.*, 233, 290, is uncertain but probably as Gsell suggests he was the chief of a small attached indigenous clan.

[32] *C.*, 16352; *At. arch. Tun.*, Ksour, 87.

[33] *C.*, 15775; *At. arch. Tun.*, Ouargha, 1.

[34] *C.*, 8813, 8814; *At. arch. Alg.*, f. 15, 78.

tribal units of a large area to which they gave the name Numidia, and were thus distinguished from the Gaetulians; a resettlement at an early date in a territory not well occupied and defined before 138 A. D. seems unlikely; Roman practice in Africa seems rather to have favored attribution or some form of limitation. Division where practised consisted in the alienation of native ranges with a portion of the population, such as occurred in the formation of the territory of the Saltus Beguensis or of Ammaedara. The difference in development between the Numidae in Mauretania and those about Thubursicum is quite evident. The western plain, now a considerable producer of cereals and of horses, then probably the chief source of Numidian horses, had been occupied during the last years of the first century. It was under Nerva that the nearby military colonies of Sitifis [35] and Cuicul [36] had been deduced. The definition [37] in 138 A. D. of lands by the procurator of the Emperor Hadrian for himself and members of the imperial family shows why he limited the tribesmen to a limited assigned territory and turned the rest of the land to a more fruitful use than the pasturage of horses. The notice in the Tabula of Peutinger of Musulamii in the region southwest of Cirta is due either to one of the mistakes frequent in the Tabula, or else to the fact that with the advancement of the

[35] *C.*, 8473.

[36] Cagnat, *Musée belge,* 1923, p. 114; *C. R. Ac.*, 1916, p. 593 ff.

[37] *C.*, 8810-2; *At. arch. Alg.*, f. 15, 82; on *definitio* and *defensio* see Rostovtzeff, *Klio,* 1911, p. 387 ff.

Roman occupation some of the nomads had themselves moved westward to preserve their freedom.[38] The Numidae of the Plaine des Zouarines and of Masculula were racial rather than tribal names.

To see a definite policy of urbanization in the developments of the first century and in the measures of Trajan and of Hadrian with regard to the native tribes seems unfounded. As nomads the tribesmen and their land were of no use to the state, and a distinct menace to the neighboring portions of the province. To stop the roving and to secure peace we find under Trajan and Hadrian that in the newly-occupied areas the tribesmen with the exception of the inhabitants of the Aurès were almost completely included in the legionary and municipal territories, or in the extra-territorial estates, while the tribes previously settled were limited to the poorer portion of their land and left to work out their own salvation, and, if they developed a tribal center to some semblance of urban life, were granted the Roman municipal form. The development itself was however the natural result of settled life and a more intensive cultivation of the soil. The civitas or municipium with its territory large or small as the case might be, was really considered by the government more as a stipendiary or tax-paying unit and put in the municipal

[38] See Toutain, *Mém. ant. Fr.*, 1896, pp. 271-94; cf. Gsell, *Mél. éc.*, 1894, p. 344; *I. L. Al.*, 1335. A spontaneous division and migration of portions of the tribe was not difficult in the case of the Musulamii since they were nomadic and organized into families or clans, see ch. III, n. 37; also n. 17.

form usual among Roman towns than as a developed urban unit. Centers like Thiges and Turris Tammalleni never achieved a brilliant urban life while in Gigthis and Thubursicum Numidarum the brilliant period dated later than the achievement of municipal status. The probable quality of the Romanization and the significance of the grant of municipal rights must be determined from a consideration of the probable social and economic conditions of the particular locality. Advancement in status indicates a development but does not necessarily indicate a great degree of Romanization or of developed urban life. This became particularly true in the time when the increase of municipal burdens, and the need of a wider basis of recruitment for the army caused the emperors to extend the bounds of Roman citizenship. The following survey of the municipal development of Africa during the second century will discuss mainly how far municipalization in the province generally may be considered a valid index of the degree of Romanization achieved.

Trajan continued the system of veteran settlements, which was basic for the development of southern Algeria. The foundation of Timgad in 100 A. D. has already been mentioned.[39] The town provided a meeting-place and market for indigenous people about it, and grew well beyond its original size. The legion may have been moved from Theveste to Lam-

[39] Gsell, *At. arch. Alg.*, f. 27, 255; Boeswillwald, Cagnat, Ballu, *Timgad; C.*, 2355 = 17842.

baesis, to a temporary camp before the death of Trajan; as in the case of Ammaedara, when the legion went away the town was given colonial status.[40] Theveste was inscribed in the Papiria, Trajan's tribe,[41] and was the patria of soldiers at Lambaesis who probably entered service in Trajan's time.[42] The conditions surrounding the development of Thelepte and its territory have already been discussed.[43] Cuicul was originally a native site on the hills above the Oued Djemila.[44] It is surrounded by steep hill slopes not impossible for agriculture. The region with the pagus Thigillavensium to the south[45] had probably belonged to the Cirtensian federation. At least a connection with Cirta appears among the priesthoods and citizens originally of Cirta were soon found in Cuicul.[46] It was a veteran colony probably

[40] *C.*, 18084, l. 52; cf. Cagnat, *Armée romaine*,[2] p. 291; Gsell, *I. L. Al.*, p. 286.

[41] *I. L. Al.*, 3141.

[42] See n. 40; Mascula and Bagai were also patriae of legionary soldiers, *C.*, 2568, 2569.

[43] Note that the Thelepte-Theveste road was Trajanic, *C.*, 10037; and that the road from Hadrumetum via Sufetula, Cillium, and Theveste was probably early and a factor in the development of these towns, Toutain, *Les cités*, p. 137.

[44] Gsell, *At. arch. Alg.*, f. 16, 233; Cagnat, *Musée belge*, 1923, p. 113 ff.; *Rev. des ét. anc.*, 1920, p. 97 ff.; Ballu, *Guide illustré de Djemila*, Alger, 1926. There may have been a fort at Cuicul during the first century A. D. to guard communications, *C.*, 20713 (a soldier of the Leg. III Aug., *moratus a Cui/clo; Ann. epig.*, 1920, no. 19.

[45] Gsell, *At. arch. Alg.*, f. 16, 269; *Bull. du com.*, 1894, p. 344, no. 17. The territory of Cuicul extended 11 miles to southward, *At. arch. Alg.*, f. 16, 295.

[46] There was no close administrative connection with Cirta; duoviri of Cuicul are found, *C.*, 20152, 147 A. D., but officials of the imperial cults were common to the two cities, *C.*, 8318, 20144; *Ann. epig.*, 1920, no. 115; 1925, no. 24.

founded along with Sitifis during the reign of Nerva.[47] It commanded one of the lines of communication with the coast [48] and became a center for the collection of grain.[49] Rich families in the town such as the Cosinii and the Crescentiani adorned it with buildings, and themselves achieved high offices in the empire.[50]

With Trajan began to appear in Africa a new type of colony and of municipium, when titular colonial or municipal rights were granted to towns of purely non-italic composition. Such were the colonial foundations of Hadrumetum and of Leptis Magna. Caesar had begun this process by granting the Latin right [51] to certain communities in Narbonese Gaul and Spain, and to the Sicilian towns, and Vespasian extended it to the peregrine communities in Spain, probably to secure a wider basis of recruitment; for the army was no longer recruited from Italy but from the provinces [52] and each legion moreover, particularly after Hadrian, tended to be recruited from

[47] See nn. 35-6.

[48] Gsell, *At. arch. Alg.*, f. 16, p. 16, on the roads about Cuicul.

[49] *Ann. epig.*, 1924, no. 38; 1925, nos. 73-4; Albertini, *C. R. Ac.*, 1924, p. 253.

[50] Cagnat, *Rev. des ét. anc.*, 1920, p. 97 ff.

[51] On the Latin right and its extension see Mommsen, *Ges. Schr.*, I, pp. 265-382, and III, p. 63 ff. (Latium Maius); Ed. Meyer, *Cäsars Monarchie*, pp. 485 ff.; Hardy, *Roman Laws and Charters*, re the Lex Salpensana and the Lex Malacitana. The Latin right under Caesar and Vespasian was the equivalent of the Latium Minus of post-Hadrianic times: Hirschfeld, *Kl. Schr.*, p. 294 ff.; see also Steinwenter, *Pauly-Wissowa*, X, art. Jus Latii.

[52] Rostovtzeff, *Soc. and Ec. Hist.*, p. 103 ff.

the area it was stationed to defend.[53] With the accession after Domitian of emperors who took a keener interest in the provinces than heretofore came these grants to peregrine communities of Roman citizenship with municipal or full colonial status.

The development of the hinterland and the increasing value of its own territory had rendered the old Punic town of Hadrumetum quite prosperous.[54] There seems to be little trace of the early settlement, which is doubtful in any case, of Julian veterans, unless it be that the cognomen Concordia [55] refers to a union or assimilation of them and their descendants to the Punic townsfolk, while the cognomen Frugifera refers to the Punic element in the town.[56] Its citizens were inscribed in the Papiria tribe.[57] Leptis Magna,[58] also an old Punic town had pre-

[53] For Africa, see Cagnat, *Armée romaine,*[2] p. 287 ff.

[54] Colonia Concordia Ulpia Traiana Augusta Frugifera Hadrumetum, *C. I. L.*, VI, 1687. Its territory may have bordered that of Thysdrus, *Corp. Agrim.*, ed. Thulin, p. 48. The organization of the patrimonial department in these regions centered about Hadrumetum, Schulten, *Röm. Grundherrschaften,* p. 62 ff.

[55] See ch. II, n. 61, and text. On the significance of the cognomen Concordia see Dessau, *Hermes,* 1914, p. 510; Cagnat, *Rev. epig.*, 1913, p. 8 ff.; Dessau, *I. L. S.*, 9469; Gsell, *Rev. hist.*, nov., 1927, p. 232; Carcopino, *Rev. hist.*, mai-juin, 1928, p. 2. Cagnat and Gsell believe it refers rather to the peace of the Roman world after Julius Caesar's victories; Carcopino to the accord between Antony and Octavian in 42 B. C.

[56] A title of Punic Baal in Roman dress, Toutain, *Cultes païens,* III, p. 19.

[57] *C.*, 3020, 3062.

[58] Romanelli, *Leptis Magna;* Bartoccini, *Guida di Lepcis.*

served its autonomy,[59] and had possessed for a while the right to coin money.[60] The Tripolis, Oea, Sabrata, and Leptis Magna seem to have been administratively separate. For Oea in 70 A. D. quarreled with Leptis on a question of territory and invited the Garamantes to help her.[61] As all three were colonies by the end of the second century A. D.[62] and Sabrata at least was of the Papiria tribe[63] it is probable that all three owe their advance to Trajan. Leptis had grown prosperous during years of comparative peace on the proceeds of her olive orchards.[64] How far a genuine Romanization extended is uncertain. A native of Leptis Magna, a Roman knight Septimius Severus, was praised by his friend Statius[65] as completely Italian, but his grandson the emperor of the same name never lost his African accent, and his sister could hardly speak Latin at all.[66] The Punic speech remained the language in general use.[67]

[59] See ch. II, nn. 35-8.

[60] Müller, *Num. de l'Afrique,* II, p. 10.

[61] Pliny, *H. N.,* V, 38; Tac., *Hist.,* IV, 50; Cagnat, *Armée romaine,*[2] p. 37 ff.

[62] The road from Tacape to Leptis was built under Nerva, *C.,* 10016; Oea and Sabrata are mentioned as colonies in the *Itin. Ant.,* ed. Parthey and Pinder, pp. 28-9. On Sabrata and Lepcis Magna, see *Riv. della Tripolitania,* 1924-5, p. 59 ff.; pp. 281-322.

[63] *Riv. della Trip.,* 1924-5, pp. 292-5; *Ann. epig.,* 1925, no. 103.

[64] Gsell, *Riv. della Trip.,* 1924-5, pp. 41-6.

[65] *Silvae,* IV, 5.

[66] *Vita Severi,* 15 and 19.

[67] Cf. Apul., *Apol.,* 98.

Other native towns were given municipal status. The communities at Avedda[68] near the head-waters of the Oued Tinn and at Sidi Abd el Basset[69] in the same region were both of the Papiria tribe and may probably be referred to Trajan. Municipal right was also given to Vallis,[70] a strong site slightly southeast of Membressa. Calama, a mixed Punic and Berber town, was advanced by Trajan.[71] Thubursicum Numidarum we have already discussed.[72] Whether or not some of these municipia possessed only the Latin right, as Gsell conjectured for Thubursicum Numidarum from the preponderance of names not obviously those of Roman citizens in the inscriptions of the town, we have not evidence to decide.[73]

The outlines of the Trajanic development are fairly evident. In the undeveloped regions of the province the settlement of veteran colonies was basic, while some native tribes were allowed to develop themselves in reservations. Trajan began the practice of advancing native towns to Roman municipal status but applied it rather sparingly. Only where we have reason to believe that there was con-

68 *At. arch. Tun.*, Tebourba, 8; *C.*, 14372; *I. L. A.*, 438.

69 *At. arch. Tun.*, Mateur, 281; *C.*, 14343.

70 *At. arch. Tun.*, Medjez el Bab, 117 and 120; *C.*, 1289, 1282, 14783, 14784, 14786, 25827 (utriusque ordinis).

71 *I. L. Al.*, 285, 280, before 143 A. D.; *At. arch. Alg.*, f. 9, 146; Gsell, *I. L. Al.*, p. 20.

72 See nn. 21-2 and text.

73 Gsell and Joly, *op. cit.*, i. Khamissa, p. 22. It is possible that the commune at Guelaa bou Atfane also possessed only Latin right at first, Gsell, *I. L. Al.*, p. 60; and nos. 571, 572, 574, 575.

siderable contact with Roman influences, and a considerable degree of prosperity do we find native towns given colonial rights, while the Trajanic municipia were situated in regions which must have had for the most part some contact with Roman people and with Roman settlements and where some degree of imitation of Roman language and custom on the part of the more prominent native families was probable. Trajan's innovation, partly the result of the need of recruits for the army and partly of the interest taken by an emperor from the provinces in provincial prosperity, is no evidence that advantages were given to encourage Romanization or that natural processes were in any degree interfered with.

With Trajan the policy of territorial expansion ended. The rest of the century was spent in consolidating and building up the new additions in southern Algeria until Septimius Severus pushed the frontiers a little farther into the desert and re-systematized the Limes.[74] It is difficult to follow the course of the development of this region from emperor to emperor. For many foundations must have been earlier than any datable evidence from them.[75]

[74] On the Severan Limes see *Pauly-Wissowa-Kroll,* art. Limes; Cagnat, *Armée romaine,*[2] p. 747 ff.; Carcopino, *Syria,* 1925, Le Limes de Numidie et sa garde syrienne. The withdrawal of the cohort from the customs station at Zarai in 202 A. D., *C.,* 2532, D, b; 4508, probably coincided with the extension of Roman occupation to the southwest.

[75] Diana was a Trajanic or Hadrianic foundation but the earliest datable inscription is *C.,* 4587, 141 A. D. Cf. Gsell, *At. arch. Alg.,*

The conditions of the country and the manner of occupation imposed a set mode of development throughout the century.

It is possible that the legion was moved to its permanent home at Lambaesis before the death of Trajan.[76] The permanent camp had just been constructed when Hadrian visited Africa.[77] The strategic value of this site near the center of the legionary territory, and close to the important passage to the desert between the Aurès mountains and the mountains of Batna is quite obvious. The military occupation had been extended westward to the Mauretanian frontier where Zarai [78] was both a military fort and a post for the collection of customs, and southwestward to watch tribesmen such as the Nicives near the Chott el Hodna.[79] The definitio of considerable areas of land by the procurator of Hadrian in 137 A. D. about Equisetum in Mauretania, and the assignation of a limited area to the Numidae in the same district shows that the Roman oc-

---

f. 27, 62. The fact that its citizens were enrolled in the Papiria tribe does not definitely date it as Trajanic. Although Hadrian and Antoninus Pius granted municipal status to many African towns, no towns in Africa are known to have belonged to the Sergian or Voltinian tribes. Hadrian seems to have inscribed his foundations in the tribe which was predominant in their respective regions.

[76] Cagnat, *Armée romaine,*[2] p. 433 ff.

[77] *C.*, 2533; the camp was in use in 129 A. D.; cf. *C.*, 2532; *Vita Hadriani.*, 13, 5; 22, 14.

[78] See n. 74; *At. arch. Alg.*, f. 26, 69.

[79] Pliny, *H. N.*, V, 30; *At. arch. Alg.*, f. 26, 161; Tubunae, a little to the south, *Atlas,* f. 37, 10, was the patria of a legionary soldier in the third century A. D., *Bull. du com.*, 1905, p. 239.

cupation had made considerable progress by that date.[80]

The development of Southern Algeria seems to have followed three main lines.[81] First, the stationing of castella or stationes of soldiers at outlying points and the settlement of bodies of veterans on the available new land continued. At Casae[82] near the northward crossing of Dj. Bou Arif some of the legionary territory was probably divided in this way. The mountains of Batna were girdled by a circle of forts and settlements, Lambiridi[83] at the entrance to the road across the mountains to the plain of Bellezma, to protect communications with Vescera to the south,[84] Lamiggiga[85] on the northern slopes to protect communications northward and westward to Diana, while to the west of the mountains the settlements of Lamsorta[86] and Lamasba[87] overlooked the plain of Bellezma where the famous irrigation inscription was found.[88] Diana Veteranorum was evidently a large veteran foundation with a considerable territory, probably Trajanic or Hadrianic in date.[89] It possessed most of the agricultural land

[80] See n. 37.

[81] The basic articles on these regions are those of Graillot and Gsell, see n. 7.

[82] Gsell, *At. arch. Alg.*, f. 27, 141.

[83] *ib.*, 120.

[84] *At. arch. Alg.*, f. 48, 9; Biskra.

[85] *ib.*, f. 27, 73.

[86] *ib.*, f. 27, 108.

[87] *ib.*, f. 27, 86.

[88] *C.*, 18587 = 4440.

[89] *At. arch. Alg.*, f. 27, 62; on its territory see *At. arch. Alg.*, f. 27, 10, 71, 26; f. 26, 73; f. 17, 387.

from the north lateral spur of the Batna mountains northward beyond the salt lakes to the plain of Mechira. Its territory extended eastward to Lamiggiga and westward halfway to Zarai and southward over the passes to the edge of the plain of Bellezma. Between Lambaesis and Thamugadi such sites as Lambafundi [90] and Verecunda [91] began as castella or as small veteran settlements in vici on the legionary territory itself. Posts also were placed at strategic points in the valleys of the Aurès, two of which at least developed to appreciable size.[92]

In the second place these centers gathered certain native and other aggregations about them. Timgad expanded after its foundation and such must also have been the case with the soldier settlements in vici, as Verecunda,[93] and perhaps Diana [94] and the town of Lambaesis [95] were termed at the outset. About the great permanent camp at Lambaesis as about all the permanent camps grew up a town whose inhabitants ministered to the various needs of the soldiery. Merchants from the older parts of the province, servants, laborers, and camp-followers

[90] *At. arch. Alg.*, f. 27, 247.

[91] *ib.*, f. 27, 240.

[92] *ib.*, f. 38, 40, Mena'a; *C.*, 17592-5; also *Atlas*, f. 38, 48 and 91. The legion built roads through the Aurès to the posts in the south, *Atlas*, f. 38, 55; *C.*, 10230.

[93] *C.*, 4199: *possessores vici Verecundensis;* cf., 4194, 4249.

[94] *C.*, 4587, 141 A. D., res publica, so a quasi-commune.

[95] *C.*, 2604, 2605; vicus may mean a quarter of a town, *C.*, 26473; *I. L. A.*, 547, 550. Lambaesis was a res publica by 148 A. D., *C.*, 18214, 18234, Curiae Hadrianae and flamines perpetui; and had decurions by 166 A. D., *C.*, 2740, 2695.

came and settled, while the soldiers cohabited with women of the region and had families in the town. The town of Lambaesis soon became a municipium of Latin right,[96] contemporaneously with the southern fort of Gemellae,[97] was a Roman municipium before 197 A. D.,[98] and probably gained colonial rank when the legion was temporarily broken up under Gordian III. The appearance of such a center as Diana as a quasi-commune [99] instead of a regular veteran colony favors the theory that a large part of the region had been legionary territory and that veterans were settled out in larger or smaller numbers in villages in this territory and that the quasi-organizations, res publicae or vici, into which they constituted themselves received municipal recognition later. Diana was a municipium by 162 A. D.[100] The settlement of the plain of Bellezma probably dated toward the end of the second century,[101] but forts through the region were needed at an earlier period. Few or no indubitably native centers are known. The natives rather mingled in the veteran settlements which provided centers for them, or lived in villages as tenants and laborers on estates

[96] *C.*, 18218.

[97] *ib.*

[98] *C.*, 18256, 197 A. D., but it possessed this status before: *C.*, 2949, 4306, cognomen of Aurelia. On the town and camp see Gsell, *At. arch. Alg.*, f. 27, 223-5 and Cagnat, *Armée romaine*,² p. 429 ff.

[99] See n. 94.

[100] *C.*, 4589.

[101] Lamasba, res publica, *C.*, 22511, 214 A. D.; Lamsorta, dates uncertain, but a Curia of Marcus Aurelius, *Bull. du Com.*, 1901, p. cl.

or in the territories of the legion or of the settlements. Doubtless there were villages in the region about the salt lakes but few traces are left; the presence of a large indigenous necropolis on Dj. Bou Arif near Casae [102] points rather to the organization of the natives about the soldier settlements, whose members themselves were by this time almost all of African birth. Such centers as Gibba,[103] Aleanenses,[104] Thauagel,[105] and the villages in a late inscription naming the Venusianenses, [M]ucrionenses and Cusabetenses [106] were connected for the most part with large estates. The native life continued largely untouched in the mountains.

The third development was here as elsewhere the formation of estates both private and imperial.[107] Ruins of farms, presses, and agricultural establishments are numerous throughout all the region [108] and we may assume that there were probably many more estates than those of which we have evidence. Within

[102] *At. arch. Alg.*, f. 27, 140.

[103] Gsell, *At. arch. Alg.*, f. 27, 149, 166; *C.*, 4363: *pedatura steratae* Gibbensium; 18548 names an imperial procurator.

[104] Gsell, *At. arch. Alg.*, f. 27, 253; *Bull. du com.*, 1901, p. ccxiv, a dedication to Commodus.

[105] Gsell, *At. arch. Alg.*, f. 27, 322; Graillot and Gsell, *Mél. éc.*, 1894, p. 34.

[106] Gsell, *At. arch. Alg.*, f. 27, 278; Graillot and Gsell, *Mél. éc.*, 1894, p. 24; *Atlas*, f. 27, 277, close by was an imperial domain. These were probably villages upon it, Graillot and Gsell, *l. c.*, p. 20, a dedication to Commodus. The stop Claudi of the *Itin. Ant.* which may have been at *Atlas*, f. 27, 334 or 337 probably refers to an owner of an estate there.

[107] See nn. 103 ff.

[108] *At. arch. Alg.*, f. 27 passim.

municipal territories such as Timgad local grandees doubtless acquired land,[109] and senatorial estates also are found,[110] but the large majority of the domains of which we have evidence were imperial.[111] Agricultural exploitation advanced also into the mountain valleys of the Aurès where along the valleys of the Oued el Abdi, Oued el Abiod, and the Oued Rassine ruins of many farms are found,[112] but as there is no evidence of the presence of the large investor we must consider that this development probably resulted from settlements of veterans from the posts placed there.[113]

In this portion of the province however the Romanization resultant upon these processes was partial and confined to the larger urban centers. It must be remembered that the soldiers of the third legion after the time of Trajan were themselves mostly Africans;[114] and that many of the soldiers

[109] *Ann. epig.*, 1909, no. 5; Mascula, *C.*, 2232.

[110] *At. arch. Alg.*, f. 39, 11-4; *Ann. epig.*, 1894, no. 84; Graillot and Gsell, *Mél. éc.*, 1893, p. 470, n. 2.

[111] See nn. 103-5; *At. arch. Alg.*, f. 27, 324, near Thauagel, a dedication by the coloni B., *Mél. éc.*, 1894, p. 37, may mark the location of an estate; *Atlas*, f. 27, 1, a column with the word tractus; on estates in the plain of Mechira, see Gsell, *Atlas*, f. 17, 386. To the eastward at *Atlas*, f. 28, 134, a procurator in the country of the Musulamii near Dj. Mesloula may refer to the exploitation of mineral resources there rather than to a large imperial estate. *Atlas*, f. 28, 163, marks the boundary between the Musulamii and an imperial estate, *I. L. Al.*, 2988.

[112] *At. arch. Alg.*, f. 37 and 38 passim.

[113] See n. 92.

[114] Note the patriae in *C.*, 2565-9, 18067-8.

previously in Africa were of eastern origin.[115] The result was that while Latin was the official language, and the military cults were kept up, the cults which spread and took root were Punic redressed in Roman names.[116] The merchants who came in were probably for the most part of Punic origin. Outside of the towns Roman influences penetrated but slightly. The inscriptions from the country hamlets are badly graven and poorly spelled, and the native names remain.[117] Large estates fail notoriously of being instruments either of Romanization or of urbanization of the villages within their boundaries. Besides, the Aurès mountains and the mountains of Batna nearby were foyers of indigenous influence, while to the south the tribes of the desert waited but the removal of the guardian corps, themselves Syrians and Palmyrians, to flood in through the pass of El Kantara.[118] When during the late empire came that resurgence of indigenous activity which masqueraded under the name of Donatism it was precisely in the region of Bagai and of Timgad that the Donatists were strongest.[119] Romanization was not a Roman policy and what there was of it centered about a few large towns, the natural result of vet-

[115] Note the soldiers from Syria and Asia Minor in *C.*, 18084; on the recruitment of the legion see Cagnat, *op. cit.*, pp. 287-302.

[116] Toutain, *Les cultes païens*, III, pp. 91, 113-9.

[117] Gsell and Graillot, *Mél. éc.*, 1893, p. 472.

[118] Carcopino, *Syria*, 1925, Le Limes de Numidia et sa garde syrienne.

[119] See Gsell, *At. arch. Alg.*, f. 27, 255; f. 28, 68, where references are cited. On Donatism see Monceaux, *Hist. litt. de l'Afrique chrétienne*, livre 8, p. 3 ff., where other literature is cited.

eran settlements and of urban life. The legion brought peace; prosperity resulted from the peaceful exploitation of the soil, but the population for the most part remained Berbers and nomads at heart.

Within the Cirtensian territory [120] a tendency toward local autonomy became more and more apparent from the time of Hadrian on. As the demarcation of the classes of land within the territory of Sigus [121] was carried out by the legate in Hadrian's time [122] it is possible that there was some reorganization of the federation in his day.[123] It is more probable however that any such change was the result of his economic program and affected only the exploitation of the land. Otherwise the form of the attribution would have been changed. It is true however that with the exception of the large pagus of Thibilis the attributed centers did not begin to appear in inscriptions until his time. Signs of development appear first in the larger pagi where economic conditions were more favorable. Roman citizens within the pagus of Thibilis had banded themselves together for cult purposes by 73 A. D.[124] and in 121

[120] See ch. II, nn. 145-80 and text; ch. III, nn. 126-35 and text; Gsell, *At. arch. Alg.*, indices; Gsell and Joly, *Khamissa, Mdaourouch, Announa,* iii, Announa, p. 12 ff.

[121] *C.*, 19132, 19134, 19133, from the ager acceptus of Cirta.

[122] Pallu de Lessert, *Fastes*, p. 352 ff.

[123] As Gsell suggests, Gsell and Joly, *op cit.*, p. 14.

[124] *Ann. epig.*, 1907, no. 6: *Divo Augusto sacrum Lare(n)ses;* cf. at Tipasa a dedication to Hadrian by the *cultores Larum et Imaginum Augusti, C.*, 17143; *Bull. du Com.*, 1896, p. 277, no. 215; see ch. I, n. 126.

A. D. a statue was erected to Hadrian by the people of Thibilis.[125] Sigus [126] and Tiddis [127] appeared as corporate entities during Hadrian's time, Celtianis [128] in 163 A. D. During the last years of the second century and the first years of the third several more pagi and castella appeared as res publicae.[129] All were regularly governed by magistri, usually but one, and had a council of decurions,[130] while the authority of Cirta was represented by praefecti pro triumviris.[131] The close relationship which they bore to Cirta is evidenced by the presence of certain Cirtensian officials among their citizens, as for instance, the mention at Thibilis of decurions, and a flaminica of the four colonies.[132] Men born in the pagi as well as in Cirta itself achieved high positions in the imperial service.[133] In the third century there seems to have been a greater assumption of the regular municipal form of organization. The term res publica is frequent after Septimius Severus.[134] The magistri of Thibilis were twice mistakenly termed duumviri in an inscription of the grotto of

[125] *Ann. epig.*, 1907, no. 7.

[126] *C.*, 19132-4.

[127] *C.*, 6706.

[128] *C.*, 19690.

[129] See ch. II, n. 175; Gsell, *At. arch. Alg.*, f. 17, p. 13, col. 1.

[130] Gsell, *l. c.*, p. 12, col. 2; there were two magistri at Thibilis, *C.*, 18896, 18900 and elsewhere; note the album of decurions at Sigus, *C.*, 19135.

[131] Gsell, *l. c.*, p. 13, col. 1.

[132] *C.*, 5534, 18909, 18912.

[133] Lollius Urbicus of Tiddis, *C.*, 6705-6; Julius Pudens, *C.*, 18908, and the Antistii of Thibilis, Gsell and Joly, *op. cit.*, pp. 17-20.

[134] Gsell, *At. arch. Alg.*, f. 17, p. 13, col. 1.

Bacax on Dj. Taya,[135] and at Sila and Uzelis the term magistratus was in use.[136] On the breakup of the federation of the four colonies it is probable that the atribution remained as before, since the pagi were attached not to the four colonies but to Cirta itself. Thibilis however and Tigisi became municipia by the fourth century.[137]

It is evident that the process of Romanization made considerable progress in the Cirtensian area. The original Sittian soldiers were far from being Roman, but the contact with the active life of Cirta which was a foyer both of Punic and of Roman influences in the two centuries we have discussed, spread considerably the knowledge of the Latin tongue. Families which became prosperous were represented in the public service, and many of their members achieved empire-wide distinction;[138] even among the minor officials of the town the proper form of the tria nomina of the Roman citizens usually appears. And when we add the contributions to Roman literature which came in the works of Fronto of Cirta, to Roman law in Pactumeius Clemens and to ecclesiastical writings in Minucius Felix it is evident that the upper stratum at least of society in Cirta

[135] *C.*, 18845 = 5515, 18842.

[136] *C.*, 5884, 6339.

[137] *C.*, 22276, 293 A. D.; 18767, fourth century A. D.

[138] Gsell, *l. c.;* note the large number of knights of Cirtensian origin. Under the Antonines there were many senators from Cirta. Pactumeius Clemens the elder was the first consul from Africa, *C.*, 19426 = 7057, 19427 = 7058. Families from the pagi shared these distinctions also, see n. 133. See Lully, *De Senatorum Romanorum Patria.*

was thoroughly Romanized. But a study of the cults adds a touch of another color to the picture. The worship of Saturn and of Caelestis remained strong,[139] as was natural both in Cirta and in the Punic towns of Rusicade and of Chullu. In Cirta she was Caelestis Sittiana.[140] The indigenous worships of Giddaba ? in the grotto of ez Zemma[141] and of Bacax in the grotto of Dj. Taya[142] continued strong to the end, the latter a cult officially carried on by the Roman citizens who were magistri at Thibilis.[143] The passage of two centuries before the majority of the pagi and castella show any tendency to autonomy shows how unforced the development was, while the presence of native remains in much of the Cirtensian area,[144] and of Libyc[145] and of Punic[146] inscriptions even near to Cirta indicates that the under-stratum of indigenous life lived persistently on in the hills, on the great estates and in the pagi and castella themselves.

In the remaining regions of Africa there was considerable municipal development during the century. The case of Utica is well known. It was advanced

[139] Toutain, *Cultes païens,* III, pp. 89 ff.; 96 ff.

[140] *C.,* 19512a; *Ann. epig.,* 1907, no. 244.

[141] Gsell, *At. arch. Alg.,* f. 17, 109; Toutain, *op. cit.,* p. 44 ff.

[142] Gsell, *At. arch. Alg.,* f. 9, 109; Toutain, *l. c.*

[143] *C.,* 5504 ff.; 18828 ff.

[144] Gsell, *Hist. anc.,* V, pp. 273-5. About Cirta one may note *At. arch. Alg.,* f. 17, nos. 41, 43, 71, 70, 89, 143, 144, 164, 178, 183, 236, 326, 327, 334, 455.

[145] *At. arch. Alg.,* f. 17, nos. 59, 99, 100, 101, 126, 152, 172, 167, 235, 277.

[146] *At. arch. Alg.,* f. 17, nos. 59, 89, 99, 126, 463.

from municipal to colonial status at its own request.[147] Hadrian also gave colonial status to Thaenae, Bulla Regia, Lares and Zama Regia. Thaenae[148] was one of the Punic Emporiae. Bulla Regia,[149] the former capital of a Numidian princeling, was close to the area of Augustan settlement about Simitthu and had long felt the influence of it. Lares[150] also was close to the area of Augustan settlement near Assuras, and adjoined the territory of Sicca Veneria. Zama Regia had been the capital of Juba I and an indigenous center of some note, probably in the region of Jama and Mactar.[151] It is clear therefore that Hadrian although he was personally desirous of widening the basis of the municipal system of the empire restricted the grant of colonial rights in Africa to indigenous communes which were prosperous, important and well accustomed to urban life. The grant probably was given as in the case of Utica at the request of the community itself, desirous of placing all its activities under the jurisdiction of Roman law.

The same principle seems to have been followed by Hadrian's successors. Before the time of Septimius Severus only Pupput, Thibiuca, and Mactar were given colonial status. Pupput was on the eastern coast near Neapolis and received its advance-

[147] Aul. Gell., *N. A.*, XVI, 13; *C.*, 1181; on Hadrian's colonies and municipia in Africa, see De Pachtère, *Bull. du com.*, 1911, p. 390.

[148] *C.*, 22797, 2568 (Lambaesis); *C. I. L.*, VI, 1685; cf. ch. II, n. 33.

[149] *C.*, 25522; *At. arch. Tun.*, Fernana, 137; see ch. I, n. 116 and text.

[150] *At. arch. Tun.*, Ksour, 70; *C.*, 1779.

[151] *C. I. L.*, VI, 1686; *C.*, 23601 at Gsar bou Fatha; see ch. II, n. 221.

ment from Commodus.[152] Thibiuca occupied a site close by the Bagradas river just above Thuburbo Minus.[153] Mactar had long been a strong Punico-Numidian center,[154] a city of Punic constitution,[155] and had decurions in the time of Trajan.[156] It received colonial status in the time of Marcus Aurelius.[157]

The Hadrianic municipal foundations fall into two types, Roman municipia and municipia of Latin right. In the hill area which divides the watersheds of the Bagradas and the Miliana rivers communities which had been free towns from the time of Augustus now gained municipal status, while other towns now appear in the inscriptions. Bisica,[158] Avitta Bibba[159] and we may add the native commune at Thuburbo Maius[160] became municipia, while the Civ . . . . . . iana (Hr. el Aluani),[161] Tepelte,[162] and

152 *At. arch. Tun.*, Hammamet, 11; *C.*, 24092, 24093.

153 *At. arch. Tun.*, Tebourba, 68; *C.*, 14291, c. 167 A. D.

154 Gsell, *Hist. anc.*, V, pp. 267-8; on the Punic and Libyc inscriptions of Mactar see *C.*, p. 2372. There are about 120 neo-Punic inscriptions from this place.

155 Suffetes in a neo-Punic inscription, Berger, *Mém. acad. inscr.*, 1901, p. 168.

156 *C.*, 11798, 116 A. D.

157 *C.*, 11801, 198 A. D.: col. Aelia Aurelia. The cognomen Aelia may refer to some favor received from Hadrian, probably not to its elevation to municipal rank, *C.*, 11799, 170 A. D., civi]tas.

158 *At. arch. Tun.*, Bou Arada, 95; *C.*, 12292: municipium Ai.., more probably Hadrianic than Severan.

159 *At. arch. Tun.*, Bou Arada, 51; *C.*, 799; previously a civitas under suffetes, *C.*, 797.

160 *I. L. A.*, 244.

161 *At. arch. Tun.*, Medjez el Bab, 219; *C.*, 23945.

162 *At. arch. Tun.*, Bou Arada, 117; *C.*, 12248.

the vicus Haterianus [163] became known to epigraphy. Abthugni [164] in the mountainous region above Enfida and Thisica [165] in the region of Mateur received municipal status, also Althiburos,[166] an old Punicized town near the main road to Theveste. Naraggara [167] in the hill country west of Sicca, on the main road to Cirta, and Zattara [168] between the territory of the Nattabutes and that of Calama mark by their advancement the progress of municipal life in these regions. In the far south the important center of Capsa [169] and Turris Tamalleni [170] the tribal center which the Nybgenii had developed were given the same advancement. Whether the tribal center of the Musulamii ever was similarly recognized we have not the evidence to say. Hadrian also created two municipia of Latin right to which he granted the newly invented Latium

[163] *At. arch. Tun.*, Bou Arada, 112; *C.*, 23125, 129 A. D.

[164] *At. arch. Tun.*, Djebel Fkirine, 52; *C.*, 11206 = 929, 23085; *I. L. A.*, 71.

[165] *At. arch. Tun.*, Mateur, 79; *I. L. A.*, 432.

[166] *At. arch. Tun.*, Ksour, 97; Gsell, *Hist. anc.*, V, p. 267; *C.*, 27775a-d, 27769, 27781.

[167] *At. arch. Alg.*, f. 19, 73. The location suits the indications given by the *Itin. Ant.*, ed. Parthey and Pinder, pp. 18 and 20, and the town was the patria of a legionary soldier who entered service under Hadrian, *C.*, 18085e, l. 8, 18085c, l. 15 ?; *I. L. Al.*, 1189: pontifex, proves the presence of municipal organization.

[168] *At. arch. Alg.*, f. 18, 233; *I. L. Al.*, 533: d(ecreto) d(ecurionum). It at least had the form of municipal organization in Hadrian's time.

[169] *C.*, 98. About Capsa where today would be arid wilderness except for the phosphate mines, the Arab writers speak of many prosperous villages!, see Bodereau, *La Capsa ancienne, la Gafsa moderne*, p. 74 ff.

[170] *C.*, 83, 84.

Maius.[171] Gigthis which probably was the tribal center of the Cinithii[172] received this status but only after two trips to Rome by one of her prominent citizens.[173] The town became a Roman municipium under Antoninus Pius.[174] Thisiduo[175] on the south bank of the Bagradas below Membressa, also gained Latium Maius from Hadrian or soon after.

Despite the number of the Hadrianic foundations we need not see in them the application of a policy of urbanization as such, nor an attempt in the interest of the empire to force upon the towns obligations and duties which they were unwilling to assume. The municipal form of organization was a natural growth in the Roman system, the natural expression of local development and activity, and the historic basis of taxation and of administration. The emperor was not interested in the advancement in status of cities as such nor in the Romanization of the inhabitants—such of that as occurred was incidental—but desired to keep the financial and mil-

[171] Hirschfeld, *Kl. Schr.*, p. 294 ff. The creation of this special form of Latin town in which Roman citizenship was granted to decurions and their families as well as to the duoviri was probably some encouragement to municipal development since Roman citizenship was desirable, but may be regarded as a mode of distributing among a larger number of people municipal responsibilities in a better developed class of provincial town where they would be more onerous. It is not a sign of the decadence of municipal life but of the emperor's desire to suit the status of a town to its condition.

[172] See n. 17.

[173] *C.*, 22737.

[174] *C.*, 22707.

[175] *At. arch. Tun.*, Medjez el Bab, 28; *C.*, 14763, *decuriones cives Romani et municipes Thisiduenses.*

itary resources of the empire sound through the accustomed machinery. The municipal form was the customary way of creating a body of local officials with whom the central government could deal and whom the central government could hold responsible. Where such organizations were practically non-existent, as among the city-less tribes of the interior, prefects or residents were appointed to exercise control but were dispensed with as soon as a settled life and the development of a tribal center made possible some approximation of the customary form. But where such organizations were provided in an anomalous form as in the federation of Cirta or in territorial attributions to municipalities the central government let natural tendencies take their course. In general therefore the tendency was to develop municipal institutions however flexible the form that these might take, and to exercise a degree of oversight which developed later into paternalism.[176] In the time of Hadrian the eagerness evinced by such towns as Utica, Gigthis and presumably others for elevation proves that the municipal honores and munera were not felt as burdens, that the town life

[176] The tendency to exercise oversight upon municipal affairs began with the appointment of curators under Trajan, but we must not assume that the conditions which Pliny's correspondence with Trajan proves to have existed in Asia Minor were general throughout the empire, Abbott and Johnson, *Munic. Admin.*, p. 189; p. 90 ff. Asia Minor was more developed than Africa, had long been exploited and often robbed, and was at this time recovering from the effects of a famine, Robinson, *Trans. Amer. Phil. Ass.*, 1925, p. 5 ff., re Antistius Rusticus. On the curatores rei publicae in Africa, see Toutain, *Les cités*, pp. 356-8.

was still economically sound, and that the greater degree of local autonomy,[177] and the wider extension of Roman citizenship in a colony or a municipium was still considered as a privilege. We have reason to believe that there was some development of corporate life and of economic prosperity before Hadrian considered the claims of the towns for advancement.

During the rest of the century the development of these areas of the province continued along the same sane and reasonably conservative lines. The elevation of towns to colonial and municipal status continued to be a trustworthy evidence of a slowly accumulating prosperity, of a developing municipal life and of a degree of Romanization. Antoninus Pius granted full municipal status to Gigthis.[178] Muzuc,[179] on the O. Marouf northwest of Kairouan and probably on one of the roads over the central massif, now appeared as a civitas. Various indigenous towns in the chief area of Hadrianic development, the Bagradas-Miliana watershed and along the edge of the central massif [180] which had probably been civitates for some time now appeared in the inscriptions.

[177] Toutain, *Mél. éc.*, 1896, p. 315 ff.; 1898, p. 141 ff.; Von Premerstein, *Pauly-Wissowa,* art., Jus Italicum, X, 1248 ff.

[178] *C.*, 22707.

[179] *At. arch. Tun.*, Djebibina, 28; *C.*, 12059; Toutain, *Les cités,* p. 142.

[180] Thibica, *At. arch. Tun.*, Bou Arada, 124; *C.*, 12228; Civitas Biracsaccar, *Atlas,* Bou Arada, 97; *C.*, 23876; castellum, late empire, *C.*, 23849; Gens Bacchuiana, *Atlas,* Bou Arada, 74; *C.*, 12331; Chidibbia, *Atlas,* Medjez el Bab, 82; *C.*, 14870; Thuccabor, *Atlas,* Tebourba, 180; *C.*, 14851.

The Aurelian list of municipal foundations included Vina[181] and Segermes[182] in the Cape Bon ridge and above the coastal plain, the municipium at Hr. Bou Cha[183] northwest of Aradi, and Furnos Maius[184] in the central massif. Sufes also may have received some favor at this time (*C.*, 11421). In 158 A. D. there was still a prefect of the 62 castella in the mountains about Mactar.[185] During the Aurelian period the inscriptions prove the presence of many civitates in the same area. Such were Urusi,[186] Vazi Sarra,[187] Uzappa,[188] Musuc (Hr. Besra),[189] Limisa,[190] and Avioccala.[191] Sululos[192] and the community of Hr. Debbik[193] in the Bagradas-Miliana watershed, Sua[194] and Chidibbia[195] in the hills just north of the Bagradas river also appear as civitates. It was during this period that the double communities of the middle Bagradas area, Numluli,[196] and

[181] *At. arch. Tun.*, Grombalia, 219; *C.*, 960, 961, 12441 = 959.

[182] *At. arch. Tun.*, Bou Ficha, 105; *C.*, 11170.

[183] *At. arch. Tun.*, Oudna, 113; *C.*, 823, time of Commodus.

[184] *At. arch. Tun.*, Jama, 187; *C.*, 12039, 183 A. D.; Sufes, *C.*, 11421.

[185] *C.*, 23599; cf. 23421, 622.

[186] *At. arch. Tun.*, Mactar, 110; *C.*, 12014.

[187] *At. arch. Tun.*, Mactar, 107; *C.*, 12004.

[188] *At. arch. Tun.*, Mactar, 153; *C.*, 11927, 163-5 A. D.

[189] *At. arch. Tun.*, Djebel Bou Dabouss, 33; *C.*, 12095.

[190] *At. arch. Tun.*, Djebel bou Dabouss, 6; *C.*, 12036, at Furnos.

[191] *At. arch. Tun.*, Djebibina, 34; *C.*, 23828, 181 A. D.

[192] *At. arch. Tun.*, Bou Arada, 21; *C.*, 23941, 168 A. D.

[193] *At. arch. Tun.*, Medjez el Bab, 169; *C.*, 14791, 182 A. D.

[194] *At. arch. Tun.*, Tebourba, 183; *C.*, 14810, 168-9 A. D., 14808.

[195] *At. arch. Tun.*, Medjez el Bab, 82; *C.*, 14870, 14874, 182 A. D; cf. n. 180.

[196] *C.*, 26121, 170 A. D., a capitol for both pagus and civitas.

Thugga,[197] show evidence of a cooperation between their component parts, and that the two portions of Thuburbo Maius united.[198] These results were the gradual outcome of a long process of contact and of mutual assimilation of the Roman citizens, many of them descended from the earlier colonists, and the more prosperous and prominent of the indigenous folk.[199]

The gradual development of municipal life and the tendency to a uniform local organization of the Roman form does not suffice to account for the sudden increase of municipal foundations under the Severi.[200] It is apparent that Septimius Severus be-

197 *I. L. A.*, 556, 138 A. D., and see *C.*, p. 2615, col. 2. The pagus however received separately the ius capiendorum legatorum, *C.*, 26528b, 168 A. D., and the civitas became the Civitas Aurelia Thugga under Commodus, *C.*, 26625; *I. L. A.*, 517, 564, 565; cf. Poinssot, *Mél. Cagnat*, p. 349 ff.

198 *I. L. A.*, 267; cf. Poinssot, *C. R. Ac.*, 1915, p. 325 ff.

199 Note as an instance of the rise of the better class of indigenous family the Gabinii of Thugga, *C.*, 26517, 48 A. D.; *I. L. A.*, 568, 569, time of Hadrian; Poinssot, *N. A. Miss.*, XXI, nos. 5, 6, 7, 8; Carcopino, *Rev. ét. anc.*, 1922, p. 31; *C.*, 26459-62.

200 The Severan foundations may be listed thus: (a) Septimius Severus, Coloniae: Thysdrus, C. I. L., XII, 686; Vaga, *C.*, 14394, 14395, a deduction in 209 A. D., but it was called a colony in 197 A. D.; municipia: Aulodes, *At. arch. Tun.*, Tebourba, 9; *C.*, 14355; Hr. Debbik, *C.*, 14793; Thubursicum Bure, *C.*, 1426, 1427, 1439; Thugga, *C.*, p. 2615; Saia Maior, *At. arch. Tun.*, Souk el Khmis, 24; *C.*, 25500, 196 A. D.; Sululos, *C.*, 12341; Thagaste is Severan at the latest, *I. L. Al.*, p. 81, and numbers 875, 880. The following civitates may be mentioned: Apisa Maius, *C.*, 777, a civitas since the time of Tiberius; Giufi, *At. arch. Tun.*, Oudna, 172; *C.*, 23993; Suturnuca, *C.*, 24004, *I. L. A.*, 302; Neferis, *At. arch. Tun.*, Grombalia, 39; *C.*, 12401; Civ........iorum, Hr. Udeka, *C.*, 15496; and the R(es ?) P(ublica ?) C(ivitatis ?) or C(astelli ?) R.. in the territory of the Nattabutes, *Ann. epig.*, 1895, no. 83. (b) Caracalla, Municipia: Musuc, Hr.

stowed special favors on his native Africa. It is noticeable also that the majority of these municipal foundations that now become known antedate the Constitutio Antoniniana of Caracalla. The grant of Roman citizenship to all free-born men within the empire does not seem to have affected the form and status of the municipal entities. The distinction even if honorary between civitas, municipium, and colonia remained and there was little appreciable change thereafter in the rate of elevation of the towns.

In order to evaluate the significance of municipal development after the age of the Antonines certain factors must be kept in mind. In almost all the various areas of the province when we subtract the territories held by developed towns or known civitates, and the territories of the imperial and senatorial estates we find that the possibilities of further development lie with small indigenous communities on barren hills or in salty plains where a prosperous life was hardly possible, or with small villages within the territory none too extensive of larger towns. Only small and unimportant communes were

---

Khachoun, *C.*, 12060-2; Furnos Minus, Hr. el Msaadin, *At. arch. Tun.*, Tebourba, 235; *C.*, 25808b; Civitas: Sustri, *At. arch. Tun.*, Oued Zerga, 104; *C.*, 25934. (c) Alexander Severus, Coloniae: Uchi Maius, *C.*, 15447, 15450, 15455, 26270, a deduction under Caesonius Lucullus of colonists, 26262; Municipia, Giufi, *C.*, 866; Thignica, *C.*, 1406; Civitates: Bencennensis, *C.*, 15447. The civitates mentioned in this list probably all existed previously as such; the above records their first appearance in the inscriptions.

left to develop in areas of comparatively poor economic resources.[201] The extension of citizenship by the Constitutio Antoniniana[202] removed one incentive to municipal development and a genuine Romanization, while the increased interference of the central government in the local affairs and finances of the municipalities removed another and helps to show how forced the further development was. Although a large indigenous population of the laboring and artisan classes must have sprung up through two centuries of peace and exploitation under the Roman rule, such inscriptions as can be shown to belong to these classes reveal that comparatively few gave up their own language, cults, and customs for

[201] The federation of Cirta formed an apparent exception, but further municipal development in this region seems to have been confined to Rusicade, Mileu, and Chullu, the contributed colonies which broke away from Cirta during the third century, and to the comparatively large and important pagi of Thibilis and of Tigisi.

[202] The actual provisions of the Constitutio Antoniniana are still a riddle. It is noticeable that in the third century the practice of writing the name of the tribe as part of the Roman name fell into desuetude, and that the terms civitas and res publica denoting municipal aggregations whatever their status became more general. Whether the measure was taken with a view to the direct benefit to the treasury, as most say, following the statement of Dio Cassius, 77, 9, 5, or to bolster up the failing municipal life in the towns, Abbott and Johnson, *op. cit.*, p. 191, by placing all members of the community on the same basis as regards municipal obligations the effect on a tendency toward a genuine Romanization would be the same. For recent studies see, Capocci, *Mem. Acad. Lincei,* 1925, vol. I, fasc. 1; De Sanctis, *Rivista,* 1926, p. 488 ff.; Bickermann, *Das Edict des Kaisers Caracalla in P. Giss, 40,* Berlin, 1926; Laqueur, *Nachr. d. Giessener Hochschulgesellsch.,* 1927, pp. 15-28, summarized *Jour. Egyp. Arch.,* May, 1928, p. 152; Lecrivain, *Rev. hist.,* 1927, pp. 403-4.

the Roman,[203] while we have evidence that under the Roman peace the use of the Punic language spread into the country and in towns remained as the language of the lower classes.[204] Further during the third century of war, disaster, barbarian invasion, and uncertain and extortionate government the civilizing arts became decadent in Rome itself.[205] These factors all tend to show that after the age of the Antonines the extension of municipal status was no longer an index of material prosperity or of a degree of Romanization. When we remember also that during this period the imperial estates steadily increased in extent at the expense of senatorial landowners and to some extent of municipal possessors until in the time of Valentinian it constituted in the Zeugitana one-fifth, in the Byzacena one-seventh of the total areas of these provinces [206] it may help us to realize what the extension of municipal status during the third and fourth centuries really meant. The age of the Antonines marks the high point of significant municipalization and Romanization.

203 Toutain, *Cultes païens,* III, ch. 1, esp. p. 96 ff.; cf. *Les cités,* p. 254 ff.

204 Toutain, *Les cités,* p. 262; Boissier, *Afrique romaine,* p. 347 ff.; *Vita Sev.,* 15; St. Aug., *Epp.,* 209, 5; Apul. *Apol.,* 98. On Greek in Africa, see Thieling, *Die Hellenismus in Kleinafrika.*

205 Rostovtzeff, *Soc. and Ec. Hist.,* ch. IX.

206 *Cod. Theodos.,* XI, 28, 13, Feb. 20, 422 A. D.

CHAPTER V

The African Estates

The extent and importance of the great landed estates in Africa warrants a separate treatment of their part in the development and Romanization of Africa.[1] The large estates which had resulted from the private exploitation of provincial land during the Republican period had doubtless in part been confiscated during the period of the civil wars, along with the land of others who had opposed Caesar or the Triumvirate, and were slain or remained unforgiven. Many of these lands doubtless came into the hands of veterans and of colonists; some may have been resold. At any rate large private estates continued.[2] What public land there was, since Africa

[1] On Roman landowning in general see Schulten, *Römische Grundherrschaften;* Heitland, *Agricola.* The inscriptions of Souk el Khmis, *C.*, 10570; Hr. Mettich, *C.*, 25902; Ain el Wassel, *C.*, 26416, and Ain el Djemala, *C.*, 25943, have added at once to our knowledge and to our problems. A full bibliography of these inscriptions may be found in Bruns, *Fontes,*[7] pp. 259, 295, 300, 302; Girard, *Textes,*[4] pp. 199, 870, 874, 876; and *C.*, ll. cc., but Toutain, *Mém. acad. inscr.*, 1897, p. 31 ff.; Schulten, *Rh. Mus.*, 1901, p. 120 ff.; Rostovtzeff, *Gesch. d. Kol.*, p. 313 ff.; Carcopino, *Mél. éc.*, 1906, p. 365 ff. and *Klio,* 1908, p. 154 ff.; Frank, *A. J. P.*, 1926, pp. 55-73, 153-70, may be especially mentioned. Van Nostrand, *The Imperial Domains of Africa Proconsularis* offers a convenient collection and translation. See also the discussion of the African estates and of the Flavian and Antonine policy in Rostovtzeff, *Social and Economic History.*

[2] See chs. I and II on the lands of the Marian area and of the Augustan colonization; on estates in the Numidian kingdoms see Gsell, *Hist. anc.*, V, pp. 208 and 269; cf. Vitruvius, VIII, 3, 24-5.

was a senatorial province, doubtless remained under the control of the provincial quaestor,[3] but the money originally due to the aerarium tended more and more to come to the fiscus.[4] A procurator of Augustus in the Byzacena,[5] and an estate of Claudius[6] near Calama may refer to a third category of land which tended to become confounded with the patrimonium, the private property of the emperor himself.[7] The confiscation under Nero supplied the great impulse toward a concentration of the African estates into imperial hands.[8] As these properties were probably extra-territorial in any case little land was withdrawn from municipal jurisdiction.[9] Vespasian took over these properties and the career of Domitian doubtless added to them in the usual way. Thus was built up the important complex of imperial estates in the Bagradas valley for which we have inscriptional evidence from the time of Trajan.[10]

Large estates also arose from one other main source, the alienation of property which had once

[3] Halgan, *Les provinces sénatoriales sous l'empire romain,* p. 335 ff.

[4] Rostovtzeff, *Pauly-Wissowa,* art., Fiscus; On the sources of imperial property and the administration of public and of confiscated land see Dessau, *Gesch. d. Kaiserzeit,* I, p. 197 ff.

[5] Pliny, *H. N.*, XVIII, 95.

[6] On the estates in eastern Numidia about Calama and Thagaste, see ch. III, nn. 103-7 and text.

[7] On the sources of the private properties of the emperors, see Hirschfeld, *Kl. Schr.*, p. 516 ff.

[8] Pliny, *H. N.*, XVIII, 35.

[9] Schulten, *Röm. Grundherr.*, p. 3 ff.; Rostovtzeff, *Soc. and Ec. Hist.*, ch. VIII, n. 33, p. 592.

[10] Procurators of Trajan who occur in the Hr. Mettich inscription reappear, *I. L. A.*, 440, at Aquae Trajanae.

been the range of indigenous nomads. Whether considered *ager publicus* in the ordinary sense or not this land became the property of the emperor or of large senatorial landowners when the natives were restricted to narrower territories or, as seems to have been the case in the region north of the Aurès, lost the ownership of practically all of their land. Such was the process which produced the saltus Massipianus, the saltus Beguensis, the estates of Valeria Atticilla and of Antonia Saturnina during the first century.[11] The *definitio* of Matidia,[12] the great-niece of Trajan, near the reservation of the Mauretanian Numidae reveals the result of a similar process farther west under Hadrian.

The mention not only of the *Tractus Carthaginiensis* but also the regions of Hippo,[13] of Theveste,[14] of Hadrumetum,[15] of Lepti Minus, of the Tripolitaine[16] and by implication also of Thamugadi[17] and of Numidia[18] show how the development and organization of the imperial estates spread over

[11] On the treatment of these tribal territories see chs. III and IV, where the limitation and occupation of the tribal land, the formation of these estates, and the definitio are discussed. How far the theory of dominium in solo provinciali was applied in these cases is hard to say. An uncultivated tribal range could not be considered in the ordinary way, see Frank, *J. R. S.*, 1927.

[12] *C.*, 8810-2.

[13] *I. L. Al.*, 285, 3992, time of Hadrian.

[14] *C. I. L.*, VI, 790, time of Commodus.

[15] *C.*, 11174.

[16] *I. L. Al.*, 3062, 3063, 211-2 A. D.

[17] *C.*, 2757.

[18] *C.*, 26582, 7053.

the whole province.[19] This complex administrative system did not grow up at a single leap but depended in some degree upon the condition of the land before the imperial estates were formed, and was extended to the later areas on the analogy of the earlier. We may thus gain some evidence as to the period at which the imperial possessions grew in size and importance in various portions of the province.

Apart from the accretions to the imperial estates from the late second century on due to the confiscations of properties belonging to provincial families which had attained senatorial rank the total amount of land which became imperial was probably already extra-territorial from an early period.[20] The private owners of estates during the period of Augustus and of the early empire, chiefly senatorial absentees, kept farm managers loosely termed procurators on their estates.[21] A portion of the estate, if it were large, seems to have been worked directly by the procurator and the slaves, since we have mention of the *familia*,[22] while the extra labor necessary in the seasons of plowing, and of harvest was supplied by

[19] On the administration of the patrimonial department, see Hirschfeld, *Kaiserliche Verwaltungsb.*, p. 124 ff.; Schulten, *Röm. Grundherr.*, p. 62 ff.; *C.*, p. 1335, Mommsen's commentary on the inscriptions from the mausolea of the patrimonial offices at Carthage.

[20] The attainment of senatorial rank brought extra-territoriality, and exemption from municipal duties. Often however people of senatorial rank such as the Pullaieni of Thugga continued to perform these duties; cf. Abbott and Johnson, *Munic. Admin.*, pp. 103-4.

[21] A procurator on the estate of Lamia, 43 B. C., Cicero, *Ad Fam.*, XII, 29.

[22] Cicero, *l. c.*

the tenants,[23] who had leased the rest. In the middle Bagradas area tenantry seems always to have been the general rule,[24] while the tenants might be either Roman citizens or indigenous.[25] How early the system of conductores who leased the domain, or contracted for the crop began we cannot say. The latter function is quite early and the former must have begun before the imperial ownership, since their relations with the tenants were governed by the law of Mancia.[26] The letting of the *vectigalia* on a senatorial private estate near Mascula [27] may be analogous but is, of course, too late to be evidence. A system of share rentals was a necessary business arrangement with the tenants from the first, since they were not likely to have money or facilities for marketing. Whether a large general organization such as flourished under Trajan was formed before Nero's day for the land which was then patrimonial we cannot be sure. Pliny mentions a procurator of Augustus in the Byzacena.[28] Bassus,[29] an imperial freedman, was a procurator of the *Tractus Carthaginiensis.* His son was named Claudius Comon but his exact date is uncertain.

[23] Such was the meaning of the operae exacted from the tenants at the seasons of plowing and of harvest.

[24] On the growth of this system of tenantry with share rents and operae, see Frank, *op. cit.*

[25] *C.*, 10570, II, l. 14.

[26] The Law of Mancia was a private regulation, Frank, *op. cit.*, p. 155; for an opposing view see Rostovtzeff, *Gesch. d. Kol.*, p. 323 ff.

[27] Graillot and Gsell, *Mél. éc.*, 1893, p. 470, n. 2.

[28] *H. N.*, XVIII, 95.

[29] *C. I. L.*, VI, 8608; Dessau, *I. L. S.*, 1485.

The Neronian confiscation and the alienation of large tracts of land in the interior from the native tribes placed Vespasian under the necessity of providing a centralized administration for these territories, particularly for the large accretion of well developed land in the middle Bagradas valley. Thus came into being the hierarchy of officials revealed for Trajan's day by the inscription of Hr. Mettich.[30] The same inscription, and the further evidence recorded in the inscriptions of Ain el Wassel and Ain el Djemala show that the legal rights and servitudes arising from the earlier private administrations of the estates were not swept away to provide a common pattern for the administration of the saltus. In the Hr. Mettich inscription the regulations governing the occupation of the *subseciva,* and the business arrangements between tenant and conductor depend on the *lex* or *consuetudo* of Mancia, one of the former proprietors.[31] The inscriptions of Ain el Wassel and of Ain el Djemala make it clear that the law of Mancia had been valid only for the Saltus Neronianus and later because of its suitability to imperial owner and tenant was in part extended in Hadrian's day to apply to the other adjoining saltus.[32] A corvée of six days' labor from the tenants on one saltus,[33] as opposed to twelve days [34] on another, favors the same conclusion.

[30] On these officials see Frank, *op. cit.,* p. 153; Rostovtzeff, *op. cit.,* p. 327 ff.

[31] *C.,* 25902 and n. 26.

[32] *C.,* 26416, II; 25943, I and II.

[33] *C.,* 25902, IV, l. 26.

[34] *C.,* 14428, at Gasr Mezuar.

In another sense it is apparent that the organization grew only as there was need for it. For the unsteadiness in the terms used to designate the various regions arose from the difference in the extent and importance between the earlier and the later period of the imperial estates in the particular regions. By Trajan's time the large complex in the Bagradas valley had a fully evolved organization as a *tractus* with its office at Carthage and was divided into *regiones,* and these again into saltus, each with their procurator of suitable grade and his body of assistants.[35] The procurator of the *tractus* was of the equestrian order,[36] but the lower procurators were often freedmen.[37] We have evidence for the regions within the tractus of Carthage, of Vaga,[38] Thisiduo,[39] Thugga,[40] Uchi ?,[41] Assuras [42] and Thuburbo Maius.[43] There may possibly have been plots of land in the Carthaginian area which lay outside of this organization. For Delius who built a *teloneum* on an estate

[35] See n. 19.

[36] From Trajan on procurators of tractus were of this order, Hadrian's systematization made greater use of the knights in the public services, Lacey, *Equestrian Officials of Trajan and Hadrian,* Princeton, 1917.

[37] The saltus were in charge of freedmen procurators; in the regiones there was some variation; cf. *C. I. L.*, VI, 790, time of Commodus and *I. L. Al.*, 3992, time of Hadrian.

[38] *C.*, 12883: adiutor tabulari a mensa Vagensi.

[39] *C.*, 13188: adiut(or) tabul(ari) ad men(sa) Thisiduensi (sic).

[40] *C.*, 12892: dispensator regionis Thuggensis; *I. L. A.*, 568: conductoris praediorum regionis Thuggensis.

[41] *C.*, 12880: ex proc(uratore) r[eg(ionis) Uchi ?] tanae.

[42] *C.*, 12879: proc. reg. Assuritanae.

[43] *I. L. A.*, 246: disp. regionis Thuburb. Maius et Canopitan.

near Bisica at his own expense was the *vicarius* of the *vilicus* of Augustus.[44] The date is unknown, but the *vilica* of the estate of Claudius near Calama is the best parallel.[45] As the nearest known regio is that of Thuburbo Maius this was probably a small area of imperial land left under a former private form of organization for a while. Two inscriptions probably of the time of Hadrian, one at Calama,[46] one near Hippo Regius,[47] honor a Titus Flavius Macer who was *proc(urator) Aug(usti) praediorum saltu(u)m [Hip]poniensis et Thevestini,* or *proc(urator) Aug(usti) a[d pr]aedia saltus Hipponi-[en]s(is) et Theve[st]ini.* The term saltus may be used to mean *tractus* here but we have no known use of the word in connection with the territory about Hippo. The imperial estates about Theveste seem to have been comparatively unimportant during this period. For the administration of them was combined now with that of the imperial land of the region of Hippo Regius,[48] now with that of the region of Hadrumetum,[49] and the independent tractus Thevestinus does not appear in epigraphy until the time of the Severi.[50] The terminology which designated the district about Hadrumetum remained un-

[44] *C.*, 12314.
[45] *I. L. Al.*, 323.
[46] *I. L. Al.*, 285.
[47] *I. L. Al.*, 3992.
[48] *I. L. Al.*, 285, 3992.
[49] *C.*, 7039; a regio, *C. I. L.*, VI, 790, time of Commodus.
[50] *C.*, 7053, and even then the duties of the procurator of the tractus of Theveste were being performed by the procurator per Numidiam.

steady, shifting from *regio*[51] to *dioecesis*[52] and *provincia*.[53] It never included the word *tractus*. The *regio* Leptiminensis and the *regio* Tripolitana[54] seem to have been separate units. The fact that the same man was at the same time procurator of the *patrimonium* in the *regio* Leptiminensis and of the *res privata* in the *regio* Tripolitana shows us where much of the private property of Septimius Severus was, and how likely the two categories of land were to merge into one again. The *tractus utriusque Numidiae*[55] of an inscription of Thibilis seems to be a non-technical term for the sphere of a special procurator to look after the public interests and in particular the grain supply throughout the regions of Cirta and of the legionary territory probably during a period of stress in the time of Marcus Aurelius. We find otherwise no mention of a *Tractus Numidiae* but during the Severan period there was a knight, a procurator *Auggg. nnn. per Numidiam*[56] who performed also the duties of the procurator of the *tractus* of Theveste. This makes Dessau's conjecture that the *f(isci) a(dvocatus) at fusa per Numidiam* (after 270 A D.) of an inscription of Thugga[57] refers to scattered patrimonial estates throughout

[51] *C.*, 11174, 7039, 23068.

[52] *C.*, 7039, 11341 = 23219.

[53] Dessau, *I. L. S.*, 1441.

[54] *I. L. Al.*, 3062, 3063; *C.*, 11105; Dioecesis Leptitana, *I. L. A.*, 135; cf. 52.

[55] *C.*, 18909.

[56] *C.*, 7053.

[57] *C.*, 26582; Dessau, *I. L. S.*, 9018.

Numidia more plausible while an inscription of Lambaesis shows that Timgad, as we should expect, became also a center of patrimonial activity.[58] It is apparent then that the organization revealed in full bloom in the inscriptions of the Bagradas valley and of the mausolea of the patrimonial office at Carthage for the time of Hadrian and of Trajan was extended to the rest of the province in an unsteady and gradual way as the imperial estates grew in extent and importance, but it was not until after the period of the Severi that the tendency to administer other portions on the same pattern became apparent. It is noticeable that in the time of Valentinian the proportion of the total area of the province taken up by imperial estates in the Byzacena was less than in the Zeugitana.[59]

The regulations of the Trajanic procurators do not evidence any definite program or policy of agricultural development. The inscription of Hr. Mettich contains regulations valid only for one estate and was intended merely to clarify the situation regarding the actual position and title of occupants who had availed themselves of the previous rule of Mancia and enclosed the *subseciva* and to enable the process to continue on the same terms.[60] Its purpose was also to confirm the Mancian regulations regarding the relations between the tenants and the conductores. The exemptions granted to occupants who took

[58] *C.*, 2757.

[59] *Codex Theodos.*, XI, 28, 13.

[60] See ch. III, n. 155.

up new land and planted it to trees were [61] not given as premiums to induce settlement but to protect the tenant from undue liability until his plantation should bear fruit,[62] just as the clause declaring a lease forfeit after notice of two years' lack of cultivation [63] was designed to protect the owner and the conductor against shiftless tenants.

The Hadrianic provisions, however, as revealed in the inscriptions of Ain el Djemala, Ain el Wassel and Souk el Khmis give evidence of a more definite policy of development. The mention of two laws, or perhaps but one, relating to wild lands, and to lands which have been left uncultivated for ten years [64] evidences definite action to stimulate agriculture. The grant of longer terms of exemption from rental [65] than those allowed in the Hr. Mettich inscription, and of heritable title in the usual legal phraseology [66] to lands occupied and put to use, points in the same direction. The Hadrianic legislation extended with these changes the regulations of the Law of Mancia regarding the occupation of wild or neglected land to the adjoining saltus. General Hadrianic legislation appears also to have regulated the relations between tenants and conductores, the share rents, and

[61] *C.*, 25902, III, ll. 2-12.
[62] Frank, *A. J. P.*, 1926, p. 164.
[63] *C.*, 25902, IV, ll. 10-22.
[64] *C.*, 26416, II, ll. 10-15.
[65] *C.*, 26416, III; *C.*, 25943, III.
[66] *C.*, 26416, II, ll. 7-10; cf. *C.*, 25903, IV, ll. 2-9; Frank, *A. J. P.*, 1926, p. 166.

the operae and was cited as a norm by the petitioners of Souk el Khmis.[67]

The extent of application, and the economic effect of the law of Hadrian regulating the occupation of wild lands and those which remained uncultivated for ten years is a debatable question. Were they general laws applicable to all land in Africa or restricted in application merely to the imperial estates? The term lex gives no clue since it is even used loosely as synonymous with the consuetudo of Mancia.[68] In the inscription of Ain el Djemala the tenants demanded permission to occupy certain adjoining plots of land on the terms of the Lex Manciana. The phrase *lege Ha(dria)na comprehensum* in the answer implies that this permission was granted in accordance with a Hadrianic regulation of wider application. But its application does not necessarily go beyond the totality of the imperial estates.[69] As far as the inscriptions are concerned only this part of the Hadrianic legislation can apply beyond the imperial estates; the rest must apply only to them, and perhaps not to all of them since the inscription of Gasr Mezuar allows twelve rather than six days operae.[70]

[67] *C.*, 10570, III, ll. 4-18. Each saltus however seems to have been regulated separately and the former arrangements, though modified in part were not swept away; see nn. 33-4.

[68] *C.*, 25903, passim; *C.*, 25943, I, l. 7; cf. *C.*, 25903, I, l. 24.

[69] The argument that Hadrian's law regarding lands which remain uncultivated must apply beyond the imperial estates, since the tenant must by the Mancian regulation forfeit his lease if his land goes uncultivated for two years may be met by the reference to the land left neglected by the conductores, *C.*, 26416, II. ll. 6-7, and the fact that the Mancian regulation applied only to the Saltus Neronianus.

[70] See nn. 33-4.

If these laws of Hadrian were province-wide in application we should expect to find them working in two different ways. Waste land wherever found might be occupied, and planted, and at the conclusion of the period of exemption returns be made to the treasury or to the conductores. Particularly in their application to the territories of the native tribes such laws would compel them either to cultivate fully what territory they possessed for fear of losing it, or to sell part of their ranges to private investors, who threatened otherwise to lease and occupy it as patrimonial property. We should expect therefore to find during this period evidence of a sudden growth of private and of imperial estates, and a sudden increase in the production of various crops.[71] We can find nothing that does not admit of another explanation.

Such estates as we have evidence for in the territory of Hippo, in the hill country of which we should expect these laws to function markedly, were not in the hills but along the edge of the plain and near the chief highways of the district,[72] while strong Libyan communities maintained themselves in the interior.[73] There is little evidence of large estates about Thubursicum Numidarum, and what there is belongs to the late empire.[74] The estates about Calama date

[71] See Frank, *Econ. Hist. Rome,*[2] p. 447 ff.

[72] See ch. III, nn. 115-20 and text.

[73] Gsell, *Hist. anc.,* V, pp. 263 and 270.

[74] Gsell and Joly, *Khamissa, Mdaourouch, Announa,* i, Khamissa, p. 29.

from the first century A. D.; those at Ain Nechma later.[75] In the Cirtensian area and in the districts near the reservation of the Musulamii the large estates of which we have knowledge were more likely formed before the Hadrianic legislation.[76] To the west in the region north of the Aurès the rise of the estates imperial and private was coincident with the attribution of much of the territory upon the occupation of the country to the support of the legion.[77] The large senatorial estates south of Theveste belong to the same class.[78] The permission to occupy land still held by native tribesmen but not in process of development is consistent with the policy of the Roman authorities up to Trajan, but we have no record of large private or imperial estates other than the mines within the tribal limits set by Trajan. Further it must be remembered that Trajan had limited the tribesmen rather narrowly and that in the case of the Musulamii and of the Nybgenii at least the lands they possessed were for the most part unattractive. It has been shown above that the natural results of the limitation and of the military fort settlements are sufficient to account for the development throughout the century in southern Tunisia.[79] There need be no talk of encouraging the growth of

[75] Gsell, *I. L. Al.*, p. 20 and nos. 323-5, 476-7.

[76] See ch. III, re Saltus Beguensis, and the estates of Valeria Atticilla and of Antonia Saturnina.

[77] See ch. IV, n. 8 and text; nn. 107-11 and text; ch. VI, re vici.

[78] See ch. III, n. 76.

[79] See ch. III, n. 50 ff. and text; n. 66 ff. and text.

the olive in these regions;[80] exploitation is impossible without it. Natural causes were making it necessary to turn some of the land in the Bagradas valley away from cereal production.[81] Not only is the development of Africa in the second century explainable on other grounds, but it is only when confronted by an emergency that we should expect the emperor to pass legislation thus overriding the rights of private individuals in the municipalities to land of which they had full ownership or thus disregarding the legal implications of the Trajanic limitation of the tribes.

It seems necessary, therefore, to consider the Hadrianic legislation as applicable only to the imperial estates. Interpreted in this light it seems similar in scope and intent to the measures he took in Egypt.[82] By remissions and exemptions, limited in amount but sufficient to be attractive, and by the grant of privileges on the use of unoccupied land he sought to encourage agriculture. Only a national emergency could have called forth the wide and sweeping legislation which has been assumed. Hadrian had a definite policy but it was designed to encourage rather than to force exploitation; it was a piece of economic opportunism which sought to benefit the situation in a natural way and bring unused

[80] Rostovtzeff, *Soc. and Ec.* Hist., p. 322.

[81] See ch. III, n. 139-40 and text.

[82] See Jouguet, *Rev. ét. grec.*, 1920, p. 375 ff.; Westermann, *Jour. Egyp. Arch.*, 1925, p. 165 ff.

land unsuited to cereals yet suitable for olives and fruit into cultivation.[83]

It seems unlikely that Hadrian's purpose went farther than an increase of production and the building-up of a body of long-term possessors upon the land and that such a policy was intended to foster *vici* which should grow into municipalities.[84] The very status of their land precluded that. The dedication from the *vicus Haterianus* was set up by a group of Roman citizens living on or near a private estate;[85] the *vicani vici Annaei* were probably similar.[86] *Vici* of course were found on most large estates private and imperial.[87] There is no evidence, however, of any *municipium* in Africa Proconsularis which developed out of the *vici* on a private or an imperial estate.[88] If such were Hadrian's purpose he had but little success.

The large estates were in general poor instruments of municipalization or of Romanization. They formed extra-territorial or extra-municipal blocks of land.[89] It is to such a situation the Agrimensores

[83] On Hadrianic policy see Rostovtzeff, *op. cit.*, ch. VIII.

[84] Rostovtzeff, *op. cit.*, p. 322.

[85] *C.*, 23125.

[86] *C.*, 23116; Poinssot and Lantier, *C. R. Ac.*, 1923, p. 197 ff.; cf. ch. VI, n. 145 ff.

[87] *Corp. Agrim.*, ed. Thulin, p. 45.

[88] Rostovtzeff, *op. cit.*, p. 589, quotes Thabbora as a municipium which arose from a vicus of coloni on an imperial estate, but *C.*, 23896 = *Bull. du com.*, 1897, p. 296, no. 13 is not sufficient evidence; cf. *C.*, 23897, and 23910; the community was in existence in the time of Vespasian and Trajan, Cagnat, *Armée romaine*,[2] p. 213, and *C.*, 23910.

[89] Schulten, *op. cit.*, p. 3 ff.; Rostovtzeff, *op. cit.*, p. 592, n. 33.

look when they declare that most litigation regarding boundaries in Africa arises between Caesar and the *municipia*,[90] while it is evident from the inscriptions of Hr. Mettich and of Souk el Khmis that the tenants of the estates depended on the imperial procurators for protection and for justice.[91] This does not assume that there was no community life on the large estates. The Agrimensores speak of the estates with a large " plebeian " population and villages as in the municipal territories.[92] For private estates we may note the *vici* and *nundinae* on the estates of Lucius Africanus,[93] and of Antonia Saturnina.[94] For imperial estates we may note the *magister* of the Hr. Mettich inscription,[95] also at Souk el Khmis,[96] and the magister,[97] and village units [98] of the Saltus Massipianus, where, however, the piece of community work was done at the bidding of the imperial procurator, a freedman Provincialis.[99] Their common position as tenants tended to assimilate the Roman citizens of the saltus of the middle Bagradas area to their indigenous neighbors. The rise of indigenous families such as that of the

90 *Corp. Agrim.*, ed. Thulin, p. 46.
91 *C.*, 10570, II.
92 *Corp. Agrim.*, ed. Thulin, p. 45.
93 *C.*, 23246 = 11451 = 270.
94 *C.*, 8280.
95 *C.*, 25902.
96 *C.*, 10570.
97 *I. L. A.*, 194.
98 See ch. VI, n. 32 ff., 127 ff. and text; ch. III, nn. 61-3 and text.
99 *C.*, 587.

Gabinii at Thugga[100] under municipal institutions offers an interesting contrast. Such organizations as continued were purely for local convenience and had no validity in law. In the rest of the province we may assume upon the estates a purely indigenous population among whom the indigenous languages, customs, and worships lived on little influenced by contact with their Roman overlords.[101] As the procurators with whom they had to deal directly were usually African freedmen, and the conductores often as we see at Thugga, were of prominent indigenous families presumably somewhat Romanized and their *vilici* less Roman yet we can imagine how slight the tendency to Romanization would be.

The system of exploitation by conductores itself tended to lower the condition of the tenants. For the conductores were important men in the region and they formed associations for which we have evidence in the regions of Thugga and of Hippo,[102] probably merely local in character but influential and bound to grow in influence.[103] We find in the time of Commodus that they were powerful with the procurator of the *tractus*,[104] to say nothing of the lesser procurators of the regions and the saltus. Between these two forces the condition of the tenants

[100] Carcopino, *Rev. ét. anc.*, 1922, p. 31; *C.*, 26517, 26459-62; Poinssot, *Nouv. arch. miss.*, XXI, p. 60.

[101] Rostovtzeff, *op. cit.*, p. 293.

[102] *I. L. Al.*, 568; *I. L. Al.*, 285, 3992.

[103] Carcopino, *Rev. ét. anc.*, 1922, p. 13 ff.

[104] *C.*, 10570; on the effect of the growing power of the conductores see Rostovtzeff, *Gesch. d. Kol.*, p. 390 ff.

steadily grew worse especially as the officials of the fully formed bureaucracy were not without their susceptibility to graft.

The conditions, however, of the times of Trajan and Hadrian were not burdensome. A share rent usually of one-third compares not unfavorably with the one-half which often obtains today. The two-year notice before shiftless tenants could be evicted is quite generous. Had the Hadrianic policy been successful the deterioration in the position of the tenants might have been averted but the mention of lands left uncultivated by the conductores shows the direction of their influence, while a desire, natural in them, for immediate profits did not encourage a settlement of the waste lands or the extension of orchards of olives or fruit. The natural tendency to a deterioration was furthered by the times of stress which followed during the reign of Marcus Aurelius and in the third century when the need of supplies particularly of grain for the capital and for the armies of the various pretenders brought increasing pressure to bear upon all strata of the patrimonial society. The coloni with none to champion them fell to a worse condition than their municipalized neighbors.

CHAPTER VI

The African Municipal Anomalies

The urban center was, particularly for Roman citizens, the normal basis of Roman organization, whether in Rome itself, or among the Romans who lived in colonies or municipia. In the growth of the Roman system the urban center was normally the unit upon which assessments were made and through which a local body of responsible officials was provided. It was but natural therefore that there was a tendency under the Roman régime to develop the forms of Roman municipal life in areas where they had not previously existed. The slow acceptance of Roman municipal forms in many regions of the Roman west and the persistence of many anomalous forms of organization prove that this process was not the result of a definite governmental policy but the outcome of a long period of assimilation, development, and adaptation. There is evidence at once of the elasticity of the Roman system, more concerned with the essentials than with the forms of power, and of the strength and conservatism of the indigenous influences. For most of the municipal anomalies which are found are the result of the incorporation into the Roman organization of previous indigenous institutions or of the adaptations of the

Romans themselves to the necessary social and economic conditions of a particular locality or period of settlement.[1] A discussion therefore of the extra-municipal units in Africa, their types, basic character, and development, of the double communities, and of the phenomena of attribution and of contribution may, even if it be necessary to repeat some of what has been said in previous sections, form a not unfitting conclusion to a study of the development of the proconsular province.

In so far as the indigenous people of Africa had any settled community life their basic unit was the indigenous village.[2] This was an autonomous unit, composed of the people, usually a few related families or a small clan, who dwelt together and tilled a small section of the surrounding territory. The natural Berber tendency to disunion discouraged larger entities. These people gathered in some spot provided with water and natural means of defence, close to their cultivated fields, and built their simple dwellings, their storehouses for grain, their defensive works, and whatever else required the co-

[1] A study of these units throughout the Roman empire has been made by Schulten, *Philol.*, 1894, pp. 629-86; *Rh. Mus.*, 1895, pp. 489-557. This study was valuable at its time and has been the basis of much useful work, but is inaccurate in a number of details and takes insufficient account of the social and institutional background of particular areas at particular periods. See also Toutain, *Dar. et Sag.*, art. pagus; *Les cités* passim; Abbott and Johnson, *Munic. Admin.*, ch. II; Reid, *The Roman Municipalities*.

[2] On the indigenous Berber village, see Gsell, *Hist. anc.*, V, pp. 238-44; on its social basis and organization, *op. cit.*, pp. 63-6, 70.

operation of many hands. Where people lived under more nomadic conditions the corresponding unit was the family of agnates, but even these spent much of the year in village strongholds, passing the rest in seeking pasture for their flocks and herds. In the same way today inhabitants of the Aurès sow their grain in the autumn, pass the winter on the edge of the Sahara and return to their mountain villages in the spring. Raiding tribesmen ever on the move had within their range strong places and towers for refuge and the storage of booty.

Such were the common types of indigenous community in Africa before the Romans came. Towns were few and were almost all due to the influence of the Carthaginian exploitation or to the encouragement of civilizing princes such as Masinissa. They almost all dwell in castella, is the statement of Pliny [3] who applies this Roman term to the indigenous fort-like village. Such were the castella which Masinissa took from Carthage [4] and the φρούρια which were numerous in the Carthaginian territory of 149 B. C.[5] The castella of the Carthaginian territory, no longer defensive in character under the Roman peace, remained as inhabited centers and in large part developed into towns first of Punic, later of Roman constitution. Such is the origin and course of development of many inland cities of the Proconsular province whose sites testify to a former need

[3] *H. N.*, V, 1.
[4] Livy, XLII, 23; App., *Pun.*, 68.
[5] App., *Pun.*, 101.

of defence,[6] whose name is indigenous, and for which the archaeological evidence favors an indigenous origin.[7] Consequently, the original indigenous village type of castellum had practically disappeared from the developed portions of the province before the period from which inscriptional evidence is frequent, and such information as we have of its actual form comes largely from certain hilly late-developed regions,[8] and from areas where special conditions tended to preserve in some measure the more primitive relationships.[9]

No indigenous village to which the term castellum was applied under the Roman régime was completely autonomous. In 146 B. C. Rome gave autonomy only to the seven free cities. The numerous inland villages, many of which were Punicized, were officially without designation or with their territories were considered as mere territorial divisions in pagi.[10] The castella dependent on Carthage about 40 B. C.[11] prove that the indigenous centers were still of inferior status. Augustus and succeeding emperors granted them autonomy and they became civitates. Many of the indigenous villages of the central massif and of the region about the Algerian border early became towns of Punic constitution under

[6] Toutain, *Les cités,* p. 46 ff.

[7] See Toutain, *l. c.;* Gsell, *op. cit.,* V, pp. 240-1.

[8] e. g., the regions bordering on La Cheffia, *C.,* 17327; and the central massif about Mactar, *C.,* 23599.

[9] e. g., the attributions to Sicca and to Cirta.

[10] *I. L. A.,* 422; *C.,* 68, 69.

[11] *C. I. L.,* X, 6104.

the influence of the Punic people who fled there in 149-6 B. C.[12] The dependent position of many of the indigenous villages about Mactar until the Aurelian period has already been noted.[13] The castella of Sicca Veneria and of Cirta seem, with the exception of Thibilis and of Tigisi,[14] to have retained their dependent position throughout.

The total area which the inhabitants of the indigenous village cultivated or pastured was with its center usually termed by the Romans a pagus.[15] Strictly speaking, therefore, the castellum was not a territorial unit, and it appears to have been used indifferently with pagus as an administrative term. Sigus, a center dependent on Cirta, was termed a castellum, but its officials were magistri of the pagus.[16] Among these castella the term res publica never was used with the word pagus but always appeared with or implied either the word castellum or the name of the inhabitants.[17]

The local administrative body of the indigenous castellum was composed of the village elders, much as in the Berber village of today, who met for discussion of matters of local interest.[18] Such were the

[12] See ch. I, n. 25.

[13] See ch. II, n. 130.

[14] See ch. IV, n. 137.

[15] See n. 56 ff. and text.

[16] *C.*, 19121, 5683, 5705 = 19114, 10860 = 19135; cf. Phua, *C.*, 6267 ff., and the mag(ister) castelli Phuensium, *C.*, 6272 = 19252, 6298, 19278; see Gsell, *At. arch. Alg.*, f. 17, pp. 12-3.

[17] Gsell, *l. c.*

[18] Gsell, *Hist. anc.*, V, pp. 63-6.

seniores in the castella attached to Sicca.[19] In these castella with the exception of Tituli, there is no evidence of a magister. His place may have been taken by the prefect sent out from Sicca.[20] A center perhaps attached to Thabraca had seniores and an annual magistrate.[21] In the castellum of Tituli the chief official was the magister of the pagus.[22] M. Gsell has noted that in the indigenous villages of to-day questions are often discussed and shaped for submission to the elders by an inner committee of the more prominent elders.[23] It is possible that the institution of the undecimprimi who are mentioned in a dedication of the Gens Saboidum at Cirta, and in several communities of a markedly indigenous area in the original province reveals the survival into towns of Punic or Roman constitution of such an organization.[24] It seems to have been an inner board

19 *C.*, 15666, 15667, 15669 at Ucubi; 15721 = 1615, 15722 = 1616 at castellum of Nebeur; cf. Theveste, Diod. Sic., XXIV, 10, 2: πρεσβύτεροι.

20 *C.*, 15726 at Nebeur; cf. Sigus, *C.*, 19135, where the praefectus pro triumviro from Cirta headed the local ordo. Sigus also had its magistri, cf. n. 16.

21 *C.*, 17327: *universi seniores Mas...rensium* .... *anno Fortunatiani mag(istri)*.

22 *C.*, 27828. Tituli (Hr. Machjouba) may have been a castellum of Sicca. Such centers as that at Hr. Koudiat Setih, *At. arch. Alg.*, f. 18, 282; *I. L. Al.*, 952, with a council of decurions and an annual magister, *I. L. Al.*, 951, and that at Hammam des Ouled Zaid, *At. arch. Alg.*, f. 18, 352; *I. L. Al.*, 928, with a magister may also belong to this type.

23 Gsell, *Hist. anc.*, V, p. 63.

24 Gens Saboidum, *C.*, 7041, in Cirta; Gens Bacchuiana, *At. arch. Tun.*, Bou Arada, 74; *C.*, 12331; Bisica, Bou Arada, 95; *C.*, 12302, 23853; Furnos, Tebourba, 235; *C.*, 25808; Hr. Debbik, Medjez el Bab, 169; *C.*, 14791; Chidibbia, Medjez el Bab, 82; *C.*, 14875; Vazi Sarra, Mactar, 107; *C.*, 12006; Sicilibba, Tunis, 74; *C.*, 14755.

selected by the ordo of decurions [25] and separate from it. Two of the centers where it appeared were themselves termed gentes.[26] The village community also had its assembly, probably composed of all its able-bodied men.[27] Such was the plebs of Tituli.[28]

The assimilation of the indigenous castella to the Roman form of municipal government went on slowly or quickly according to the regions in which the particular castella were situated. The former territory of Carthage was ready for autonomous institutions before Rome granted them, and when granted assumed for the most part those of Punic type. The change to Roman forms came largely in the second century A. D. The mountainous regions about Mactar and the Algerian border developed later in the century.[29] Areas like that of La Cheffia near Hippo Regius were always markedly indigenous. The non-Roman term seniores prevails in the castella about Sicca. Those of Cirta from their first appearance in epigraphy termed their council the ordo of decurions and had magistri.[30]

Many of the indigenous villages developed as villages upon private or imperial estates. We have seen in the discussion of the inscription of Phileros

[25] *C.*, 14791 (Hr. Debbik); cf. 12006, not equivalent to flamen perpetuus.

[26] Gens Bacchuiana, and the Gens Saboidum where the dedicant is both princeps and undecimprimus, *C.*, 7041.

[27] Gsell, *Hist. anc.*, V, p. 63.

[28] *C.*, 27828.

[29] Cf. n. 13.

[30] See Gsell, *At. arch. Alg.*, f. 17, pp. 12-3.

that the possibility that some of the castella were centers of estates whose lands were subject to a vectigal cannot be completely excluded.[31] Of these villages upon estates we may distinguish two types. Where considerable areas populated by indigenous people were alienated and became private or imperial land many of the indigenous people were kept to cultivate it, now reduced to the status of tenants. On the Saltus Massipianus, the Saltus Beguensis and similar areas taken from the territory of the indigenous tribes, the inhabitants seem to have been left in their natural groupings.[32] Evidence of the use of the word castellum for these indigenous villages is lacking in the Proconsular province,[33] since the Romans tended to use the word vicus already customary in Italy for villages upon estates or in municipal territories.[34] The second type is the central villa of an estate which with its settlement about it required special protection in a land not yet free from hill-men's raids long after the Roman occupation.[35] Such may have been some of the πύργοι to which the inhabitants fled while the Romans harvested the Carthaginian grain fields in 149 B. C.[36] The fortified villas mentioned in the Bellum Africanum exemplify

[31] See ch. II, n. 92 ff. and text.

[32] *C.*, 587; see *At. arch. Tun.*, Thala.

[33] Note the praesidium on the saltus Philomusianus, *C.*, 14603.

[34] Thala was also a praesidium during the war with Tacfarinas, Tac., *Ann.*, III, 21, but the natives were governed by seniores in the time of Septimius Severus, *I. L. A.*, 195.

[35] Cf. *C.*, 14603.

[36] App., *Pun.*, 101.

the type,[37] but the comparative security of the proconsular province prevented the extensive use of the term castellum for the villas [38] and villages on the estates there. In Mauretania villages of both types upon estates were commonly so designated.[39] These types are of little importance for the development of the proconsular province since none are known to have achieved municipal status.[40]

The military fort was a type of castellum of surpassing significance in the development of the southern and interior portions of the province. Detachments of soldiers were stationed in forts at vantage points to preserve peace and order and to compel the settlement within limited boundaries of the nomadic tribes of the steppes.[41] Since they were necessarily placed on sites which possessed a supply of water, means of defence, and a command of communications, they probably succeeded older native refuges. These forts were suitable nuclei about which a series of Roman towns developed from the settlements of Roman soldiers [42] and the accretions of indigenous folk.[43] As the area of occupation increased the system was extended westward to the regions north of the Aurès and the Batna mountains, and southward

[37] *Bell. Afr.*, 67, 2; 65, 1.

[38] *C.*, 25902, Hr. Mettich.

[39] See Schulten, *Röm. Grundherr.*, pp. 45-9.

[40] See ch. V, n. 86 and text; also n. 125 ff. and text below.

[41] See ch. III, n. 38 ff. and text.

[42] The presence of a detachment of Roman citizens from the outset explains civi castelli Suf., *C.*, 11427, at Sufes.

[43] See ch. III, n. 38 ff. and text.

to the edge of the desert.[44] Such is the probable origin of Sufetula, Sufes, Cillium, Thelepte, Mascula, Vazaivi, Bagai, Lamasba, Lamsorta, Lambiridi, Diana, and perhaps of Timgad, Lambaesis and other towns. In the south Thiges and Turris Tamalleni were probably forts of the Limes at the outset, and on the edge of the Sahara towns grew to some importance at Vescera[45] and Gemellae.[46] The legionary forts carried town life as far as it could go into the Sahara.[47]

The term pagus always referred to the rural canton or neighborhood, and was territorial in significance,[48] not however as a unit of measurement but rather like the parish as a local grouping of the country people about their shrine.[49] Vestiges of a paganal organization existed about the city of Rome itself[50] and the term was applied to pre-Roman country cantons which Rome subdued.[51] It is usually a designation for a rural neighborhood within a municipal territory,[52] but the term was applied at Capua to the

[44] See ch. IV, n. 1 ff. and text; 81 ff. and text.

[45] *At. arch. Alg.*, f. 48, 9.

[46] *At. arch. Alg.*, f. 48, 39 and 65; *C.*, 18218, at Lambaesis, 17950, cf. 2482.

[47] Fabricius, *Pauly-Wissowa-Kroll*, art., Limes, XIII,[1] pp. 660-7.

[48] Schulten, *Philol.*, 1894, pp. 631 ff.; Abbott and Johnson, *op. cit.*, p. 14; Toutain, *Dar. et Sag.*, art., Pagus; Frank, *A. J. P.*, 1926, p. 62, n. 16.

[49] Schulten, *op. cit.*, p. 635.

[50] e. g., the pagi Sucusanus, Montanus, Aventinensis, Janicolensis, and Lemonius.

[51] Note Toutain, *l. c.*; Schulten, *l. c.*

[52] Note the census formula: in qua civitate et in quo pago sit, *Dig.*, L, 15, 4.

organizations of Roman people from whom municipal rights had been withheld,[53] and in the Table of Veleia to rural territorial divisions which crossed the boundaries of several municipal territories.[54] In Gaul pagus signified a division of a large tribe.[55] The term therefore in its extended application kept its basic connotation of a rural territorial division but cannot be more closely defined.

The African pagi may be divided into two main classes, pagi of indigenous people, and pagi of Roman citizens. The indigenous pagus was merely the indigenous castellum or village with its surrounding territory. The Romans applied the term as a territorial designation but it was used to designate the administrative unit also.[56] The pagi Muxsi, Gususi, and Zeugei in the original Roman province were mere territorial designations for the stipendiary native communities and their territories.[57] The communities which they typified appear as castella about 40 A. D.[58] and as civitates in the early empire.[59] At Gurza an inscription of 12 A. D.[60] named three civitates stipendiarii which were associated in a single

[53] Livy, XXVI, 16; Mommsen, *C. I. L.*, X, p. 366.

[54] *Tab. Vel.*, V, 70, pagus Salutaris.

[55] Livy, V, 34; Caes., *Bell. Gall.*, I, 12; I, 27; Pliny, *N. H.*, III, 124; cf. Hirschfeld, *Kl. Schr.*, p. 112 ff.; Jullian, *Hist. de la Gaule*, IV, p. 352 ff.

[56] See nn. 15-6 and text.

[57] See ch. I, nn. 55-65 and text.

[58] *C. I. L.*, X, 6104.

[59] See n. 169 ff. and text.

[60] *C.*, 68. The relation between these villages and Pliny's oppidum stipendiarium unum, Uzalis, is unknown.

pagus. All were in the region of Hadrumetum, and one, Uzitta, was termed oppidum in the Bellum Africanum.[61] These were therefore three closely associated villages in an area where the indigenous communities had probably long since been Punicized, and had been treated by the Romans as a unit. The whole reappears in the first century A. D. as a civitas.[62] The pagi Cirtenses were the castella with their territories all attached to Cirta.[63] The castellum of Tituli, probably attached to Sicca, termed its chief official the magister of the pagus.[64] The pagus of Aubuzza upon the territory of Sicca was probably an association of Roman citizens.[65] The ultimate origin of these attributions to Cirta and to Sicca remains unknown, but must go back to a quite early date. Even under quite primitive conditions the individual castellum was limited in some degree by its relationship to the tribe.[66] It is probable that where possible the Numidian chieftains strengthened such relationships and that the development of the towns of Cirta and of Sicca Veneria gathered to these towns the attachment of the units which had been included in a former tribal territory or a principality.[67] The influence of the Sittian organization and of the Sittian soldiers settled there must be taken into account

[61] 41, 1; 58, 3, and elsewhere.
[62] *C.*, 69.
[63] See chs. II, III, IV, sections re Cirta.
[64] *C.*, 27828.
[65] *C.*, 16367.
[66] Gsell, *Hist. Anc.*, V, pp. 70 ff.
[67] See n. 81 ff. and text.

before the final organization of the Cirtensian territory can be explained,[68] while at Sicca the addition of a body of veterans or a group of colonists during the Augustan period is not impossible.[69]

The settlement of Roman citizens in pagi on the Campanian land[70] is a possible precedent for the early paganal settlements of Roman citizens in Africa. Capua, upon its recapture during the second Punic war, was deprived of all city organization. Its landed population was dispersed, and the land, now public land of the Roman people, was let out to renters from Rome. These appear to have had no regular municipal organization, but to have been organized in pagi with a considerable degree of autonomy about shrines, and joined with collegia of people who probably represent the artisan population of the older Capua to care for their shrines and other buildings. Whether this system in its entirety dated from the destruction of Capua or not it was in full operation in 111 B. C.

In Africa the annulment of the charter of Colonia Junonia reveals the same jealous determination to disallow any regular municipal organization as the Roman government had evinced at Capua, but the colonists were granted the ownership of their land viritim by the provisions of the Agrarian Law of

[68] See ch. II, n. 148 ff. and text, and below n. 276 ff. and text.

[69] *C.*, 16367.

[70] On the Campanian pagi and magistri, see Mommsen, *C. I. L.*, X, pp. 366-7; Boak, *Cl. Phil.*, 1916, p. 25 ff. is still bound by the view of the conventus which Schulten and Kornemann expressed.

111 B. C.[71] What organizations they formed for the transaction of local business we do not know, but it is probable that Marius used the precedent of the previous agrarian legislation to settle his veterans with a viritane assignment.[72] As in the Campanian pagi the paganal associations formed by the veterans took the place of the municipal organization which was denied them. Unlike the settlers in Campania these owned their land. There is no evidence that they were organized about shrines like the pagus Herculaneus at Capua.[73] Even in the case of the Augustan pagi Mercurialis and Fortunalis we do not know whether the veterans were grouped about the shrine of an eponymous deity or not. We do not know what organization the Marian pagi possessed during the first century B. C. In the later period the magistri which were so prevalent in the territory of Capua were comparatively few here amid a relatively large number of inscriptions.[74] This may be due to an inclusion of all previously established bodies of Roman citizens in this area in the newly-founded colony of Carthage in 44 B. C.[75] We find therefore no close resemblance between the Marian pagi and those upon the Campanian land. It is possible however that the latter were a precedent for the Marian settlement but that the difference in the local conditions was such as to prevent any correspondence

[71] See ch. I, n. 33 and text.
[72] See ch. I, n. 82 and text.
[73] *C. I. L.*, X, 3772.
[74] *C.*, p. 2615.
[75] See ch. II, n. 85 ff. and text.

in detail. The inhabitants of the Marian pagi were probably enrolled in the colony of Carthage as citizens. The further development of these pagi will be discussed below.[76]

The Augustan paganal settlements at Medeli and at Sutunurca seem to have developed no further. They were still pagi in the time of Septimius Severus.[77] The titles Fortunalis, Mercurialis, and Minervius in the case of a probably similar pagus near Hippo Diarrhytus[78] offer a parallel to the Herculaneus at Capua, and to the titles Veneriensis, Minervia, and Sarnensis in the colonies of Rusicade, Chullu, and Mileu. The latter three may possibly have been important pagi in the Sittian kingdom.[79] The pagus Veneriensis[80] near Sicca may be similar to the Augustan pagi but the cognomen may rather mark its relationship to Sicca Veneria and the pre-Roman deity which was worshipped there.

The African gens was the indigenous tribe.[81] Occasionally we find the words natio[82] and populus[83] used in the same way. The word tribus seems to have referred to a smaller division or clan within

[76] See n. 237 ff. and text.

[77] *C.*, 885; *I. L. A.*, 301.

[78] *C.*, 25423.

[79] See ch. II, n. 152 ff. and text; below, n. 304 ff. and text.

[80] *C.*, 27763; Poinssot, *C. R. Ac.*, 1913, p. 424 ff.

[81] Known large tribes are regularly termed Gentes in the African inscriptions; cf. Pliny, *H. N.*, V, 17, 21.

[82] Pliny, *H. N.*, V, 30; *C. I. L.*, V, 5267; *C.*, 22729.

[83] Pliny, *H. N.*, V, 1. In V, 29, *populos* includes all forms municipal and extra-municipal units alike.

the tribe,[84] and familia is used in a similar sense.[85] As M. Gsell has shown,[86] the African tribe must not be imagined as the compact self-contained unit which it was among other peoples, notably in Gaul. The primary unit in Africa was the family of agnates among the nomadic people, and correspondingly, the indigenous village or castellum wherever agriculture was practised. These primary units jealously guarded their autonomy, but associations were made necessary by the needs of self-defence or by the natural conditions of various regions. In general it is from these associations that the tribal divisions of the country appear to have arisen. They were also the basis of whatever authority the princes and nobles of the Numidian kingdoms possessed. But since these associations were constituted of units so individualistic revolts were frequent, and any strength they had depended on the personal ascendancy and success of the chieftain.

The variations in the development of the different gentes were due to the natural conditions of their sites, and to the order and manner in which external influences and authority were imposed upon them. Within the territory occupied by Carthage and later by Rome in 146 B. C. the tendency to divide the indigenous people into their own village units merely supplemented the natural separatistic tendency of

[84] *I. L. Al.*, 138, 156, 174, 2836, 2853, 3144.

[85] Pomponius Mela, I, 42; Pliny, *H. N.*, V, 17; *I. L. A.*, 107; *I. L. Al.*, 3869.

[86] Gsell, *Hist. anc.*, V, ch. I, pt. III to end; ch. II.

the Berbers themselves.[87] Consequently, the Gens Bacchuiana,[88] the Gens Severi at Thimida Regia,[89] and the gens at Thuccabor, if such existed,[90] must be interpreted as a survival into the Roman system of smaller native communities, the village or castellum, under this name. The presence of undecimprimi among the Gens Bacchuiana corresponding to the same official in several civitates of the same area supports this interpretation.[91]

Beyond the limits of the Carthaginian occupation and of the original Roman province a different set of conditions prevailed. The two chief national divisions, the Numidae [92] and the Gaetuli, correspond to the division between areas whose people adapted themselves more early to agricultural life and the areas which continued to be ranged by nomads. Wherever agricultural conditions became general the inhabitants could be attached to an authority outside of their local units with a greater degree of permanence, and the tribal constitution or princely author-

[87] See above re castella. The Burenses if these were a tribe in the middle Bagradas area can be traced only in the cognomina of the towns Thimida Bure, Thigibba Bure, and Thubursicum Bure and in the probable ethnicon of *C.*, 15335.

[88] *C.*, 12331.

[89] *C.*, 883 = 12386. It is an inscription of the third century A. D. and may not refer to an African gens but to some honor paid to the family of Septimius Severus.

[90] *C.*, 14853: dedicatione(m) congentilibus et sacerdotib[us] viscerationem et epu[lum].

[91] *C.*, 12331; see n. 24.

[92] We must distinguish between Numidae as a national term, see ch. IV, nn. 32-8 and text, and the tribe of the Numidae which centered about Thubursicum Numidarum.

ity, as the case might be, had a better chance to be perpetuated. It is possible that the attributions of indigenous villages and their territories to Cirta and to Sicca Veneria arose in this way, and were later incorporated with little change into the Roman system.[93] The majority of the gentes therefore which continued as such until and after the Roman conquest lived in the mountainous region of eastern Algeria, and in the steppes of southern Tunisia and Algeria, where the influence of Carthage remained unfelt and the power of Masinissa and his successors was more nominal than real.

Deducting the colonies, oppida civium Romanorum, and oppida libera from the 516 populi of the Augustan list which Pliny used 462 populi are left. The majority of these, he declares, are rightly to be called nationes.[94] In estimating the significance of this statement it must be remembered that the majority of these nationes were probably village communities of related people, or small clans. He lists however a few tribes almost all of which reappear in the epigraphical evidence.[95] The effort of the Roman author-

[93] On Sicca we have no evidence; it was a town of some importance in the third century B. C., Polybius, I, 66. The territory about Cirta was the principality of Masinissa, a vassal of Juba, App., *Bell. Civ.*, IV, 232. The meaning of the trib. Iar. Gentis, *C.*, 16368, at Aubuzza and presumably dependent on Sicca is not clear.

[94] Pliny, *H. N.*, V, 29 and 30.

[95] Nattabutes, Capsitani, Musulamii, Sabarbares, Massyli, Nicives, Vacamures, Cinithii, Musunii, Marchubi (cf. Macurebi in Mauretania), and all Gaetulia to the river Niger, perhaps the modern Oued Djedi, *At. arch. Alg.*, f. 48, 29.

ities during the first period of advance and occupation in Gaetulia seems to have been directed toward a settlement of the tribes upon their ranges and a stoppage of the customary raiding and seasonal migration. The resultant war with Tacfarinas was a general conflagration, since his genius seems to have united all the Gaetulian tribes from the Tripolitaine to Mauretania, and perhaps included the Numidae about Thubursicum. His death ended the resistance and resolved the union into its component tribes again. Since there were no urban centers to which to attribute them, and the tribesmen had but little villages of their own, they were left for convenience of administration under the control of the commander of the legion, restrained within limited territories and overawed by the distribution of detachments of soldiers in forts at strategic positions.[96] The authority of Rome was represented within these tribes by a military prefect.[97] It is not known whether there was a chief prefect for all the tribes with sub-prefects for particular tribes or not. We find a prefect of the six Gaetulian tribes in Numidia who also had a military command,[98] a prefect of the Gens Numidarum,[99] a prefect of the Musulamii who was previously duovir of Ammaedara,[100] and a prefect of the Gens Cin-

[96] See ch. III, n. 40 ff.
[97] See ch. III, nn. 31-6 and text.
[98] *C. I. L.*, V, 5267.
[99] *Ann. epig.*, 1896, no. 10.
[100] *I. L. Al.*, 285, 3992.

ithiorum who had previously held a military command.[101]

The settlement of the tribes hastened the development of tribal centers, especially in the case of the Numidarum whose territory was suitable for agriculture. As soon as the tribal center was sufficiently developed it tended to be transformed into a civitas. The former territory of the tribe probably became the territory of the civitas and the military officer was removed. Such seems to have been the case of Thubursicum Numidarum [102] and of Gigthis. [103] From the territory of the Nattabutes two centers seem to have developed.[104] In southern Tunisia the Trajanic limitation of the Nybgenii seems to have hastened the development of the settlement about Turris Tamalleni [105] which had probably been a fort of the Limes of the first century. The further development of the Musulamii after the Trajanic limitation is unknown.[106] The Sabarbares southwest of Cirta, also limited by Trajan, seem to have remained a gens.[107] In the region north of the Aurès any tribal areas

[101] *C.*, 10500. There is no proof that the Sabarbares were attributed to Cirta. The Gens Salass., *C.*, 19923, *At. arch. Alg.*, f. 8, 139, were apparently a gens in the hilly region north of Cirta under a non-military prefect.

[102] See ch. III, nn. 94-9 and text; ch. IV, nn. 21-2, 72-3 and text.

[103] Ch. IV, n. 17.

[104] See ch. III, nn. 100-2 and text; ch. IV, 23-31 and text.

[105] See ch. IV, nn. 14-7, 169-70 and text.

[106] The ruins at Morsot point to a town of no great importance.

[107] *C.*, 10335, 8270, a defensor gentis; Col. Tutcensium is unexplained. See ch. IV, nn. 18, 19, 20 and text.

which existed seem to have been disregarded [108] and the people attached to the legionary foundations.[109]

It was not Roman policy to compel municipal development among the tribesmen, nor to interfere with their customary form of internal organization. The small tribe of the Musunii Regiani remained on their territory near Thelepte and kept their original clan organization.[110] Traces of similar clan organization appear south of Theveste [111] and among the Musulamii,[112] where in one case the name of the gens and of the clan is given on the same inscription.[113] Similar traces also appear in the strongly indigenous area about Thullium, southeast of Hippo Regius.[114] The indigenous principes or chieftains remained a while under the Roman régime. The princeps familiae Medid. among the Musunii,[115] the princeps et undecimprimus of the Saboides,[116] the principes noted at Thubursicum Numidarum,[117] the principatus of the town at Guelaa Bou Atfane,[118] and perhaps the princeps at Calama [119] prove the tolerance of the Ro-

[108] The Nicives about Ngaous, *At. arch. Alg.*, f. 26, 161 were probably treated like the other large tribes.

[109] See ch. IV, n. 81 ff. and text.

[110] *C.*, 23195; *I. L. A.*, 102, 103, 107.

[111] *I. L. Al.*, 3869; *At. arch. Alg.*, f. 40, 154.

[112] *I. L. Al.*, 2836; *At. arch. Alg.*, f. 18, 526; *I. L. Al.*, 2853; *At. arch. Alg.*, f. 18, 513.

[113] *I. L. Al.*, 3144; Perhaps also in *I. L. Al.*, 174: Sadavis f. Numida, Misic///.

[114] *I. L. Al.*, 138, 156.

[115] *I. L. Al.*, 107.

[116] *C.*, 7041.

[117] *I. L. Al.*, 1297, 1341.

[118] *I. L. Al.*, 561.

[119] *I. L. Al.*, 233, and p. 20.

man organization for the customary native officials. Changes which came were unforced, the natural result of the development under the Roman authority of the native units themselves.

Vicus seems primarily to have meant the village, Italian or Roman, considered not as a territorial unit but as a place of residence or as a collection of dwellings.[120] Consequently we find that there were wide differences of composition and status between various vici. Some vici were composed of Roman citizens, others of indigenous people. Some had political significance, others had not. Some had a constitution of their own, others had no constitution of their own but their inhabitants ranked only as citizens of the larger center in the territory of which the vicus lay.[121] Some were established by Rome for special purposes,[122] others were merely market-places like the fora.[123] Some were merely villages on large estates. In Gaul the term was applied to the urban centers within the territories of the large tribes.[124] The significance of the vicus depends therefore very largely upon the conditions of settlement in particular localities and on the previous organization of the people.

[120] Walde, *Lat. Etymol. Wörterbuch;*[2] Schulten, *Philol.,* 1894, p. 656 ff.

[121] See Schulten's discussion; cf. Festus, ed. Thewrewk de Ponor, p. 562; vici are listed among the municipal units of the Lex Rubria, *C. I. L.,* I, 205; Abbott and Johnson, *op. cit.,* no. 27.

[122] e. g., the viasii vicani, *Lex Agraria* of 111 B. C., §11.

[123] Festus, *l. c.*

[124] See Hirschfeld, *Kl. Schr.,* p. 112 ff.; Jullian, *Hist. de la Gaule,* IV, p. 352 ff.

In Africa we must distinguish first between vici composed of indigenous people and those composed of Roman citizens, also between those which were on large estates or municipal territories and those which achieved some independent status. The indigenous village was ordinarily termed a castellum.[125] As a result the vicus within a municipal territory hardly ever appeared.[126] Instead appeared the castellum and its pagus, as in the territories about Sicca Veneria and about Cirta; these differed moreover from the ordinary vicus within a municipal territory in that they were not part of Sicca or of Cirta but perpetuated under their own officials the independent character of the indigenous village.

On the large private estates so numerous in Africa it is probable that for the most part the indigenous people lived on in their ordinary groupings, but their land was extra-territorial and their villages had no political significance. In the Agrimensores is mentioned the large plebeian population and the villages about the villas of the private estates just as if they were municipal territories.[127] The people on

[125] See re castella above.

[126] I have not found a proven instance of this use in the proconsular province. Thala, which may have been in the territory of Ammaedara, was a castellum, *I. L. A.*, 195, and the cultores Iovis Optimi Maximi who built a paganicum at Sidi Mohammed ech Chaffai in the same area may be a pagus of Roman citizens. The Turratenses near Theveste, *At. arch. Alg.*, f. 29, 96; *I. L. Al.*, 3517 should, judging by their name, be a castellum; cf. *C.*, 11470, a vicus in the plain of Foussana.

[127] *Corp. Agrim.*, ed. Thulin, p. 45.

both the senatorial estates and the imperial saltus formed an extra-territorial society.[128] Their villages, though for the most part really indigenous castella, were generally termed vici in the proconsular province from the analogy of the Italian vici.[129] Such was the vicus Casae upon the Saltus Beguensis, where the owner instituted a market-day by senatorial permission for the convenience of his tenants.[130] The vicus and nundinae on the estate of Antonia Saturnina is another example.[131] South of Theveste the villages of Thesecthi [132] and Vesat.[133] were probably vici upon a senatorial estate. The Vicus C . . . at Ain Maja, east of Thala, was probably similar.[134] On the imperial estates the same conditions prevailed. The presence of Roman citizens among the tenants in the middle Bagradas area complicated the situation there.[135] Vicus Augusti of the Tabula of Peutinger seems to preserve the name of a village nearby or on an imperial estate in this region.[136] Bordj el Arbi is on the site of the central village of the Saltus Massipi-

128 Schulten, *Röm. Grundherr.*, pp. 3-13.

129 In Mauretania where conditions were less peaceful we find castella upon estates more common; see Schulten, *op. cit.*, p. 35.

130 *C.*, 270 = 11451 = 23246.

131 *C.*, 8280; *At. arch. Alg.*, f. 17, 386; cf. *At. arch. Alg.*, f. 17, 384, on the nundinae among the Emadaucapenses, and *C.*, 6357, on the nundinae in the castellum of Mastar.

132 *I. L. Al.*, 3625; *At. arch. Alg.*, f. 40, 2.

133 *I. L. Al.*, 3636; *At. arch. Alg.*, f. 40, 11.

134 *I. L. A.*, 198.

135 In the Saltus Burunitanus, *C.*, 10570, and probably elsewhere in the region.

136 *Tabula Peutingerana,* ed. Miller.

anus.[137] In the region north of the Aurès Gibba was probably a vicus on an imperial estate.[138] Lambafundi is uncertain;[139] but the three villages Venusianenses, [M]ucrionenses, and Cusabetenses[140] of a late inscription were probably similar. Evidence of other vici on estates in the region is probably preserved in the station Vicus Aureli of the Tabula of Peutinger on the road from Theveste to Diana, and in the station Claudi of the Itinerary of Antonine.[141] It is probable that some of the vici on large estates appointed officials and used quasi-municipal forms. A magister is found on the Burunitan Saltus,[142] and also on the Saltus Massipianus[143] but whether he was magister of a particular vicus or of a whole saltus is unknown. The former seems more probable since the whole was directly under the authority of the procurator of the saltus.[144]

In the class of vici upon estates but different in character from the above were the Vicus Annaeus and the Vicus Haterianus. Quintus Geminius An-

[137] *At. arch. Tun.*, Thala, 73; *C.*, 587; cf. *I. L. A.*, 194.

[138] *At. arch. Alg.*, f. 27, 149 and 166; *C.*, 4364 = 18547, 4363 = 18548.

[139] *At. arch. Alg.*, f. 27, 247; *C.*, 2438 = 17941.

[140] *At. arch. Alg.*, f. 27, 277-8; Graillot and Gsell, *Mél. éc.*, 1894, pp. 24-8.

[141] *Itin. Ant.*, ed. Parthey and Pinder, p. 14. For names of other vici drawn from these sources see Schulten, *op. cit.*, p. 22. The character of the vici such as the vicus Gemellae of the Tab. Peut. between Theveste and Capsa we have not evidence to discuss. The character of the vicus of *C.*, 11470, mentioned in an epitaph from the plain of Foussana, is unknown.

[142] *C.*, 10570, IV, also at Hr. Mettich, *C.*, 25903.

[143] *I. L. A.*, 194.

[144] *C.*, 587.

naeus, the owner of an estate near Semta[145] who served with distinction in various military commands under Vespasian and Trajan, left orders in his will presumably along with a bequest, for the erection of two statues to him by the Vicus Annaeus, a village on or near his estate.[146] The name Annaeus appears at Semta once more in the late empire,[147] when it became a municipium,[148] but in the time of Trajan it was no more than an indigenous civitas. The inhabitants of the vicus appear to have been Roman citizens under an annual magister Decimus Annaeus Advena, who was enrolled in the Arniensis, the tribe of Carthage. We may presume therefore an association of Roman citizens, probably conventual in character, who came from Carthage and elsewhere for commercial purposes and located themselves near the estate of Annaeus and the indigenous community of Semta. The fact that it seems to have possessed the right of receiving legacies is surprising since that right was not generally accorded to vici before Marcus Aurelius[149] and was even then a beneficium caeleste for a Roman pagus.[150] The vicus Haterianus seems to be a similar association of Roman citizens,

145 *At. arch. Tun.*, Djebel Fkirine, 9.

146 Poinssot and Lantier, *C. R. Ac.*, 1923, p. 197 ff.

147 *C.*, 23116.

148 *C.*, 23114-5.

149 *Digest*, XXX, 73; Gaius mentions the rescript *nostri imperatoris*.

150 *C.*, 26528b. On the grant of full corporate right to communal organizations, see Buckland, *A Text-book of Roman Law*, p. 176 ff.

conventual in character,[151] which made a dedication to Hadrian.[152]

The vici on the legionary territory were quite different in character. They were settlements of veterans on the legionary territory of southern Algeria. Bodies of veterans were settled in colonial foundations such as Timgad and bodies of soldiers were also stationed out in forts. But there were also settlements in vici which were not given complete autonomy as communes, although the particular settlers were given full possession of their land. The best instance is Verecunda,[153] the inhabitants of which were practically all soldiers or veterans. An inscription of 149 A. D.[154] mentions the possessores of the vicus who probably are the same as the incolae which a later inscription implies.[155] In honor of Marcus Aurelius and of Verus the town termed itself Vicus Augustorum Verecundensium.[156] It quickly assumed the municipal form, calling itself a res publica by 162 A. D.[157] and decurions appeared early.[158] It possessed full municipal status at the latest by the time of Carus.[159] Although the word

[151] See ch. I, nn. 118-26 and text.

[152] *C.*, 23125.

[153] *At. arch. Alg.*, f. 27, 240.

[154] *C.*, 4199 = 18493.

[155] A personage who was municeps of the town from which he came was incola, flamen perpetuus, and princeps at Verecunda, *C.*, 4194, 4249.

[156] *C.*, 4205 = 18495, 160-1 A. D.

[157] *C.*, 4206, 162 A. D.

[158] *C.*, 4232, shortly after 162 A. D.

[159] *C.*, 4220.

vicus is never applied to Diana,[160] the development of the town followed a similar course. It was a res publica in 141 A. D.[161] but still under the legion which built works there in 161 A. D.[162] It received municipal status the following year.[163] Centers such as Lambiridi, Lamiggiga, Lamasba, and Lamsorta were probably in origin forts to guard against the tribesmen of the mountains of Batna and of the territories to the southwest rather than vici on the legionary territory. In any case the soldiers in these centers had a degree of communal life under magistri and as at Lamasba were probably given assignations of land in full ownership.[164]

The one representative in Africa of the vici canabarum near the great northern camps is the town of Lambaesis. It is not certain whether the vicus found on two inscriptions there refers to the town or to wards within the town.[165] The camp naturally attracted the merchants and camp-followers necessary to the business of supplying the wants of the soldiers and the requirements of the army. From this beginning the town is found to have a communal form of organization by 162 A. D.[166] It subsequently secured

160 *At. arch. Alg.*, f. 27, 62; see ch. IV, nn. 89 and 100.

161 *C.*, 4587.

162 *C.*, 4590.

163 *C.*, 4589.

164 See ch. IV, nn. 83-8 and text; *C.*, 18587.

165 *C.*, 2604, 2605; cf. *C.*, 26473; *I. L. A.*, 547, 550, at Thugga; *C.*, 23398, at Mactar; *Ann. epig.*, 1907, no. 8, at Thibilis.

166 *C.*, 2740, 2695, 164 A. D.

the Latin right,[167] and was a municipium by the time of Commodus.[168]

In Africa civitas was normally opposed in meaning to vicus and to pagus. The civitas was the autonomous peregrine community. Under the Roman system it was one of the successors of the Berber village, of the Berber tribal area, and of the Punic commune. The few known towns and the village castella among the Berber people had a large measure of autonomy.[169] We have already discussed the castella.[170] Traces of the former Numidian constitution of the town appear at Thugga dating from the time of the Numidian kingdoms,[171] and urban institutions of some sort, whether Punic or Libyc were in operation in Cirta,[172] Vaga,[173] and Theveste.[174] How far the Berber villages retained their constitutions under Carthage is unknown; it is also unknown whether Carthage tended to impress the Punic constitution upon them.[175] The towns of the littoral, which were

167 *C.*, 18218.

168 *C.*, 18247; cf. 18256, 197 A. D.; see ch. IV, nn. 95-8.

169 Gsell, *Hist. anc.*, V, p. 130 ff.; many towns had the right to issue a coinage. Besides certain coast towns it is sure for Cirta and probably for Thagora, Gsell, *op. cit.*, p. 131.

170 See n. 1 ff.

171 On the bilingual inscription of Thugga, see Gsell, *op. cit.*, pp. 133-4; Chabot, *Punica*, p. 208 ff.

172 Gsell, *op. cit.*, pp. 132 and 134; Livy, XXX, 12, 8; a suffete ?, Gsell, *l. c.*, n. 8.

173 Gsell, *op cit.*, p. 131-2; App., *Numidica*, p. 163 (Didot); Sall., *Jug.*, 66, 2.

174 Diod. Sic., XXIV, 10, 2; Gsell, *op. cit.*, p. 132; πρεσβύτεροι= seniores ?

175 Gsell, *Hist. anc.*, II, pp. 301-2.

Tyrian or Carthaginian colonies, and probably Punic inland towns such as Tunis and Neferis had the Punic municipal organizations under suffetes similar to Carthage itself.[176]

The Roman organization of the province of 146 B. C. granted autonomy only to the seven Punic cities on the coast.[177] The suffetes mentioned on a Punic inscription of Thinissut, a town whose name is Libyan, may date before the destruction of Carthage;[178] those at Hr. Avin in 91 B. C.[179] point to the local organization of a special settlement in the Miliana valley.[180] Otherwise the stipendiary people lived on in pagi with their indigenous institutions unrecognized.[181] The vicissitudes of the Jugurthine war, in which Vaga was destroyed,[182] and of the settlement of Marian veterans in the middle Bagradas valley either modified or destroyed the previous constitution of Thugga, since the native town reappeared in the time of Claudius as a town of ordinary Punic constitution.[183]

The participation of several of the seven free cities against Caesar in the civil war probably cost them their immunity, if not their autonomy.[184] To

[176] Gsell, *Hist. anc.*, II, p. 193 ff.

[177] See ch. I, nn. 4, 55, and 56.

[178] Merlin, *Notes et documents,* IV, 1910, pp. 22-3; Gsell, *Hist. anc.*, II, p. 106, n. 4, and p. 302.

[179] *C.*, 24030; Gsell, *Hist. anc.*, VI, p. 115.

[180] See ch. II, nn. 138-44 and text.

[181] See ch. I, nn. 57 ff. and text.

[182] Sall., *Jug.*, 69.

[183] *C.*, 26517.

[184] Note the fines levied on the towns, *Bell. Afr.*, 97.

Theudalis only was immunity granted or continued [185] by Augustus but all were guaranteed their autonomy and Utica became a Roman municipium.[186] The Punic coast towns which were annexed from Numidia kept their customary institutions.[187] The numerous oppida libera mentioned in Pliny exemplify the Augustan policy for the development of the cities of the province. The continuance of the process is proven as more and more autonomous communities appeared during the first two centuries A. D. The civitas of Gurza has already been discussed.[188] It was composed of three Punicized villages which had previously been associated as a pagus. How far the adoption of the Punic constitution under suffetes by a number of the indigenous communities within the boundaries of the original province [189] was a direct legacy of the past cannot be stated, and moreover the constitution of the Punic coast cities and of the peregrine town which existed for a while beside the Roman colony of Carthage provided models for them

[185] Pliny, *H. N.*, V, 23: immune oppidum.

[186] See ch. II, n. 214 ff. and text.

[187] e. g., Leptis Magna where suffetes are found, *C.*, 7; cf. Sall., *Jug.*, 78, 4; 77, 1.

[188] See nn. 61-3.

[189] The following communities may be noted: Thaca, *C.*, 11193, 11194; Thibica, 12228, one sufete; Gales, 23833; Gor, 12422, su[fete ?]; Biracsaccar, 12286 = 23876, found at Bisica but probably suffetes of Biracsaccar; Hr. Bou Aradi, 23867; Tepelte, 12248; Avitta Bibba, 797; Thugga, 26517, with senatus and plebs; Apisa Maius, *C. I. L.*, V, 4921; Siagu, *C. I. L.* V, 4922; Thimiliga, *C. I. L.*, V, 4920; Themetra, *C. I. L.*, V, 4919; Carthage, Müller, *Num. de l'Afr. anc.*, II, p. 149, nos. 319-20; Curubis, *C.*, 10525; Thuburbo Maius ?, *I. L. A.*, 228. The sites of Thimiliga and Themetra have not been identified.

to follow.[190] To the influence of an admixture of Punic or Punicized people who fled from Carthaginian territory before the Roman invaders is due the development of active Punic institutions in the mountains of the central massif about Mactar and of the Algerian border regions.[191] In these regions neo-Punic inscriptions are numerous and many civitates of Punic constitution are known.[192] Suffetes appear even so far south as Capsa.[193] The names of many civitates such as Thullium,[194] Thagaste,[195] the civitas of Ain Nechma,[196] and others can be mentioned in which no sign of the Punic constitution has appeared but the general distribution of the towns of Punic constitution within the proconsular province is such that we cannot be certain of the passage of indigenous village centers to the status of civitas without the mediation, direct or indirect, of Punic influences.

The settlement of the indigenous tribesmen of the interior called into being a civitas more territorial

190 Gsell, *Hist. anc.*, II, p. 302.

191 Gsell, *Hist. anc.*, V, pp. 267-70; Punic was long spoken about Mactar, pp. 132-33; cf. intro., n. 33 and text.

192 The term suffete passed into the indigenous tongue, and as at Thugga may not always have meant a municipal magistrate. In these regions suffetes are found in the following places: Mactaris, Limisa, Althiburos, Masculula, Calama, and perhaps at Bir el Abiod, south of Calama, *At. arch. Alg.*, f. 18, 365. See Gsell, *op. cit.*, V, pp. 132-3.

193 It is possible that the power of Carthage penetrated to this important strategic center but unlikely, *C.*, 22796; Gsell, *op. cit.*, II, pp. 98-9; V, pp. 278-9.

194 *I. L. Al.*, 137.

195 Pliny, *H. N.*, V, 30.

196 *I. L. Al.*, 469.

in significance and with some faint resemblance to the Gallic type. The settlement of the nomadic tribes on a limited territory caused them to build up urban centers. As soon as any semblance of urban life was possible the Roman government for convenience of administration withdrew the military official who was previously in charge of the tribe[197] and granted the central town the status of a civitas with a territory coterminous with the territory previously assigned to the tribe. Such in effect was the process but its application varied. The Nattabutes seem to have developed two centers instead of one.[198] At Thubursicum Numidarum the principes or tribal chieftains remained probably as honorary officials for a while.[199] The Cinithii about Gigthis,[200] and the Nybgenii who after their limitation by Trajan quickly developed to a municipium under Hadrian[201] exemplify the type. How far the Musulamii developed is unknown.[202] The Sabarbares may have developed a center in Col. Tutcensium,[203] but it is uncertain. The Nicives probably centered about the site of modern Ngaous.[204]

In none of the civitates whatever their type was it Roman policy to compel an acceptance of the Roman municipal form. The logic of their position, the

[197] See n. 81 ff.
[198] See ch. IV, nn. 23-31 and text; n. 104 above.
[199] *I. L. Al.*, 1297, 1341; civitas, 1244, 1239; see n. 102.
[200] See ch. IV, n. 17.
[201] See ch. IV, nn. 14-17, 169, 170, and text.
[202] See ch. IV, nn. 11-2.
[203] *C.*, 8270; see ch. IV, nn. 18-20 and text.
[204] See n. 108.

slow processes of contact and assimilation, and the Romanization of the more ambitious citizens combined to produce this effect. The ubiquitous flamen of the imperial cult also contributed his part, and the accession of emperors in the second century A. D. who were particularly interested in the well-being of the provinces led to the advancement of many of the civitates to municipal status as soon as some degree of development had been achieved.[205] In those which were not thus advanced the tendency to use Roman terms to designate their administrative officials grew constantly stronger. The ordo of decurions may mean the body of elders of an indigenous civitas,[206] or the seniores of a castellum.[207] The civitas of Thugga had its senatus and plebs in 48 A. D.[208] and there was even earlier a senatus and populus with suffetes in Curubis.[209] The Constitutio Antoniniana did not affect the relative status of the municipal entities. Missua, which was important enough to have a place in the building of the corporations at Ostia,[210] is known to African epigraphy only as a civitas of the fourth century.[211] In the late empire the term civitas seems to have been applied to municipal foundations regardless of status. An

[205] See ch. IV, n. 147 ff. and text.

[206] e. g., Chiniava, *C.*, 25450; Sululos, *C.*, 23941.

[207] Sila, *C.*, 5884; Arsacal, *C.*, 6041.

[208] *C.*, 26517.

[209] *C.*, 10525 = *C. I. L.*, I,[2] 755. The type of constitution within the African towns varied from aristocratic to democratic without following any observable regional principle, Toutain, *Les cités,* p. 352.

[210] Calza, *Bull. comm.*, 1915.

[211] *C.*, 989.

aqueduct of the Lambaesitana civitas was repaired by the patron of the colony.[212]

In origin the African double community [213] was not a double community at all but two communities fortuitously located at or near the same site. In each case one was a community of Roman citizens and therefore of superior legal and social status, the other a Punic or Libyan community of peregrine right. The two had no duties or obligations toward each other. Community of location brought a certain community of interest. Assimilation followed tending to bring the peregrine community up to the Roman model. Cooperation between the two sections of the community increased and after the Roman constitution and citizenship began to be granted to peregrine communes the two portions sooner or later coalesced.

Such were the general outlines of the process of development without regard to special types and particular variations. There were three types of double community, the first of which may be termed the

[212] *C.*, 2661.

[213] Barthel did much to correct Kornemann's view of these organizations, but inscriptions giving more information about them have since been found. The discussions of Poinssot, Merlin, Cuq, Chatelain, Dessau, and others, have gone far toward a solution of the problem. Gsell's masterly description of the Carthaginian and indigenous backgrounds must form the basis of any study. See Kornemann, *Philol.*, 1901, pp. 402-426; Barthel, *Zur Gesch. d. röm. Städten in Africa;* Rostovtzeff, *Soc. and Ec. Hist.*, p. 281 and p. 580, nn. 59 and 60. Other literature will be cited in the notes below. An early parallel to these double communities may perhaps be the Roman citizen colonies of three hundred citizens, where necessarily a small body of Romans was settled among people of inferior status.

colonia and civitas. The most important example of this class was Carthage where Augustus granted freedom in 28 B. C.[214] to a Punic town beside the Roman colony.[215] The sea-port towns of Curubis,[216] Clupea,[217] Neapolis,[218] and perhaps Hadrumetum [219] and the inland town of Thysdrus,[220] where Caesar settled detachments of soldiers are reported in Pliny as oppida libera.[221] The towns of Carpis, which was a Colonia Julia,[222] and its consanguineous Hippo Diarrhytus [223] are termed oppida but were probably similar. Augustus evidently followed his grant of freedom to Carthage with a grant of freedom to the Punic portions of these towns. Thuburbo Maius is a clear case of this type of double community. A colony of Augustan or perhaps Julian veterans [224] was settled about a native community which had its own constitution and its own temples and cults in its own portion of the town.[225]

214 Barthel, *op. cit.*, pp. 19-20; Consularia Constantinopolitana for 28 B. C. in Mommsen, *Chronica Minora*, I, p. 217; Consularia Italica, *ibid.*, p. 276.

215 See ch. II, nn. 66-77 and text.

216 Duovir, 45 B. C., *C. I. L.*, I,[2] 788 = *C.*, 977; suffetes, *C. I. L.*, I,[2] 755 = *C.*, 10525; Col. Julia, *C.*, 980, 24100.

217 Duovir about 40 B. C., *C. I. L.*, X, 6104.

218 Col. Julia, *C.*, 968; a Roman town, *C. I. L.*, VI, 29539, an epitaph.

219 *C.*, p. 2319, C. I. H. on tiles.

220 *C. I. L.*, VI, 3884, 5, 4.

221 Pliny, *H. N.*, V, 23-4.

222 *C.*, 25417; building by Balbus, 43 B. C., *C.*, 24106.

223 *C.*, 25417.

224 Pliny, *H. N.*, V, 29; cf. ch. II, n. 134.

225 See Merlin, *Le Forum de Thuburbo Maius*, 1922; Poinssot, *C. R. Ac.*, 1915, p. 329; Ritterling, *Pauly-Wissowa-Kroll*, art., Legio, XII,[1] p. 1240, has confused the evidence from Thuburbo Maius and from Thuburbo Minus.

The Punic sea-port towns, which were well developed, and filled with a population, Roman and Punic, which was actively engaged in commerce tended to assimilate quickly the disparate elements of their population. Thanks to Concordia [226] the two communes at Carthage had united before the date of Pliny's source.[227] The other sea-port towns followed the same course but more slowly. The cognomen Concordia in the Trajanic colony of Hadrumetum may preserve the memory of some such assimilation.[228] A coin of Hippo Libera dating from 6 B. C. is known.[229] Thysdrus is referred to in Severan times both as a Julian [230] and a Septimian town.[231] At Thuburbo Maius where conditions were agrarian and differences were less easily overcome development was slower. The indigenous population was probably more primitive and the difference in title between veterans who had been assigned land in Quiritary right and the native cultivators who held theirs probably iure precario constituted a barrier.

[226] Tertullian, De Pallio, 1; Barthel, *op. cit.*, pp. 23, 34-5, 40; for an opposing view, Gsell, *Rev. hist.*, 1927, p. 232; Carcopino, *Rev. hist.*, mai-juin, 1928, p. 2, n. 2. Note the frequent appearance of C(olonia) C(oncordia) I(ulia) K(arthago) in the inscriptions; cf. Cagnat, *Rev. epig.*, 1913, p. 4 ff.; Heinze, *Hermes*, 1914, p. 510; Cagnat, *C. R. Ac.*, 1915, p. 318, no. 3. Note also the dedication to Concordia Augusta by the civitas Bencennensis on the occasion of the promotion of Uchi Maius, *C.*, 15447, 230 A. D.

[227] As a result the free city of Carthage is not mentioned; see Gsell, *l. c.*, and p. 239.

[228] See ch. IV, n. 55.

[229] *C.*, p. 2520.

[230] *C. I. L.*, VI, 3884, 5, 4.

[231] *C. I. L.*, VI, 3884, 3, 21; XII, 686.

The civitas [232] was elevated to municipal status [233] by Hadrian,[234] and the two portions cooperated in the building of a capitol in the time of Marcus Aurelius.[235] They coalesced under Commodus to form a single colony.[236]

The second type of double community was the pagus and civitas. Our best examples are found in the area of Marian colonization in the middle Bagradas valley. The pagi of this area were associations of Roman citizens dating from the Marian settlement [237] and were probably included in the newly founded colony of Carthage in 44 B. C.[238] It is uncertain whether the Marian annexation broke up whatever organizations the indigenous villages and towns of this region may have had. The indigenous commune of Thugga, the constitution of which had contained Libyan elements,[239] reappeared in the ordinary Punic form under suffetes in the first century A. D.[240]

The pagi in the towns of this area are probably to be considered as associations of proprietors of scattered pieces of land rather than of the large

[232] *I. L. A.*, 235, 254, 255.

[233] *I. L. A.*, 244, 247, 277, 278.

[234] *I. L. A.*, 277, 278.

[235] *I. L. A.*, 244.

[236] *C.*, 848; *I. L. A.*, 281; on the development of the town see Merlin, *C. R. Ac.*, 1919, p. 368.

[237] See ch. I, nn. 84 ff. and text.

[238] See ch. II, nn. 78-91 and text.

[239] Gsell, *Hist. anc.*, V, pp. 133-4.

[240] *C.*, 26517; note that the office of flamen Divi Augusti was the highest honor.

blocks originally assigned. The natural processes of sale and lease and the probable confiscations of particular holdings would divide a block of land originally assigned.[241] Imperial estates are found at various scattered points throughout the region as well as in the large imperial saltus.[242] It is certain that the territory of the civitas of Thugga extended considerably to the south and east and that on the border of the imperial estate adjoining it no sign of territory of the pagus appears.[243] For both units however Thugga was the residential center, and both could intervene separately in the affairs of the town. One of the chief buildings, the porticus of the forum, was given to the pagus only.[244] However the territory was apportioned, the pagus must be treated as an association. Complete recognition of its status as a juristic person did not come until the time of Marcus Aurelius.[245]

The fact that a large majority of the inscriptions of this region come from Thugga while the evidence from the other double communities is scanty makes it necessary to assume that their development followed in outline the same course at that of Thugga.

241 Note the phrase, centuriis elocatis, in the inscription of Ain el Djemala, II, ll. 9-11; Ain el Wassel, II, ll. 1-2; cf. Frank, *A. J. P.*, 1926, pp. 61-2.

242 See ch. I, nn. 109-10.

243 *C.*, 25988; Poinssot, *C. R. Ac.*, 1907, pp. 468-75; *C.*, 27417.

244 *C.*, 26524.

245 *C.*, 26528b; Poinssot, *C. R. Ac.*, 1911, p. 496 ff.; the civitas had probably possessed this right from the time of Nerva; cf. Buckland, *op. cit.*, p. 178.

A factor which delayed the cooperation of the two portions of these communities may be the differing status of their land, one class held iure Quiritium, the other iure peregrino. It may be that the development and application of the theory of dominium in solo provinciali during the second century A. D.[246] aided the natural tendency toward a degree of assimilation. Further, as prominent indigenous families such as the Gabinii of Thugga [247] became Roman citizens they would tend to associate with the members of the pagus. Roman authorities moreover during the second century A. D. favored the elevation of the indigenous towns. It was not until the time of Hadrian that any marked evidence of cooperation between the pagus and the civitas appeared although the patron of the pagus had been previously called upon to perform honorific functions for the civitas.[248] After Trajan patrons common to both and cooperation in the erection of public buildings were quite general, though not universal.[249] There was no actual union of the two organizations, although the decurions at times acted together.[250] The pagus of Thugga separately received the right of receiving legacies from Marcus Aurelius,[251] and the civitas received from Commodus the cognomen of Aurelia.[252]

246 Frank, *J. R. S.*, 1927.
247 Carcopino, *Rev. ét. anc.*, 1922, pp. 31-2.
248 *C.*, 26517.
249 *C.*, p. 2615; cf. *C.*, 26579, 26534, 26598.
250 *C.*, 26482, 26590, 26591, 26597.
251 *C.*, 26528b.
252 *C.*, 26534, 26598; *I. L. A.*, 564, 565.

They were united to form a municipium under Septimius Severus [253] but some memory of their former state is retained in the phrase decuriones utriusque ordinis in the municipium of Thugga.[254] The other double communities of the area followed a similar course of development but its stages cannot be dated as precisely as those of Thugga.[255] It must be remembered also that not all the communities of this area were double but only those in which the accidents of colonization had originally placed two separate organizations of people of differing status. There is no evidence that the native towns of Thubursicum Bure, Thimida Bure, Thigibba Bure, Sustri and Geumi ever were double communities. The pagus of Roman citizens moreover at Uchi Maius [256] was raised to colonial rank [257] without including the civitas Bencennensis, probably situated near it, which celebrated the advancement of Uchi Maius with a dedication to Concordia. Of the Augustan pagi only one so far is known to have been double. The pagus Fortunalis at Sutunurca [258] was situated beside an indigenous civitas [259] but there is no evi-

[253] *C.*, p. 2615.

[254] *C.*, 26591, 26622.

[255] Thignica, *C.*, 1413d, 15212, 1406, municipium under Septimius Severus; Numluli, 26121, 26125, municipium in 26129; Avensensis, 26157; Thibaris, 26176, [civi ?] tas; 26179, 198 A. D., a pagus, 26181, municipium Marianum; Agbia, 1548, Antoninus Pius, 1552, a municipium.

[256] *C.*, 26252.

[257] *C.*, 15447.

[258] *I. L. A.*, 301.

[259] *C.*, 24004; *I. L. A.*, 302; the flamen perpetuus of *I. L. A.*, 300, 303, 304, and the decurio of *I. L. A.*, 304 probably belonged to the civitas.

dence as to the relations and further development of the two units which were separate in the time of Septimius Severus.

The third and less significant type of double community was the result of the settlement in an unorganized way of small groups of Roman citizens in peregrine communities for commercial or other purposes. These formed separate associations, probably conventual in character.[260] Such were the associations of Roman people at Thinissut,[261] the cultores Larum et Imaginum Augusti at Tipasa,[262] the cives Romani at Sua,[263] and at Masculula,[264] and the inhabitants of the oppida civium Romanorum mentioned in Pliny at Chiniava, Thibica, and Vaga.[265] The Roman citizens in the Vicus Haterianus[266] and the Vicus Annaeus[267] may be listed here. It is possible that the Lare(n)ses of an inscription of Thibilis of 73 A. D. are the Roman citizens of the pagus.[268] Evidence of cooperation between the organizations of Roman citizens and their indigenous neighbors appears at Sua,[269] and at Masculula Numidae were included in the association.[270] The mode of development

[260] See ch. I, nn. 118-26 and text.

[261] *I. L. A.*, 306.

[262] *C.*, 17143.

[263] *C.*, 25850.

[264] *C.*, 15775.

[265] See ch. II, nn. 204-10 and text.

[266] *C.*, 23125.

[267] Poinssot et Lantier, *C. R. Ac.*, 1923, p. 197 ff.

[268] *Ann. epig.*, 1907, no. 6; see Gsell and Joly, *Khamissa, Mdaourouch,* Announa, iii, Announa, p. 13.

[269] *C.*, 25850.

[270] *C.*, 15775.

of these associations is unknown. The spread of Roman citizenship swallowed them up and the Constitutio Antoniniana deprived them of a reason for existence.

The castellum of Thiges of 97 A. D.[271] beside a civitas of 83 A. D.[272] was probably a fort of the Limes of the first century [273] near or in an oasis which was the center of a tribal territory. The castellum and civitas of Biracsaccar near Aradi is not a parallel. The civitas belongs to the time of Antoninus Pius.[274] Its appearance as a castellum in the late empire [275] reflects the insecurity of the later times.

Within the Roman organization of the provinces villages, towns, and smaller tribal areas were sometimes attached for ease of administration to some nearby town which became responsible for them to the Roman government, collected their dues, and had administrative power over them. Such a relation was termed an attribution of the smaller to the larger center.[276] Instances are found in Cisalpine Gaul in the relations of the Genuates to the castellum Vituriorum [277] and of the Anauni to Tridentum.[278] Other cases were found in the east.[279] The attributed ter-

271 *C.*, 23166.

272 *C.*, 23165.

273 Fabricius, *Pauly-Wissowa-Kroll,* art. Limes, XIII,[1] p. 665.

274 *C.*, 23876.

275 *C.*, 23849.

276 Marquardt-Mommsen, *Staatsverw.* I, p. 16, where the instances are all from the east; Abbott and Johnson, *Munic. Admin.,* p. 10 ff.; Barthel, *op. cit.*, p. 40 ff.; cf. Isidor, *Orig.*, XV, 2, 11.

277 *C. I. L.*, I,[1] 199 = V, 7749; Abbott and Johnson, *op. cit.*, p. 262 ff.

278 *C. I. L.*, V, 5050; Abbott and Johnson, *op. cit.*, p. 347 ff.

279 Marquardt-Mommsen, *l. c.*

ritory was not considered a part of the territory of the city to which it was attached, but it is evident from the edict of Claudius concerning the Anauni that in that case the attachment had resulted in a virtual union. In other cases however the attributed portion developed separately and became an autonomous unit.[280]

The relation of the pagi and civitates of the middle Bagradas region to Carthage does not therefore constitute an instance of attribution. The civitates were autonomous communes[281] and the pagi were composed of Roman citizens not of inferior right but probably full citizens of Carthage from its foundation.[282] The inscription of Phileros however proves the attachment of a large number of indigenous villages of the region to Carthage during the first few years of its existence but the Augustan policy of granting autonomy to African towns broke up this attribution.[283]

It is probable that Mactar, though itself but a civitas,[284] was the administrative center for a considerable number of indigenous villages in the central massif of Tunisia. The 62 c(astella?) of an inscription of 158 A. D. at Gsar Bou Fatha[285] were under a prefect, and a prefecture perhaps that of the same

[280] Marquardt-Mommsen, *l. c.*, n. 3.

[281] Barthel, *op. cit.*, p. 43; cf. *C. I. L.*, III, 388, a dedication by the 44 civitates of Africa to a tribune who was probably the governor's assistant in a census.

[282] See ch. II, nn. 85-91 and text.

[283] See ch. II, nn. 92-129 and text.

[284] Till 170 A. D. at least, *C.*, 11799.

[285] *C.*, 23599.

man is evidenced by an inscription of 157 A. D.[286] at Mactar. It is not until the time of Marcus Aurelius that the civitates of the central massif begin to appear in the inscriptions.[287]

The praefecti, quite numerous in the African towns,[288] are no valid indication of an extensive use of attribution since the majority of them seem to be municipal officials such as are provided for in the charter of Urso,[289] to perform by delegated authority the functions of the elective municipal magistrate. The cursus honorum, aedile, quaestor, praefectus iure dicundo, duovir is quite frequent with slight variations[290] and in many cases it is stated which official the prefect replaces.[291] It is possible that the praefectus iure dicundo at Thysdrus[292] is evidence of the attachment to Thysdrus of the almost desert

[286] *C.*, 622; the prefect of 23421 was a city official.

[287] See ch. IV, n. 185 ff. and text.

[288] There are at least thirty-three known exclusive of those which occur in the territories of Cirta and of Sicca. The praefecti iure dicundo of which there are four instances in the middle Bagradas region may be merely officials of Carthage, *I. L. A.*, 390, *C.*, 12585 at Carthage; *C.*, 26185 at Thibaris; *C.*, 15456 at Uchi Maius; *C.*, 26615, *I. L. A.*, 520 at Thugga.

[289] See Dessau, *I. L. S.*, 6087, 93, 94, 95; cf. *Corp. Agrim.*, ed. Thulin, p. 124.

[290] *I. L. A.*, 390, at Carthage; *C. R. Ac.*, 1915, p. 316, nos. 1 and 2, at Cuicul; *I. L. Al.*, 3007, 3064, 3069, at Theveste; *I. L. A.*, 451, 458, at Bulla Regia; *I. L. A.*, 282, Thuburbo Maius; *C.*, 12018 at Zama (Sidi Amor Djedidi); *C.*, 15585 at Sidi Abd er Rebbu near Mustis; *I. L. Al.*, 1294 at Thubursicum Numidarum; *I. L. Al.*, 572 at Guelaa Bou Atfane.

[291] e. g., for duovir when Antoninus Pius was honored with this position, *C. R. Ac.*, 1915, p. 316, n. 3, at Cuicul; for duovir, *C.*, 4580, 4597, 4600, at Diana.

[292] *C.*, 2343; cf. 2406.

hinterland between it and Sufetula and Capsa where no Roman sites are known. Diana had a considerable territory but the praefecti [293] there are as certainly magistrates of the town as are those of the much smaller territory of Timgad.[294] The office of prefect seems to be part of a regular municipal cursus honorum at Theveste [295] which was probably an administrative center for much of the territory to the south. The attachments of the pagus Trisipensis and the pagus Mas . . . rensium are unknown but it is probable that they were attached to Thabraca. Hippo Regius had a considerable territory but we have no evidence as to the way in which units within it were related. Thullium was an autonomous civitas and the castellum Fussala adjoined but was not in the territory of Hippo.[296]

The origin of the attachment of various pagi and castella to Cirta and to Sicca is uncertain. It is possible that the areas thus defined had been tribal areas or principalities under the Numidian kings and remained as administrative units under the Roman régime. Given the attribution to Cirta the cognomen of Nova Cirta may not be without significance in explaining that to Sicca. The castella of both seem to have been originally indigenous villages. The fact that those of Cirta appear to be more developed at the time when they become known to epigraphy may be due to the Sittian settlements, the

[293] See n. 291.
[294] *C.*, 2400 = 17911; 17838; *Ann. epig.*, 1901, no. 191
[295] *I. L. Al.*, 3007, 3064, 3065, 3069, 3070, 3141.
[296] See ch. III, n. 108 ff. and text.

influence of which for the rest is more apparent in the contributed colonies, but it is uncertain. The organization of these castella has been described.[297] Officials of Sicca had their homes out among the castella[298] and the prefect of one of them had first been duovir at Sicca.[299] The magistrates of the colony of Cirta exercised a general oversight over the attributed pagi and castella. The authority of the colony was actually represented in them by praefecti pro triumviris probably delegated with judicial functions by the magistrates of Cirta.[300] One of these appears at the head of the album of decurions at Sigus.[301] The office seems to have been held regularly after the aedileship of Cirta and before the triumvirate of the four colonies.[302] Whether the praefectus pro triumviris served one or many pagi at once is uncertain, but the latter case is more probable. As the historic attachment of these centers was to Cirta their condition remained unaffected by the severance of the union of the four colonies.[303]

The only case of contribution, the joint administration of communities of equal legal status by common officials, in the proconsular province appears in the Cirtensian area. The origin of the contribution

[297] See ch. II, n. 145 ff. and text; ch. III, n. 126 ff. and text; ch. IV, n. 120 ff. and text; also above re castella and gentes.

[298] *C.*, 15669.

[299] *C.*, 15726.

[300] Gsell, *At. arch. Alg.*, f. 17, 126, p. 13, col. 1; Barthel, *op. cit.*, p. 46.

[301] *C.*, 19135.

[302] *C.*, 19489, 7986, 10867.

[303] Probably about the middle of the third century A. D., *C.*, 8210.

remains obscure. The cognomina of the three colonies, Veneria Rusicade, Minervia Chullu, and Sarnensis Mileu, particularly the latter, are certainly early and go back to the settlement made by the Campanian Sittius, but Mileu is not mentioned in Pliny, and Rusicade and Chullu are merely termed oppida.[304] The triumviri usual in the confederation do not appear at Cirta during the first years of the colony but duumviri and quattuorviri instead, and the forms of the letters and the spelling of the words upon the significant inscriptions are early.[305] We may note that the pagi of Augustan veterans probably settled about 29 B. C. had similar cognomina. It is probable however that the union of the towns with Cirta was original, that their importance[306] as settlements of Sittians now Roman citizens brought them colonial status, but that they remained in the attachment which their historical and national background favored and worked out a system of federal municipal government.

From the end of the first century on the contribution is certain.[307] Triumviri, aediles, and decurions of the four colonies are frequent. Various priesthoods were also common to all. The administrative center was Cirta but the administration of justice in the three contributed colonies was entrusted to

[304] See ch. II, nn. 152-163 and text.

[305] *C.*, 7099, 7117, and perhaps 7110; see Gsell, *l. c.*, pp. 11, col. 2.

[306] Chullu and Rusicade were old Punic trading-posts, and Chullu had a dye industry, while Rusicade was the port of Cirta, *At. arch. Alg.*, f. 8, nos. 29 and 196.

[307] *C.*, 7986.

praefecti iure dicundo, who could have jurisdiction in three colonies or two or a single colony, who might repeat the office or be prefect in each of the colonies in turn.[308] Contrary to Mommsen's view,[309] Gsell's opinion [310] that the praefectus iure dicundo held this office subsequently to his triumvirate seems best. The confederation continued until late in the third century, and then was dissolved we know not why or exactly when.

This study of the municipal organizations of the province in their local setting and historical evolution reveals at once the persistence with which the indigenous people clung to their own natural associations, and the tolerance and flexibility of the Roman system. From the many types of communities which appear we can trace the course of an evolution as Roman and native communities adapted themselves to each other; while the natural processes of assimilation and harmonious contact did more to build up a prosperous and civilized life than the imposition of set forms of the Roman type could have done. The municipal anomalies, the double communes, and the phenomena of attribution and of contribution show how unlikely it is that the Roman government ever determined to follow a set policy of urbanization or of Romanization in Africa, and how much more they were interested in maintaining the essentials of organized administrative activity than wedded to any particular form.

[308] See Gsell's summary and discussion, *l. c.*, p. 12.

[309] *Hermes,* I, 1866, p. 58 ff.; *C.*, p. 618.

[310] Gsell, *l. c.*

CONCLUSION

Our study of Roman Africa has brought us from the time of Rome's entrance over the ruins of Carthage to the period of the Severi, when the province was most prosperous. In retrospect the story of the Roman development seems largely to be a story of Roman adaptation to the social and economic conditions of the country coupled with a Roman insistence upon orderly settlement and effective exploitation. The Roman legion brought security; a Roman colonization fostered agricultural and municipal development particularly in the more fertile regions where Carthage had already begun the process. But in other regions insistence on settled life and enforcement of peace compelled the natives to find out the best possible adaptations to their unpromising climate and resulted in a prosperous urban life in regions formerly desolate, while the establishment of soldiers in forts and in veteran settlements gave them centers about which to develop. Rome insisted on peace, order, and security, on a settled, producing, tax-paying people and in so doing gave Africa the means of civilizing herself.

For the development of Africa was primarily a native development. The social basis was never appreciably changed. Only in the Bagradas valley was the Roman colonization sufficiently extensive to affect the general mass of the population, which even there much outnumbered the dominant Romans. After the first century A. D. the soldiers who served in the Third Legion and settled in the country were almost all Africans by birth. Such Romanization as occurred was the result of the slow acceptance through a process of long contact and assimilation by native people of the Roman forms and was particularly noticeable only in the sphere of municipal government.

The degree of urbanization was not a complete index to the degree of Romanization. Carthage had accustomed a portion of the country to a measure of urban life, and Punic influences had tended to extend it, while the provincial prosperity which had resulted from the Roman peace naturally resulted in the development of urban centers. As the towns grew in prosperity Roman influences, felt in commercial and official relations, the use of the Latin language for official purposes, the insistence on the worship of the imperial cults, and the ambition of the leading indigenous families, tended to draw the towns and their people to the Roman forms.

Urbanization, particularly urbanization on the Roman model, was not a Roman or an imperial policy. The long continuance of indigenous organizations and the anomalous institutions which arose through the contact of Roman and of indigenous people prove the tolerance and flexibility of the Roman administration, the conservatism of the indigenous influences, and the slow adaptations which they made to each other. Only in the insistence upon the acceptance everywhere of the imperial cults as the symbols of authority, and in the treatment of the nomadic tribes do we see an active policy on the part of the Roman government. And in the case of the nomadic tribes the withdrawal of the military officials and the grant of municipal institutions as soon as their enforced settlement had produced some semblance of an urban center was not due to a policy of urbanization but to the recognition of the fact that they now had a body of citizens who could be held responsible. One can still question how urban such centers as Thiges and Turris Tamalleni ever were.

Moreover the rise of the great private and imperial estates created a society but slightly Romanized and but slightly urbanized which assimilated even Roman tenants downward to their indigenous neighbors. The capitalistic agricultural exploitation which was a feature of the Roman régime from the beginning at first made Africa famous for her glorious harvests, but ended in the production of a society of unprivileged serfs.

Despite the urban development to the Roman municipal forms the process of Romanization did not penetrate deeply. The more prosperous and ambitious families assimilated themselves with the descendants of the Roman colonists and became quite

Romanized. The wide extension of Roman citizenship to the towns of the province marks in some degree the advance of this process. A municipal aristocracy was thus formed to whom much of the African contribution to Roman civilization is due, but the ways of the mass of the people never changed. They still worshipped, if sometimes under Roman names, their ancestral gods in their ancestral way until the coming of Christianity, another Semite religion. The Punic language, far from being supplanted, spread out under the Roman rule into the country to supplant the Libyan tongues, and remained the speech of the common people. Mountain areas, little touched by outside influences, continued the ancient ways ready to spread indigenous influences again; and in the late empire when the legion weakened, and security was gone, and the religious struggle between Catholic and Donatist masked an awakening of the indigenous people, Africa shed its exotic veneer of Roman civilization until it seemed but for its stone memorials almost as if it had never been. The Romans adapted themselves to Africa; they gave her peace, and made her prosperous, but they never made her Roman.

INDEX